The Impact on Philosophy of Semiotics

The Impact
on Philosophy
of Semiotics

The Quasi-Error of the External World
with a Dialogue between a 'Semiotist' and a 'Realist'

John Deely

ST. AUGUSTINE'S PRESS
South Bend, Indiana
2003

1 2 3 4 5 6   09 08 07 06 05 04 03

Library of Congress Cataloging in Publication Data
Deely, John N.
    The impact on philosophy of semiotics : the quasi-error
of the external world with a dialogue between a
'semiotist' and a 'realist' / John Deely.
        p. cm.
    Includes bibliographical references and index.
    ISBN 1-58731-375-8 (hardcover : alk. paper)
    1. Postmodernism. 2. Semiotics. 3. Realism. I. Title.
B831.2 .D437 2003
121'.68 – dc21   2002151648

∞ *The paper used in this publication meets the minimum requirements of the American National Standard for Information Sciences –
Permanence of Paper for Printed Materials, ANSI Z39.48-1984.*

This book in three parts is likewise dedicated:

Part I to
Sonny McDonald,
for making the Umwelt of carpentry
accessible to a philosopher

Part II to
Sebeok, Thomas A.,
9 November 1920–2001 December 21
friend and founder of semiotics as a global network

Part III to
extending the insight of Thomas Aquinas
repositioning realism
vis-à-vis
the difference between speculative and practical objects of knowledge

Contents

PART II.
THE QUASI-ERROR OF THE EXTERNAL WORLD

PART III.
DIALOGUE BETWEEN A 'SEMIOTIST' AND A 'REALIST'

Part I.
The Impact on Philosophy of Semiotics

Chapter 1

The State of the Question

In the conventional wisdom, as Descartes was the father of modern philosophy in the early 17th century, so Ferdinand de Saussure was the father of semiology in the early 20th century, and Charles Peirce the father of semiotics in that same time-frame. The picture is fair enough.

But if we ask what has been the impact of semiotics upon philosophy over the course of the 20th century, early in the 21st century to answer anything beyond "marginal" would be an exaggeration. This situation, as I read it, is about to change dramatically. In the less than a century of dominance enjoyed by so-called "analytic philosophy" in English-speaking and Hispanic academic worlds of the late modern twilight, it was the custom regularly to issue "promissory notes" on philosophical programs, usually epistemological in character, never realized in detail. As modernity and postmodernity reach the stage of passing one another in the night, the first receding in its twilight as the other moves toward a brilliant dawn, I would like to give a passing example of a reverse procedure. Instead of going from a brief programmatic statement to a grand project never to be fulfilled, I want to present instead an abstract of an already completed larger project,[1] a setting of contemporary semiotics fully within the horizon and context of philosophical history as a whole, from its origin in ancient Greek Ionia to its latest manifestation as semiotic, the doctrine of signs.

Of course, I could be wrong in my belief that the philosophy establishment will not be able much longer to avoid refurnishing its house along semiotic lines – but I have gotten so used to being wrong, especially in prophecies, that the prospect hardly daunts me. And this time, wrong or not, I can tell you for sure from personal experience that, even though the situation has begun to change over the last two decades particularly, semiotics has been and still is at the margins of philosophy. Analytic philosophy in particular, after all the dominant paradigm in academic departments of philosophy throughout the English speaking and Hispanic worlds, has not been receptive to semiotics, though superficially you would have expected a proclaimed linguistic perspective in philosophy to be receptive of the semiotic point of view, particularly when you consider that the dominant model for the study of signs in the 20th century, to wit, semiology, has

[1] The "completed project" in question is the thousand-page book, Four Ages of Understanding. The first postmodern survey of philosophy from ancient times to the turn of the twenty-first century (Toronto, Canada: University of Toronto Press, 2001), referred to hereafter as the Four Ages (Deely 2001). The present brief version of the story is based on my December 1, 2000, presentation, "The Impact of Semiotics on Philosophy", at the first Annual Hommage à Oscar Parland at the University of Helsinki, toward the close of my semester there as the first Visiting Professor of Semiotics.

emphasized the linguistic paradigm for studying even signs in general. But this superficial impression would be belied by the fact that the conception of language itself within analytic philosophy has been that of a self-contained whole, even as a system of signs. By contrast, semiotics has insisted from the first that linguistic semiosis, the action of signs within human language, is far from a self-contained universe of discourse. On the contrary, according to semiotics, the action of signs exceeds the boundaries set by the human use of signs, and the human use of signs would not be even possible except in constant collaboration with and on the basis of an action of signs at many levels surrounding linguistic usage and rendering it successful whenever and to whatever extent it does succeed (which of course is far from always).[2]

---

[2] The human use of signs is commonly referred to as "anthroposemiosis", or the action of signs within the sphere of human thought, feeling, and activity. Whence the term "anthroposemiosis", in sharp contrast to all variants on the Greek root "psyche", connotes both "the self/nature correlation" and "powers of the unconscious" requisite to convey "a sense of the relationship between human forms of semiosis and semiotic cosmology as a whole", denoting precisely "the human order and its unique forms of semiosis" according to an overall perspective wherein, as Corrington (2000: 86–7) puts it, "semiosis is the genus of which particular orders of semiotic interaction are species." Somewhat oddly, in the very course of saying all this, Corrington suggests that we opt rather for the term "psychosemiosis" to convey "some of the drama of the internal work on the unconscious with a sense of the relationship between human forms of semiosis and semiotic cosmology as a whole". But here his preoccupation with the idea of 'psychoanalysis' as connoting (ibid.) "something confined to the human process, something at once private and too linked to a dyadic structure of analyst to analysand", which he wants to "get beyond", has led him into a trap. For the suggestion of 'psychosemiosis' as the "natural replacement term" for psychoanalysis hardly moves us as far as we need to go. Not only is the root term "psyche" too generic for the purpose, even in the context of ancient

Indeed, within semiotics, the open question is not whether the action of signs is broader than any construal of language, but rather how far the paradigm for the action of signs extends. There is general agreement by now that the action of signs, "semiosis", extends at least as far as awareness or cognition occurs, which includes the entire domain of animal sign usage, or "zoösemiosis". This already defeats the proposal Saussure embodied in the semiological model of sign which would have made of the study of signs a variant of modern idealism (the philosophical doctrine distinctive of modernity according to which the mind knows only what the mind itself constitutes or makes[3]). In the model of sign operative within semiotics, every sign consists in a relation connecting three terms, one of which performs the vehicular function of other-representation (and which Peirce calls accordingly the "representamen"[4]), a second of which performs the function of self-representation or objectification

thought (cf. Deely 2001: 85n57); the corruption of the root in modern context guarantees an ongoing misunderstanding. For the 'replacement' of 'psychoanalysis' with 'psychosemiosis' all too naturally connotes the mind-body dualism of modern philosophy as a whole wherein psychoanalysis took root, and this connotation is only reinforced when we try to take 'physiosemiosis' under the genus as well. After all, a "psycho", whether semiotic or not, is not the way one spontaneously describes an individual in whom integration and balance of natural processes is exhibited.

[3] See the Four Ages (Deely 2001), Chap. 16.

[4] A term habitually mispronounced, as my students know, by the Anglophile Peirceans as a consequence of their general ignorance of Latin. In 1992 I launched, by way of a footnote (Deely 1992: 157n), my quixotic crusade to correct the pronunciation of contemporary Peirceans of the term "representamen", which I may as well continue here. Since it is a question of pronunciation, an audial form, and here my sole medium is scriptal, my foray remains no doubt doubly quixotic. Nonetheless, here goes (again). The term "representamen"

(which Peirce calls the "object signified", a somewhat redundant expression, as we will see[5]), and the third term of which performs the function of relating within the signification itself – even when the representamen or sign-vehicle is a natural event, such as a volcano belching smoke, as we will see – the representamen to the significate, thus completing the triad on the basis of which Peirce, following his Latin predecessors (so difficult for his late modern followers to acknowledge) from whom he learned the fact, identified the sign strictly so called with a triadic relation. Thus Peirce, exactly as did the Latins before him, Poinsot in particular,[6] distinguished between signs *loosely so-called*, which are strictly representamens, and signs *strictly so-called*, which are the triadic relations themselves and as such, in contrast to each and every one of the three terms united within the sign,[7] and in contrast to the objects related within the web of sign relations.

The "open question" within semiotics today, thus,[8] is not

is derived from the Latin for "to represent", or "a representation", more specifically understood in context as an "other-representation" in contrast to a "self-representation". In accordance with this etymology, the term should not be pronounced, as by the Anglophile Peirceans, "represént-a-men", but rather as "represen-tá-men".

5   In Chap. 3 below, p. 44.

6   Poinsot was the first author to establish (just a year before the Galileo debacle quite eclipsed the Latin epistemology that had been developing along semiotic lines over the last two-and-one-half Latin centuries) the unity of the subject matter a doctrine of signs undertakes to investigate: see his *Tractatus de Signis* of 1632 (Poinsot 1632a, in the References), Book I, Question 1.

7   See the "hard distinction" discussed in Part III below, pp. 166, 196–97, 200–201, and 202.

8   So, for example, the international colloquium recently held in Germany (Nöth 2001) on "The Semiotic Threshold from Nature to Culture" as the pressing question for semiotics opening the new millennium.

whether semiology is co-ordinate with or subaltern to semiotics, but only whether semiotics is broader even than zoösemiotics, and on this question two positions have emerged. There is the comparatively conservative position which would extend semiotics to the whole of living things, plants as well as animals. This extension was first formally proposed and argued in 1981 by Martin Krampen under the specific label "phytosemiotics", the study of an action of signs in the realm of vegetable life, a powerful case quickly ridiculed, but one which I, initially among the skeptics of the proposal, wound up early defending.[9] The conservative faction in the matter of whether the action of signs, and hence the paradigm of semiotics, can be extended beyond the sphere of cognitive life has rallied around the generic label of *biosemiotics*.[10]

The more radical faction (chief among which must be counted Peirce himself) does not quarrel with the inclusion of phytosemiotics along with zoösemiotics under the umbrella of biosemiotics, but argues that even this extension leaves something out, namely, the physical universe at large which surrounds biological life and upon which all life depends. Heretofore the development of the physical universe as able to spawn and support life has been studied under the rubric of *evolution*. The radical faction in semiotics today argues that what is distinctive of the action of signs is the shaping of the present, and hence of the past in its pertinence, on the basis of

[9] Krampen 1981; Deely 1982b. See the reprintings in Deely, Williams, and Kruse 1986: 83–103.

[10] Three whole issues of *Semiotica* have been devoted to this topic in recent years: Vol. 120–3/4 (1998), thirteen reviews of Hoffmeyer 1996 with a rejoinder; Vol. 127–1/4 (1999), a Special Issue titled "Biosemiotica"; and Vol. 134–1/4 (2001), a Special Issue on Jakob von Uexküll Guest-Edited by Kalevi Kull. See the capsule summary of the matter in Sebeok 2001: 31–43.

future events.[11] On this accounting, the action of signs (or "semiosis") can be discerned even in the rocks and among the stars – a veritable *physiosemiosis*, theoretical justification and practical exploration of which marks the final frontier of semiotic inquiry, "final" only in the sense that there is nowhere left in the universe of finite being for semiosis to be looked for, it having now been found to occur (if the notion of physiosemiosis be finally vindicated) wherever finite beings interact, and so to justify Peirce's proposal that the universe as a whole, even if it does not consist exclusively of signs, is yet everywhere perfused with signs.

In this debate between the conservative biosemioticians and the radical proponents of the correctness of Peirce's fundamental intuition of the permeation of finite being by semiosis the "philosophers of language" have been left in the dust, as it were, of the intellectual race which turns out to have carried philosophy itself beyond modernity and the paradigm of knowledge that modernity embodied as its very identity as a distinct philosophical epoch.

Let us consider this situation, for without a clear idea of modernity in philosophy it is bootless to quarrel over the meaning or lack of meaning in the label *postmodernity*.

---

[11] See the further discussion in Part III, pp. 168 and 203–4.

Chapter 2

Demarcating Modernity within Philosophy

Fortunately, though the means seem not to have occurred to many among our historians of philosophy, to identify modernity as a distinct epoch or age within the general history of philosophy is actually not that difficult, at least not when we look back with, so to speak, a semioticized eye. We need only to consider the defining assumption by which modernity can be sharply and accurately *distinguished*: on the side of its far boundary ("early modern philosophy", in the fashion of end-of-the-century parlance), *from* both Latinity and the mainstream schools of ancient Greek philosophy (setting aside only Skepticism, which is not as much a philosophical school as a determined attitude of mind which can be found in every epoch without exceptions); and, on the side of its near boundary, *from* semiotics itself as a quintessentially postmodern phenomenon of intellectual culture.

I.2: Demarcating Modernity within Philosophy

The far boundary first. The Greeks and the Latins were agreed that there is found within human experience a dimension within objects experienced that does not reduce to our experience of these objects, and that this dimension, labeled *ov* by the Greeks and *ens reale* by the Latins, gives a "hardcore" sense to the term "reality". To be sure, there were major disagreements among the Greeks, and between the Greeks and Latins, over the exact demarcation of this dimension – mainly (as between Plato and Aristotle) over whether the dimension of experience directly and essentially revealed by sense perception ought to be directly included in the inventory of "the real". But *that there is* a reality which the human mind does not make and which is what it is regardless of the opinions, beliefs, and feelings of humankind was, among the Greeks and Latins, a point of common agreement.

The decisive point uniting the mainstream Greek and Latin schools went one better than this. Those schools further agreed that this dimension of reality in its proper constitution could be reached in human thought, that is to say, *known*, not perfectly, to be sure, but gradually, and more and more, an optimism they embodied in an Aristotelian maxim taken over by the Latins and everywhere acknowledged among themselves: *anima est quodammodo omnia*, "the human mind is able to become all things". Nor was there a single formula for this conviction, but many, celebrated in the later medieval doctrine[1] of the transcendental properties of being, that is to say, the properties consequent upon the fact that being and intelligibility, "communication and being",[2] are coextensive (*"ens et verum convertuntur"*, and so also *bonum* and *res*, etc.).

---

[1] A doctrine that received its first formulation, as it happens, when the great Aquinas was but a newborn babe (Philip Cancellarius c.1225/8; Deel 2001: 253 n. 10).

[2] As Petrilli and Ponzio (2001: 54) exactly put it.

Now just this is what the early moderns began by denying. What is remarkable is that their initial denial of the coextensiveness of being and intelligibility was inconscient, a matter not explicitly visualized as such but merely embodied in a common assumption which they never came to examine, an assumption that came through its consequences to define modernity in its epistemological development as *philosophy*, in contrast with that other distinctively modern development we now recognize as *science* in its own right. The fatal assumption blindly made concerned the identity or lack thereof of fundamental means at work in the shaping of sensation, on the one hand, and sense perception, on the other.

Debated among the Latins had been a basic distinction between *sensation* ("sentire") and sense *perception* ("phantasiari"). The debate[3] concerned the formation and role of mental images (*conceptus* or *species expressae*) in consciousness: are they part and parcel of the awareness from its very beginnings in sense, or do they arise only as sensations are incorporated within and transformed into objects experienced as this or that (something to be sought, avoided, or safely ignored)? Positions taken on this question separated the Thomists and Scotists from the Ockhamites and Nominalists generally as the Latin Age entered its final three centuries. According to the Thomists and Scotists, we ought to take note of the fact that only sometimes are objects given in experience which are not present at all in the physical surroundings. We ought to take even greater note of the further fact that even objects present in the immediate physical surroundings are not "given" in just the way that they are experienced as being.

---

[3] See Poinsot's *Treatise on Signs* (1632a), esp. Book II; but this Latin debate took root much earlier, at least as early as Aquinas: see "The problem of being-as-first-known" in *Four Ages of Understanding* (Deely 2001: 341–50).

I.2: Demarcating Modernity within Philosophy

It is not "in itself" that the cry of a wolf is attractive or repulsive, but only according as I am a sheep or a fellow wolf hearing that howl. So perception needs to be distinguished from sensation as a stimulus which does, as distinct from one which does not, involve an element of subjective interpretation to manifest it for "what it is". In sensation, subjectivity, the bodily type of the organism, only *selects* (and prescissively at that) what can be detected. But perception *interprets* what has been selected by *adding to it* objective relations of the mind's own devising. This element of subjective *interpretation* is precisely what the Latins called a "concept" or *species expressa*,[4] the moderns a "mental image", or we today call a "psychological state" or even, in a more current fashion,[5] a "cognitive type". It is part and parcel of subjectivity, understood as what serves to separate any one cognitive organism from the rest of the universe.

Now however much Descartes and Locke disagreed over the role of sensation in the origins of distinctively human knowledge in spawning "Rationalism" vs. "Empiricism" as the intellectual currents internally distinguishing philosophical modernity, one idea that never seems to have occurred to either side was the possibility of tracing a level within human awareness which did not of itself depend upon subjective interpretive responses expressed in the form of "mental images" or ideas. In short, forgetting the medieval Latin debate, the moderns simply presumed the losing side. Both Rationalists and Empiricists began by embracing the assumption that representations formed in and by mental activity are the birth of awareness *tout court*. The further consequence that, if this be true, then there is no way out of objects in their

---

4   See Poinsot 1632a: Book II, Question 2.
5   See "Cognitive Types and Nuclear Content" in Eco 2000: Chap. 3, 123–223; see also Deely 2001: 347.

mind-dependent aspects, no path that leads from objects into structures of *ens reale* as part thereof, no way to justify an apprehensive grasp of *ov* in its character as prejacent to and independent of human belief: this consequence never fully and clearly dawned on either Rationalists or Empiricists. To the extent that the consequence did dawn on the early modern founders, both Descartes and Locke devoted the whole of their considerable speculative genius to evading it. To Kant fell the privilege of systematizing and embracing without cavil the modern assumption whose consequences others sought in vain to work around.

So far did the late medieval debate over the prescissive difference between sensation and sense perception slip from the modern consciousness that, by the time we reach Hume, not a trace of the memory remains.[6] "No man, who reflects," Hume assures us,[7] "ever doubted, that the existences, which we consider, when we say, **this house** and **that tree**, are nothing but perceptions in the mind." Indeed, as early as 1710, thirty- eight years in advance of Hume and a bare seventy-eight years after Poinsot's demonstration of the semiotic character of sensation

---

[6] For a summary of the Latin debates and a clear statement of the reasons for rejecting the very view deemed by Hume as never doubted by anyone, see Poinsot's *Tractatus de Signis*, Book III, Question 2, "Whether a Concept Is a Formal Sign", esp. pp. 309/47–312/6, with cross-references to the books commenting on the *De Anima*, namely, Poinsot's *Philosophiae Naturalis Quarta Pars* of 1635, Q. 6, Art. 1, "Whether It Is Necessarily the Case That an Exterior Object Be Present Physically In Order To Be Sensed", 170a38–177a47, esp. 172b13–173a30, and Art. 4, "Whether the External Senses Form an Icon or Expressed Specifying Form In Order To Cognize", 192a18–198a16, esp. 195a5–46. Lengthy citations from these cross-referenced texts are incorporated in the critical apparatus of the 1985 Deely edition of Poinsot 1632a.

[7] Hume 1748: 152 par. 9.

(in contrast to that of perception) as a naturally determined web of sign-relations linking physical environment with cognitive organism on the basis of the nature of the organism sensing, Berkeley had already been able to deem it:[8]

> . . . an opinion strangely prevailing amongst men, that houses, mountains, rivers, and in a word sensible objects have an existence natural or real, distinct from their being perceived by the understanding. But with how great an assurance and acquiescence soever this principle may be entertained in the world; yet whoever shall find in his heart to call it in question, may, if I mistake not, perceive it to involve a manifest contradiction. For what are the forementioned objects but the things we perceive by sense, and what do we perceive besides our own ideas or sensations; and is it not plainly repugnant that any one of these or any combination of them should exist unperceived?

And so the stage was set for the peak development of modernity, the mighty *Critiques* of Immanuel Kant, who, awakened by Hume from a dogmatic slumber, found it a scandal to philosophy and affront to reason that the existence of a world external to human representations had yet to be salvaged from the sea of doubt with which Descartes had managed to flood the philosophical landscape of modern times. But it did not occur to Kant to reconsider the collapse of the real distinction medievals had essayed between sensation prescissively[9] considered as such and sense perception in its distinctive character as interpretive of the sensations selectively presented by the organs of exteroception but semiosically

---

[8] Berkeley 1710: *The Principles of Human Knowledge*, Part 1, Sect. 4.

[9] See the terminological remarks in Chapter 3, note 12, p. 37, below.

organized there by the nature of the physical factors, environmental no less than organismic, at work in the interaction.[10]

Instead, with the modesty characteristic of modernity, Kant presented us with "the only possible proof" of an external world, by introducing not so much a distinction as a veritable *diremption* between the "thing-in-itself", externally real but intrinsically unknowable, and the "phenomenon" wholly constituted on the basis of representations made by the organism under the influence of these unknowable "things" and subsequently "formed" (in the human case, for zoösemiotics was no part of the Kantian purview) by the understanding itself so as to restore from the side of reason what Hume's analysis had shown to be lost forever on the side of "things", namely, those concepts underlying the necessity upon which scientific knowledge claims an objective causality of interconnections that cannot be reduced to custom.

Of course, one had to be careful. Concepts themselves could get out of hand, might, in unguarded analytical moments, go on holiday. In that case, "noumena" would arise, empty concepts not proportioned to and based upon the "intuitive" representations of sense. To block this other door to the unknowable, Kant arrived at his famous maxim: "Gedanken ohne Inhalt sind leer, Anschauungen ohne Begriffe sind blind" – concepts without percepts are empty; percepts without concepts are blind.[11] In this manner the enterprise characterized in later Greek and in Latin tradition as "metaphysics", to wit, a knowledge of *ens reale* that could in principle not be brought under the intuition of sense, was

---

[10] The detailed semiotic analysis of sensation compared with the early modern approach undertaken in *New Beginnings* (Deely 1994a: 77–88), is much expanded in Chaps. 10, 12, and 13 of *Four Ages of Understanding*.

[11] Kant 1787: 75: "If the *receptivity* of our mind, its power of receiving representations in so far as it is in any wise affected, is to be entitled

shut down – again, with characteristic modern modesty – in Kant's 1783 *Prolegomena to Any Future Metaphysics*.

Kant himself was so enamored of his "only possible proof" of a world beyond or external to our representations of objects that he thought his leaving it intrinsically unknowable was a mere detail. Against idealism, he thought, he had vindicated realism as a *transcendental* idealism. For realism, he thought, the affirmation of an unknowable world independent of our representations was enough – never mind its intrinsic knowability (or, rather, lack thereof). And just this "realism" is advanced today from within analytic philosophy, by Putnam and others, as a triumph of "scientific realism" over

sensibility, then the mind's power of producing representations from itself, the *spontaneity* of knowledge, should be called the understanding. Our nature is so constituted that our *intuition* can never be other than sensible; that is, it contains only the mode in which we are affected by objects. The faculty, on the other hand, which enables us to *think* the object of sensible intuition is the understanding. To neither of these powers may a preference be given over the other. Without sensibility no object would be given to us, without understanding no object would be thought. Thoughts without content are empty, intuitions without concepts are blind. It is, therefore, just as necessary to make our concepts sensible, that is, to add the object to them in intuition, as to make our intuitions intelligible, that is, to bring them under concepts. These two powers or capacities cannot exchange their functions. The understanding can intuit nothing, the senses can think nothing. Only through their union can knowledge arise."

Whence it is ironic that Jakob von Uexküll, the great pioneer of zoösemiosis, took his original inspiration for the animal Umwelt, precisely a world without human concepts, from the Kantian theory of mind; for surely, in a wholly logical world, the study of the purely perceptual intelligence of animals would have been rather the inspiration for the jettisoning of Kantianism in the philosophy of mind. History, as we have seen, has its ironies. Consult "Jakob von Uexküll" in Deely 1990: 119–124; and compare the discussion of the relation of understanding to sense intuition in Poinsot 1632a: Book II, Questions 1 and 2.

modern idealism, as if modernity before Kant were any different in principle from modernity after him. For where is the triumph? Triumph requires a distinction with a difference. Here we have only a distinction without a difference, for the quintessence of modern idealism was to make the passage from mind to nature a "no passage", and Kant does not change that situation at all.[12] Semiotics does – but let me not get ahead of the story.

Let us deal, summarily if briefly, with the claim that an epistemological position consistent with Kantian philosophy of mind can legitimately lay claim to the title of "realism", in order to show that, words being what they are, such a claim can be uttered, but the utterance perforce rings hollow. Of course, modern philosophy from the start has embraced and embodied nominalism, as Peirce so trenchantly put it.[13] Under nominalism, all general terms are a *flatus vocis*, a "vocal fart". So why not "realism"? Why not, indeed. What's in a name? If what passes for "realism" in the late modern analytic philosophy is realism, "bark" is the noise trees make when the wind blows through their branches, or is the protective coat on dogs to shield them from the elements. We are here dealing with a "realism" that is neither naive nor critical, but hollow: *hollow realism*.[14]

Consider carefully the beginning of modern philosophy, the break with the Latin Age as far as mainstream development

---

[12] See the remark of Schrader below, p. 24 n. 25 below.

[13] Peirce, "Lessons from the History of Philosophy", 1903a: CP 1.19. The point was noted independently in Maritain 1959.

[14] In the *Four Ages*, I could only think to call this variant "anemic" or "sterile" realism (cf. the Index entry REALISM, p. 975); but I think the qualification "hollow" better carries the point that it is only by abusing nominalistically the ancient and medieval senses of "realism" that the term can have a modern mainstream philosophical appropriation at all.

would be at issue. As Galileo and Descartes experienced their situation, the new learning, "modern" philosophy, was to be a turning away from authority based on the interpretation of linguistic texts ("commentaries" on secular and religious authorities alike) to establish a new authority based on experimental results expressed in mathematical form, all based on a reading directly of the "book of nature" written by God. At the beginning the two tried, as it were, to walk arm in arm, to stand shoulder to shoulder in a war to delegitimize the mentality and methods bizarrely canonized centuries after the fiasco of the 1616 condemnation of Copernicus in the person of "saint" Robert Cardinal Bellarmine,[15] Rome's own Torquemada of early modern times.

But soon enough, in spite of themselves, the followers of these two giants found themselves parting ways. No one saw it so at the time, but what in fact was underway was the establishment of a whole new enterprise of human understanding: ideoscopic knowledge thematically pursued, in contradistinction to the cenoscopic "sciences"[16] of traditional philosophy which could provide no more than a framework, never a substitute, for such pursuits. The line of Galileans, in moving

---

[15] See the discussion in Deely 2002: 57 n. 13; and Blackwell 1991.

[16] Here I advert to Peirce's adoption (e.g., c.1902: CP 1.242, 1.278) of a strange but useful terminology from Jeremy Bentham (1748–1832, in a work of 1816), according to which Peirce divides science into *idioscopic* (perhaps better spelled *ideoscopic*, a variant I will adopt) – what are ordinarily called the experimental sciences as requiring special experience to determine the sense of their propositions – and *cenoscopic* (also "coenoscopic"), what are dependent on observation only in that sense which is available to a mature human organism at any time. Thus Aristotelian physics is a coenoscopic science, and so was medieval metaphysics a coenoscopic science. But physics after Galileo, modern physics, is rather a definitely ideoscopic science. The ideoscopic sciences are scientific in the modern sense, but the coenoscopic or philosophical ones are rather doctrinal in the Latin sense

physics to a new, ideoscopic base, was to lead to Newton, Einstein, and Mission Control in Houston placing men on the moon and ships bound for the far stars; the line of Cartesians, the line defined by the assumption shared between Locke and Descartes in the matter of the origins of knowledge in mental representation, was to lead rather to Hume and Kant and a reluctant conviction that the universe of reality prejacent to and independent of the human mind is a universe forever unknowable "in itself", in its own being, in its physical subjectivity, as *ens reale*. Modern philosophy, in short, came to play Mr. Hyde to the Dr. Jekyll of modern science,[17] which remained convinced in its practitioners that reality was just what was being revealed and brought more and more under the arts of human practical knowledge, exactly as the medieval Aquinas had expressed it: that the speculative understanding of the being of nature becomes by extension practical when human beings find the means to turn that understanding of nature to use.

Locke, of course, had tried to intervene in the Cartesian and modern development to give credit and credence to the role our senses play in feeding the growth of human understanding. But his intervention was without avail for deflecting the main trajectory of the mainstream modern development in philosophy as a kind of semiotic lapse. For, by accepting Descartes' reduction of objects to representations made by the mind, he accepted foreclosure of the only avenue by which

---

which separates itself equally from theological dogma and scientific hypothesis to constitute the interpretive horizon of objectivity within which the relative autonomy of all three types of discourse can be verified and vindicated, both in general and as each admitting of a variety of further subdivisions.

[17] See "The Strange Case of Dr. Jekyll and Mr. Hyde" in *Four Ages of Understanding* (Deely 2001: 540ff.).

the understanding moves back and forth in its grasp of objects between the realms of nature and culture, considering the last, as Vico said,[18] to be our own construction, even as the former comes somehow from the hand of God, as the moderns mainly assumed.

To be sure, the Latins had only themselves to blame for being consigned in turn to the flames of modernity. A decent interval had to pass before the outrages of the Latin authorities in their abuse of philosophy and theology[19] could fade into the oblivion of that ever-present-minded consciousness of the living generations. It was probably inevitable that, along with the healing of the wounds of that memory, the speculative achievements of the late Latins in illuminating both the nature of the workings of properly human understanding and the semiotic structure of the experience upon which understanding depends and feeds (as we now realize looking back) should also for a time suffer oblivion. But the hour has come to separate in this matter the chaff from the wheat, and to go back over the fields of Latin philosophy and civilization to see what might be retained or rehabilitated in the area of the philosophy of being – still, after all, the most ample of the interpretive horizons ever achieved within philosophy; and arguably the one most proper to the nature of understanding itself as the linguistic dimension of the human

---

[18] Vico 1744: par. 331.

[19] Think not only of the infamous condemnations of Copernicus in 1616, renewed and extended in that of Galileo in 1633, but of the burning alive in 1600 of Giordano Bruno, and of the more gruesome if, after a fashion, less cruel "burning dead" of the Archbishop Marco Antonio de Dominis on 21 December 1624. (Having died and been buried in September of that year, his body was exhumed for display during the trial of his spirit for "relapse into heresy". Convicted *in absentia*, his body was tied to a stake and set aflame. Still, he must have suffered incomparably less than did Bruno eight years before.)

modeling system[20] whereby alone a relative freedom from or transcendence over the perceptual horizon of sensation is achieved within our experience of objects not all of which reduce to our experience of them.

In this task, the work of Kant and his successors, mighty though it be in the modern line, is no help, but rather adds to the chaff in need of being separated. Like the followers of Saussure who tried to have it both ways – to revive the concept of sign and yet leave epistemological matters to stand where Kant left them[21] – so the would-be "realists" of contemporary philosophy (naive, critical, and hollow alike)[22] are missing what is at issue. Alike, these thinkers are *late* modern, even *ultra*modern, but definitively not *post*modern. For postmodernity (in philosophy) is what comes *after*[23] idealism. A postmodern philosophy is neither *realism* in the sense that preceded modernity – "scholastic realism", as Peirce called it – nor the *idealism* that confines knowledge to the products of representation wholly fashioned by mind, such as Kant imagined. Postmodernism in philosophy is precisely the adoption of a standpoint that, like pragmaticism in contrast

---

[20] The distinction between language as modeling system (Innenwelt) adaptively and species-specifically human, and language as linguistic communication ("language" in the vulgar sense), also species-specifically human but exaptively so and constitutive of anthroposemiosis in its difference from all pure forms of zoösemiosis, is foundational to the *Four Ages* and developed throughout it. But the insight itself I got from Sebeok, who sets it forth in several places, such as Sebeok 1987 among others. The distinction between exaptation and adaptation comes originally from Gould and Vrba 1982.

[21] See the *Four Ages* (Deely 2001), esp. Chapters 15 & 16.

[22] The interlocutors in Part III of this work may be taken to illustrate the point, though not as fully as it needs to be illustrated.

[23] Not what went before, even if something of what went before is retrieved in the process.

to pragmatism,[24] essentially incorporates, but does not reduce to, vindication of a capacity of the human mind to discriminate within objects radically distinct aspects. For we experience in the objective world aspects that pertain to physical as well as to objective being, and we distinguish these aspects – fallibly, to be sure – through critical control of objectification from yet *other* aspects that pertain to objective being *alone* and have no reality apart from objectivity. Further, we experience aspects that, while pertaining to both orders, seem to belong as realities *more* to objectivity than to physicality – like the rector of a university, or the pastor of a church, or an officer of the state. The one standpoint that has thematically emerged as capable of accommodating this radical diversity of experimentally objective aspects in a theoretical unity is the standpoint of semiotics, the standpoint of the being proper to signs as able to pass back and forth between nature and culture in first establishing experience and then feeding through experience the understanding wherein and whereby symbols grow.

Like the land surveyor who can quite well, thank you, distinguish in the public realm, and not just in the privacy of his own mind, between the cliffs of Dover and the legal boundary of Britain as between what is physical as well as objective and what is only objective, and without having to deny that geologists have some genuine grasp of the intrinsic structure, the very subjectivity objectified, of the composition of Dover's

---

[24] Here I refer to pp. 13–24 of the "red book", entitled "The Beginning of Postmodern Times or: Charles Sanders Peirce and the Recovery of *Signum*", prepared for The Metaphysical Club of Helsinki in November, and available through my University of Helsinki colleague, Erkki Kilpinen. I refer in particular to what Peirce called (1905: CP 5.428) the "complete rupture with nominalism" required by the semiotic roots and ambience which distinguishes pragmaticism from its surrogates in pragmatism. Cf. *The Four Ages*, Chapter 15, on which the Red Book was principally based.

cliffs; so the semiotician is able to distinguish between those sign relations one of whose arms includes roots that antecede human experience (the case of so-called natural signs, such as smoke bringing awareness of fire) and sign relations whose arms embrace only the human world of conventions and culture (the case of so-called customary signs, such as flags bringing awareness of national states). Neither *ens reale* nor *ens rationis*, mind-independent nor mind-dependent being, are excluded from the purview of semiotics as it comes to terms with objectivity, the fallible condition of the human knower.

What distinguishes semiotics from the philosophies that preceded modernity is to include *ens reale* without being exclusively ordered to or preoccupied with that order of being. Semiotics is not a mere revival, recovery of, or return to *realism*. Yet neither, in embracing *ens rationis* under its rubric of the action of signs establishing an objective world of experience, does the doctrine of signs exclude *ens reale* as "unknowable". Thing-in-itself and unknowable are incompossible notions in the action of signs, exactly as Hegel – that semiotician manqué of the modern evening – said in exposing for all to see the severed nerve of scientific inquiry left by the scalpel of the Kantian *Critiques*.[25] Hegel was an abortive attempt at establishing a postmodern perspective, yet his work remains a harbinger of what was to come, an owl of wisdom who flew

---

[25] Kantian commentators such as Schrader (1967: 188) are quite right in thinking that Kantian epistemology "cuts the nerve of philosophical inquiry"; but they are curiously reluctant to accept the full consequence of that realization, which ought to be the relegation of the "critical philosophy" in which modernity culminated to the museum for the history of discredited notions, along with the proofs that bees can't fly, that flying machines are impossible, or that the human body would fly apart if subjected to speeds above sixty miles per hour.

toward evening. Yet it could not be, that prospective postmodern future of philosophy, in the Kantian line; for the Kantian line drew precisely and rather the boundary of modernity itself in matters epistemological, that is to say, in all that concerned philosophy in becoming aware of its difference (originally not recognized) from the enterprise of modern science.

"Like the captives of Philippi", Stevenson said of Jekyll's transformation into Hyde,[26] "that which stood within ran forth." We may agree completely with Arthur Collins[27] that "Kant's thinking needs no modernization and has immediate application to our own philosophical problems". But the reason for this situation is just the opposite of what Collins would have us think. Collins thinks[28] that since "Kant's radical subjectivism is not a commitment to the mental status of objects of apprehension", this is enough to move his work beyond idealism *tout court*, to make of his work a veritable "basic anti-idealistic philosophy".

Let Collins stand representative for that valiant band of contemporary thinkers who would vindicate Kant as a "realist", a "scientific realist", an "analytic realist", as is recently wont to be said, as if the adjective "scientific" (such are the powers of nominalism) somehow magically vindicated an epistemology irredentistly modern in erecting a "no passage" barricade between phenomena based on representations of mind and things antecedent external to and independent of those representations. Watch the tragic if heroic charge of philosophy's light brigade in realism's modern struggle against psychological variants on idealism.

Here is the argument. Both Descartes and Locke identified the objects of immediate experience with ideas as subjective

---

[26] Stevenson 1885/6: 65.

[27] Collins 1999: 14.

[28] Ibid. p. xiv.

mental states. Kant, to the contrary, separates the objects of immediate experience from the mental states of subjectivity and gives those objectivities a relational, necessary structure as truly objective and "public", in the restricted sense of being opposed to the subjective mental states on the basis of which they exist suprasubjectively as objects. This warrants concluding that Kant's thinking can be "liberated from idealistic interpretation".

Here is why the argument fails. The contrast Collins draws between the subjectivism of Descartes and Locke, on the one side, and the objectivism of Kant, on the other side, is accurately drawn as far as Collins draws it. But the contrast in this particular is not enough to efface the deeper idealist bond. For the 'essence of idealism' is not that "the things we immediately apprehend in experience are realities that exist in our own minds" as mental states thereof (*pace* Collins);[29] but that whatever we apprehend *in all that we apprehend of it* is a product, whether directly (as "ideas" in the mind) or indirectly (as "objects" terminating idea-based relations), of our mind's own working in the fashioning of representations. That the things we immediately apprehend in all that we apprehend of them the mind itself makes (be they regarded à la Kant as objectively opposed to the subject, or be they regarded à la Descartes and Locke as subjective modifications of the one knowing), in contrast with whatever it be that exists or may exist external to and independently of those workings: that is the true essence of modern idealism.

Poinsot neatly skewered this central point early[30] in what were to prove the formative years of the classical mainstream development, only to be ignored on the point by his Cartesian

---

[29] Ibid. p. xiv.
[30] Poinsot, *Tractatus de Signis*, 1632a: 312/3–6.

contemporaries.[31] With idealism's central tenet thus properly understood, no liberation of Kantian thought is possible – as a matter of principle. Kant's philosophy needs no modernization because it is quintessentially modern, root and branch. If the implications of Kant's thought are anywise unacceptable in the framework of postmodernity, that is precisely because of their thoroughly modern character. Poinsot was an evening star marking the passage into the Latin night of medieval philosophy. But his stand on these matters make him as well a morning star for postmodernity as Peirce brought its dawn. Even Frege might have approved, had he been so lucky as to have his logical universe invaded by that semiotic light of the postmodern dawn.

---

[31] Thus the theme of my book, *New Beginnings. Early Modern Philosophy and Postmodern Thought* (Deely 1994a), was precisely to survey the speculative horizon of Latin thought in the lifetime of Descartes in order to see what, if anything, of enduring interest might have been overlooked in the inventory made by the classical early moderns, i.e., the thinkers of the time (beginning with Descartes and Gassendi) who successfully fed into the mainstream of what would become mainstream modern philosophy down to the twentieth century's end.

Chapter 3

Why the Doctrine of Signs Is Not Modern

With Peirce, in recovering from the Latins the general notion of sign,[1] and in advancing that notion both by naming distinctively its third term and by shifting the focus from the being to the action of signs (so that it is well understood that, in that spiral of semiosis[2] we call experience, representamen, significate, and interpretant are constantly changing places as abductions give way to deductions and deductions to retroductions provenating yet further abductions, and so on, in a semiosis that *would be* infinite did not death intervene to curtail the process in the individual case), what we were handed was precisely a new set of categories.[3] This "new list",

[1] Beuchot and Deely 1995; Deely 1994b.
[2] See the Diagram in Part III, p. 164 below.
[3] Peirce 1867: CP 1.545–59.

like the categories of Aristotle, purported to contain modes of being as able to exist independently of mind and able to be known precisely in that dimension of their being; *but unlike* Aristotle's were not restricted to that order of prospective existence, "ens reale". *Like* Kant's categories, the new list purported to reveal the input of mind into objectivity; *but unlike* Kant's was not restricted to the mind-dependent dimension of what is consequently known, "ens rationis". In short, by revealing how mind-independent and mind-dependent being *interweave* in the constitution of experience as a semiotic web of relations whose nodes, reticles, or interstices precisely present to us an objective world *both* natural and cultural in its provenance and knowability, the new list of categories carries us forward beyond modernity and not simply back to some older viewpoint ("realism") adequately presaged in both ancient Greek and medieval Latin thought.

In short, semiotics proves for philosophy neither a question of premodern (though it draws on ancient discussion of relation as much as on medieval discussion of sign) nor modern, but precisely postmodern in its positive essence. For semiotics enables us to see clearly what, for philosophy, modernity consisted in, and why modern philosophy proves wanting when it comes to the analysis of science, language, and knowledge – to matters epistemological generally. For all thought is in signs, and signs are sustained by their distinctive action, which is exhibited in but cannot be confined or reduced to language, as semiology and late modern analytic thought (after the "linguistic turn") beguiled their followers into believing.

Semiotics Is More than Peirce

I pointed out that, in separating itself from Latin tradition, modern philosophy at first made an ill-fated attempt to ally itself with the project of modern science, which I have personified as Dr. Jekyll, only to learn, belatedly and reluctantly, and in spite of itself, that it harbored and belonged to another persona entirely, the pathological persona of Mr. Hyde. The sophisticates of modern philosophy at first were content to snicker at the naivete of those who contrived to believe that science could reveal something of the way things are in themselves. Later in modernity, as the prestige of science waxed and that of the prestidigitators of "the problem of the external world" waned, the philosophers sought nominalistically and vainly to recover their importance, as it were, by borrowing the adjective "scientific" to clothe the nakedness of their attempt to steal the term "realism" without relinquishing their irredentistly idealist tenets.

I have said that Peirce was the first to embody the truly new spirit of what alone could constitute "postmodernism" in philosophy as anything more than a hollow term of fashion bandied about with sound and fury signifying nothing. But Peirce was not alone in rending the phenomenal veil of late modernity. He was alone in being of full consciousness a semiotician, a traveler on the way of signs fully in contrast to the way of ideas. But he was not alone in being a traveler on the new way of signs. There were others along that path, pioneers who saw, to be sure, neither as deeply into the underbrush as Peirce nor as clearly the requirements of the new way, but who trod it half blindly, mayhap, yet surely, advancing in their own manners the postmodern enterprise for those who would come after them and could benefit by their work. Sebeok has called such workers *cryptosemioticians*,[4] and has even identified among them a *primus inter pares*, the German biologist of Estonian birth and upbringing, Jakob von Uexküll (1864–1944).[5]

---

[4] Sebeok 1976: x.

[5] See Sebeok 1977, the discussion in Deely 1990: 119ff., and the series of

I.3: Why the Doctrine of Signs Is Not Modern

It was my privilege, while teaching at Helsinki University in the Fall of 2000, to give some lectures in Estonia at the University of Tartu , but before that to visit, thanks to Kalevi Kull, the very house on the Baltic shore where von Uexküll wrote his celebrated *Bedeutungslehre*, wherein he introduced for postmodernity to savor what would prove to be one of its central tenets: the Umwelt, the objective world in contrast to the subjective universe of psychological states, on the one hand (the Innenwelt), and the physical universe of things-in-themselves, on the other hand.

From the Baltic shore which lay beneath the window of the house in which von Uexküll wrote, I carried in my coat pocket a stone I fished from beneath the shore waters. This stone, thus, carries a twofold story. There is the natural one a geologist might verify. Yes, this is indeed a stone from the Baltic region. And a second story which forever eludes the geologist, the story that this stone comes from within the Umwelt wherein von Uexküll brought to light the structure of experience shared by all the animals, a structure which differentiates them as such from the plants, and which is true of human animals as well. Both stories are true (or false). The Umwelt provides the best starting point to explain the human use of signs in its uniqueness, better even than the New List of Categories handed us by Peirce, even if it eventually leads to them and, as it were, semiotically presupposes them. The two stories associated with my stone as their vehicle well symbolize the dual structure of the Umwelt as an interweaving of relations which reduce on one side to mind-dependent

sessions on "Neglected Figures in the History of Semiotic Inquiry" in the Semiotic Society of America Annual Proceedings Volumes, esp. after 1983. In this regard, the pioneering works of A. Russell (1981–99) on Collingwood bears particular mention. And I would emphatically add Heidegger to the late-modern list of seminal cryptosemioticians (as indicated in Deely 2001: *passim*).

being, and on another side to mind-independent being, but which only together constitute this stone as an item of the Lebenswelt of semiotics today, and of our role as participants in the development of that Lebenswelt within a nascently postmodern intellectual culture.

For I know of no better way to demonstrate how decisively semiotics today revives the old Latin epistemological debates concerning prescissive differences between sensation and perception and between perception and understanding (or language) that went into the formation of the original coalescence of semiotic consciousness, than to tell the story of the establishment of the term Umwelt as a technical term of contemporary semiotics at the outset of the 21st century AD, the first full century of the postmodern era in philosophy.[6]

Umwelt, an apparently German term, has become in fact a technical term within semiotics, and is also destined (such is my guess) to become in its semiotic sense a term of general use in philosophy and intellectual culture. If this guess is correct, then the term is too important to be left to scholars, etymologically inclined ones in particular. Still less is it enough to rely on existing German-English dictionaries to render the term, for the notion of Umwelt as it has come to be established in the usage proper to semiotics as the doctrine (in contrast to "science" or "theory") of signs admits of no full predecessor, least of all one dependent on the thoroughly modern, even "ultra-modern", epistemological paradigm developed in the work of Kant, so much admired by Jakob von Uexküll.[7] For

---

6   For a focused discussion in detail of the traditional sense/intellect distinction in semiotic terms, see Deely 2002, itself the fulfillment of the 'promissory note' in Deely 1982: 117 middle paragraph. To that discussion these remarks on Umwelt form an Appendix.

7   If we look simply to everyday German in order to grasp the semiotic sense of the term Umwelt we do not get very far. Since about 1970,

I.3: Why the Doctrine of Signs Is Not Modern

semiotics has its own epistemological paradigm, albeit under-developed, namely, that proper to the sign; and for the sign, as Poinsot early intimated,[8] the perspective proper to realism in philosophy is only a little less inadequate than the perspective

the term has been used in the political context of German "green" politics to signify the physical environment, which the Umwelt emphatically is not (even though it includes elements and aspects thereof objectively). Even as a German term, "Umwelt" seems to date back only to 1800, making its first appearance in the poetic context of an ode in German concerning Napoleon. The author of this ode, a bilingual Dane named Jens Baggesen (1764–1826), moved in the literary circles of Schiller, Goethe, Fichte, Mme de Staël; so it is not surprising that his coinage (Baggeson 1800: 102), unspecific as it was, yet found enough resonance in intellectual culture to enter the dictionary. "The funny thing is", Frederik Stjernfelt wrote me (in a correspondence dated 24 February 2001, to which I owe most of the information in this note), "that the great Danish dictionary *Ordbog over det danske Sprog* takes Danish 'omverden' to be translated into Danish from German by Baggesen. So it seems that he is the progenitor of the German as well as the Danish version of the word." Hippolyte Taine (1828–1893) gave the term a sociological sense in the nineteenth century, and in the early twentieth century the term acquired psychological and pedagogical overtones as well.

The seed for the term Umwelt in its distinctively semiotic sense, however, was not planted till the early twentieth century, in the biological investigations of Jakob von Uexküll (1864–1944). By comparison with usages existing at the time of his work, von Uexküll's originality in deploying the term Umwelt theoretically to illumine his biological research into the life cycle of animals can hardly be overestimated. Yet while Von Uexküll's work would prove seminal for semiotics, that it was less von Uexküll himself than Thomas Sebeok's reading of von Uexküll that gave the term its mainstream semiotic currency, as we will shortly see. In Sebeok's writings, Umwelt appears principally not at all as a German word but as a technical expression clarifying the requirements for the doctrine of signs pertaining to the life of animal organisms; and it is just these requirements that concern me here.

8 Poinsot, *Tractatus de Signis* 1632a: 118/6–9.

proper to idealism in the modern sense. For the sign performs its task at the crossroads or intersection of nature and culture, as well as internal to those respective realms separately considered. For though signs mark paths variously deep into both realms, the sign itself in its proper being is native to neither realm, always "mixed" in its ontogeny – at least as it comes to be a reflexive instrument within anthroposemiosis, where alone we first and initially grasp it as such.

The thematically semiotic usage of the term Umwelt, then (I eschew here placing this term in quotation marks, for, as I have tried to insist, it is not a "foreign" word, but a term indigenous to the developing doctrine of signs), began with Thomas A. Sebeok's reading[9] of the work of Jakob von Uexküll.[10] Von Uexküll himself (1864–1944), as we remarked above, was a "cryptosemiotician" rather than a semiotician

---

[9] See, for a quick conspectus, Sebeok 1977: esp. p. 193.

[10] See J. von Uexküll 1899–1940, esp. 1920, 1934, and 1940; also T. von Uexküll 1981, 1982. Beyond the bare remarks in note 7 above, I have no intention here to document the historical sources upon which Jakob von Uexküll drew, but only those works of von Uexküll himself within which the concept of Umwelt as Sebeok took it up for semiotics were introduced. Beyond this, I have restricted my references to those very few works directly quoted or cited in the course of my remarks; for my aim here is not etymology or scholarly illustration in the full sense, but simply and directly to explicate and influence the *usage itself* of the term Umwelt within semiotics as a contribution to the establishment, little by little, of an epistemological paradigm "home grown" from reflection directly on the being and action proper to signs as the fundamental and universal vehicles by which experience grows and on which knowledge within experience depends. For this is the line of intellectual development most promising for the foreseeable future of semiotics, at least if semiotics provides, as Locke obscurely prophesied, a "new sort of Logick and Critick" – to wit, a definitive breaking out of and moving beyond the confinement of modern philosophy that resulted from its adoption (up to and including Kant and his progeny) of an epistemological

proper. He did not see himself from within (or even know of) the perspective of semiotics. He thought of himself rather in terms of research in biological science, early ethology, some might put it. It took a semiotician, Sebeok in particular, as it happened,[11] to see that von Uexküll's work, in its central application of the expression "Umwelt" (here let it be for a moment a "German" term, and hence "foreign"), concerned "biological foundations that lie at the very epicenter of the study of both communication and signification in the human animal".

And every other animal, for that matter. For the Umwelt belongs first of all to zoösemiotics, and to anthroposemiotics only from there. In other words, the Umwelt is first of all, even within semiotics, a vehicle for expressing especially the role of biological heritage in the use and function of signs, rather than for expressing what is species-specifically human in the use and function of signs. Now the philosopher who best understood (or misunderstood) the limiting functions of psycho-biological constitution upon knowledge was Immanuel Kant. So it is not wholly surprising that von Uexküll saw himself indebted philosophically to Kant above all in his creative research within biology.

What von Uexküll uniquely realized was that the physical environment, in whatever sense it may be said to be the "same" for all organisms (we are speaking, of course, of the environment on earth, though much of what we say could be applied, *mutatis mutandis*, to biospheres on other planets should such eventually be found), is not the world in which the members of any given species as such actually live out their life. No. Each biological life-form, by reason of its distinctive

---

paragigm which precludes that very intersection of nature with culture which semiotics takes as its distinctive "point de départ".

[11] Sebeok 1976: x.

bodily constitution (its "biological heritage", as we may say), is suited only to certain parts and aspects of the vast physical universe. And when this "suitedness to" takes the bodily form of cognitive organs, such as are our own senses, or the often quite different sensory modalities discovered in other life-forms, then those aspects and only those aspects of the physical environment which are proportioned to those modalities become "objectified", that is to say, made present not merely physically but cognitively ("apprehensively") as well.

What needs to be stressed, then, is the limited and partial aspect of the physical environment of which the organism becomes aware in sensation. When I look out over a rich meadow on a beautiful day, I see what might be loosely described as "an infinite variety of colors". That will do for the poet or even the practical man, but the careful thinker will realize that such expressions are but shorthand for our limitations: we see not all colors possible, but only those that, under given conditions of light and shade, fall within the range of our type of eye. Nor is "our type of eye" the only type of eye. That same meadow will appear variegated quite differently to the eye of a bee, a beetle, or a dragonfly, however much we may suppose an underlying common "physical" being which is "the same" no matter who or what species of individual happens to be beholding the meadow. A rose by any other name may still be a rose. But what a rose is will not be the same to a bee and to a human suitor.

But that is only the starting point in the construction of an Umwelt. For an Umwelt is not merely the aspects of the environment accessed in sensation. Far more is it the manner in which those aspects are networked together as and to constitute "objects of experience". No doubt there are relations among items of the physical environment that have no dependency upon the awareness of beings in that environment. No doubt too that, given the type and condition of my eye, what colors will appear to me when I look in a certain direction will not depend upon my evaluation of anything that is there. If we presciss (in Peirce's usage[12]) sensation as such within our perceptions of the world, it is quite evident that our bodily constitution filters and restricts, but does not by itself determine, what we will become aware of in sensation. If my eyes are normal and a traditionally equipped classroom is lighted, I cannot fail to see the black rectangle against the lighter background that I will interpret as a blackboard affixed to a wall. But what my eyes objectify and what my mind makes of that vision remain as distinct as sensation as such in contrast to perception. Perception it is that transforms sensations into objects experienced, like dark rectangles against lighter surfaces "seen" to be blackboards on walls.

The bee unfortunate enough to fly into the classroom will not see a blackboard. The beetle will likewise fail to apprehend what is so obvious to me, such as the purpose of the blackboard, or of the student desks. What objects will the bee or the beetle, or the dragonfly, for that matter, encounter in this same classroom?

That is the question (or type of question) which guided the *Umwelt-Forschung* pioneered by Jakob von Uexküll. Von

---

[12] Peirce 1905a: CP 5.449: "If we desire to rescue the good ship Philosophy for the service of Science from the hands of lawless rovers of the sea of literature, we shall do well to keep prescind, presciss, prescission, and prescissive on the one hand, to refer to dissection in hypothesis, while precide, precise, precision, and precisive are used so as to refer exclusively to an expression of determination which is made either full or free for the interpreter [in removing vagueness from the use of an expression]. We shall thus do much to relieve the stem 'abstract' from staggering under the double burden of conveying the idea of prescission as well as the unrelated and very important idea of the creation of *ens rationis* . . . but which gives mathematics half its power." See the discussion in the *Four Ages* (Deely 2001), p. 310 n. 125 and *passim*.

Uexküll uniquely saw that the difference between objects of experience and elements of sensation is determined primarily not by anything in the physical environment as such but by the *relation* or, rather, network and set of relations, that obtains between whatever may be "in fact" present physically in the surroundings and the cognitive constitution of the biological organism interacting with those surroundings here and now. Nor are those relations primarily of the type that antecede and hold independently of any such interaction. To the contrary. The relations in question are not mainly between the organism and what is sensed (those limited and partial aspects of the physical surroundings which are proportioned to and activative of the limited range of this or that sensory channel in combination with however many other cognitive channels the organism in question is biologically endowed with). No. The relations in question concern above all how the limited and partial sensory aspects of the physical environment are connected among themselves so as to constitute *objects of experience*, and this constitution depends above all on the constitution of the organism doing the sensing. For it is the interests of that organism, not the "independent" nature of the source of the sensory stimuli, that is at issue in the perception as such that the organism finally acts upon and uses to orientate itself within the environment for the purposes of its life and wellbeing.

In other words, the organism does not simply respond to or act in terms of what it senses as sensed, but rather in terms of what it *makes* of that sensation, what it *perceives* to be sensed, rightly or wrongly. The female wolf responds to the male's howl differently than does the sheep, regardless of gender. Thus, whereas sensation prescissed and taken as such actively filters but passively receives incoming stimuli, perception by contrast actively structures sensation into things to be sought, things to be avoided, and things that don't matter one way or the other. Yet what constitutes a pattern of stimuli as desirable and to be sought or menacing and to be avoided depends less on the stimuli than upon the biological constitution of the organism receiving the stimuli. Thus, the pattern of stimuli, in perception as contrasted to sensation as such, is actively woven, not passively determined or "received". Between and among sensory elements of stimulation, the organism itself weaves a network of subsequent relations which obtain only in the perceiving, not prior to and independent of it. It is the pattern of this network of relations within perception, not any prior pattern within sensation alone, that determines and constitutes the objects of experience so far as they are distributed into the categories of desirable (+), undesirable (−), and neutral, or safely ignored (0). Perception does no more.

In this way, each species constructs and lives within *its own* lifeworld. The whole process is executed by means of signs, but the perceiving organism does not think of the matter in that way. It simply uses signs, as Maritain best put it,[13] without realizing for a moment that there are signs. For whenever one element of experience makes present something besides itself, be that other "real" or not (for example, the danger perceived only through an erroneous amplification in perception of the stimuli of sense), the element in question is functioning as a vehicle of signification, a "representamen". This is why Sebeok so aptly speaks of experience as "a semiotic web", that is to say, a web woven of sign relations, at whose nodes alone stand the objects of experience as experienced, whatever be their further status as "physical" or "real" independently of or prior and external to the experience within which they are given.

---

[13] Maritain 1986: 53: "Animals make use of signs without perceiving the relation of signification."

So it is clear that experience, for any organism, does not simply consist of anything that is "there" prior to and independently of the experience, but only of "what is there" within and dependently upon the experience, which normally includes objectified features or elements that were indeed prior and independent and external but have *now* become as well internal to, part and parcel of, an integral experience strands of which await untangling – both in further perception and, above all (in the case of human animals) by that critical control of objectification we vulgarly call "reason". So, however many or few relations within the experience may *also* obtain external to and independently of the experience, these relationships have *meaning* only insofar as and *as* they are incorporated with that larger network of relations constituting perception in contrast to (while inclusive of) sensation, upon whose pattern the appearance of objects as such depends. And this larger network involves, zoösemiosically, relations which would not obtain but for the biological constitution of the perceiving organism acting as interpretant even of what is given in sensation along with – indeed, *within* – the perception of objects as objects, as it further involves, anthroposemiosically, relations which would not obtain but for the cultural setting sustained by a given human social group to which the individual has been assimilated through upbringing or habitation.

So there is a great difference between an object and a thing, however confusedly the two notions are made to play in popular culture. For while the notion of thing is the notion of what is what it is regardless of whether it be known or not, the notion of object is hardly that. An object, to be an object, requires a relation to a knower, in and through which relation the object as apprehended exists as terminus. A sign warning of "bridge out" may be a lie, but the thing in question, even in such a case, is no less objective than in the case where the sign warns of a "true situation".

So we see plainly that while nothing precludes an object from *also* being a thing, nothing necessitates that a given object *also* be a thing. And a thing that is one kind of object for one kind of organism (a wolf, say) may be quite a different kind of object for another kind of organism (such as a sheep), and for a third kind of organism may be not an object at all;[14] even without getting into the question of mistakes organisms make about what kind of object a thing is or is not,[15] mistakes which may cost life or limb, or which may in the end "make no practical difference".

To say that an object may or may not be a thing and to say that a thing may or may not be an object sound like simply inverse sayings, but they are not. For to say that a thing may or may not be an object is merely to say that any given element in the order of what exists independently of finite knowledge ("things") may or may not *be known*, whereas the inverse saying that an object may or may not be a thing is to say that *what is not known is not an object*, or, equivalently, to

---

[14] In an earlier version of these Umwelt remarks circulated at the University of Tartu in October of 2000, Vahir Puik, "a humble student of geography" at the university there "who is interested in semiotics", pointed out to me that I had unwittingly, in effect, reversed my own usage of "object" and "thing" in writing: "And an object that is one kind of thing for one kind of organism (a wolf, say) may be quite a different kind of thing for another kind of organism (such as a sheep)." The wording changed above reflects Mr. Puik's perceptive reading, even as my original wording reflected the much earlier, more subtle observations by Aquinas (c.1254/6: *Commentary on the Sentences* 1. dist. 2. q. 1. art. 5 ad 2) and Poinsot (1632: 594a1–2) that "'thing' can be used as a transcendental term".

[15] Or, in the distinctive case of anthroposemiosis, what kind of thing an object is or is not! Again with thanks to Mr. Puik.

say that *whatever is known is an object*, regardless of its physical status or lack thereof. And since whatever exists as an object does so only within that network of relations (what Sebeok characterized as "a semiotic web" and von Uexküll called an "Umwelt") indifferently from nature and from cognition (yet according to a mixture or pattern wherein those relations within and from cognition itself tend to predominate in the presenting of an object *as* this or that), we see at once that "what an Umwelt is" amounts to *a species-specific objective world*, with elements of the physical environment made part of a larger, "meaningful" whole or "lifeworld" wherein the individual members of a given species live and move and have their being *as* members of *that* species rather than some other.

We see then how different and richer is the concept of Umwelt than the subalternate concept of "environmental niche". The concept of environmental niche simply identifies that part of the environment as physical upon which a given biological form mainly depends in deriving the physical aspects of its sustenance. The concept of Umwelt, by contrast, shows us how a given "environmental niche" is merely the physical part or lining of a larger, objective, not purely physical, whole which is, as it were, fully comprehensible only from the perspective of the particular lifeform whose world it is, whose "environment" is meaningful in the specific ways that it is thanks only to an irreducible combination of relations many of which have no being apart from the lifeworld and all of which contribute to the contrast between the physical environment as neutral or common respecting all organisms, on the one hand, and parts of that same physical environment interpreted and incorporated within a meaningful sphere of existence shared by all the members of a species, on the other hand. Only things which are objects make up part of these species-specific worlds, but within these worlds are many objects which also are not things apart from the worlds.

I.3: Why the Doctrine of Signs Is Not Modern

Von Uexküll compared each Umwelt to an invisible bubble within which each species lives. The bubble is invisible precisely because it consists of relations, since all relations as such, in contrast to things which are related, are invisible. The objective meaning of each world and each part within each world depends less on physical being than it does on how the relations constituting the Umwelt intersect. The difference between objects and things makes mistakes possible, but it is also what makes for the possibility of meaning in life, and different meanings in different lives.

There is yet another way of putting this matter, one which brings more immediately to the fore the dominance of semiotics as the perspective proper to the problematic traditionally called "epistemological", as well as to the new era called "postmodern". Relations among things always directly presuppose physical existence; but for relations among objects as such, physical existence is presupposed only indirectly. To hit a tree with my car I have to have a car and there has to be a tree. But to discourse about my car hitting a tree I need neither a car nor a real tree. The reason for this anomaly traces back to a little noticed yet fundamental point for epistemology: the status of objects as objects presupposes directly the action of signs, whereas the status of things as things does not (although I would argue that even the status of things presupposes the action of signs indirectly, as a "physiosemiosis"[16]). In Peirce's terms, of course, this is but to say that things belong to the category of secondness, while objects involve always thirdness. But we need not deviate into a technical discussion of these semiotic categories in order to make the point that relations among things always suppose two existents, whereas relations among objects suppose only one existent

See Deely 1990: Chapter 6; 1997; 1998; 2001b.

necessarily, namely, the interpreting organism. For even when the sign vehicle (the "representamen") is a physical mark, sound or movement external to the organism, that which it signifies need not be physical, when the organism is mistaken, for example, or thinking of a state of affairs that is possible ("this hotel robbed") but not yet actual, and so on. As when a beaver sets out to build its dam. So we realize that what we have heretofore called objects, and what are yet commonly confused with things, in fact are, as a matter of principle and in every case, significates. To say "object" and to say "object signified" is to say exactly the same thing. The two-word expression merely makes explicit what the one-word expression implies and – all too often – serves to quite effectively conceal from the one using the expression.

To preclude this concealment,[17] and all the philosophical errors attendant upon the failure systematically to distinguish objects from things, we need only to realize that signs are what every object as such immediately presupposes. Without signs there are no objects. For signs are those very irreducible relationships that comprise the semiotic web, and the semiotic web is precisely that network of suprasubjective relationships which constitute objects as such as publicly accessible elements of the Umwelt shared by every member of each biological species.

In Poinsot's time (the late 16th and early 17th centuries), the distinction between objects and things and the status of objects as signifieds was explained in terms of the difference between physical relations, which in principle link two subjects (or are "intersubjective", connecting two or more elements physically existing), and sign relations, which in principle link minimally three elements of which one at least

---

[17] Which was the point of the 27th Presidential Address to the Semiotic Society of America (Deely 2001e), in this work Part III.

(namely, the object signified), need not exist physically at all, or not in the way that it is represented as existing physically. Later on, in the early 20th century, Peirce would succeed in expressing this situation in terms we may reduce to a terse formula, or maxim: sign relations are irreducibly triadic, whereas physical relations as such are only dyadic.

We see then how truly Sebeok characterized the species-specific objective worlds which von Uexküll labeled *Umwelten* as concerning "biological foundations that lie at the very epicenter of the study of both communication and signification in the human animal", and, as I said, every other animal, for that matter. I think it is not too much to say that, insofar as there is any one single concept that is central to the study of zoösemiotics, that would be the concept of Umwelt,[18] the invisible bubble or species-specific objective world within which every biological organism that is an animal dwells.

But the concept has one shortcoming – is, we might say, as a biological concept, inadequate in one particular to explaining

---

[18] This is a judgment in which Sebeok heartily concurs (2001: xxi): "By the early 1970s, it was clear to me that restricting semiotic inquiry to our species was absurd and that its field of reference had to be extended to comprehend the entire animal kingdom in its maximum diversity. I designated this expanded field *zoösemiotics*. I could envisage the outlines of a fact-finding program, but what zoösemiotics sorely lacked, I thought, was a sound theoretical basis. This uninformed belief, as I soon discovered, or, in fact, rediscovered by the end of that decade, was totally mistaken. The theory was there, in theoretical biology, and it was called Umwelt-research." I beg the readers' indulgence in my not forebearing to modify Sebeok's original coinage and own usage by adding the umlaut over the second "o" in the word, in order to obviate the need for distinguishing (among English speakers) between the study of communication among captive animals ("zoosemiotics") and the more general study of animal communication ("zoösemiotics") without respect to whether the animals are wild, captive, or domestic.

the human use of signs. For when it comes to the human being, it is true but not enough to say that we live in a bubble wholly determined by our biological constitution. True, our body, no less than the body of a snail, alligator, bee, or armadillo, determines the range and type of physical environmental aspects that we can directly objectify; and our perception, so far as it depends upon sensation, is quite bound by those limits, just as is the perception of a dog, dolphin, or gorilla. But the human modeling system, the Innenwelt underlying and correlate with our Umwelt, is, strangely, not wholly tied to our biology. The first effectively to notice this anomaly in the context of semiotics was again Sebeok.[19] When we are born, or, indeed, when our genotype is fixed at fertilization in the zygote from which we develop, what we can see or sense in any direct modality is established and determined, just as is the case with any animal life form. But what language we will speak or what we will say in that language is far from so fixed and determined. Sebeok was the first effectively to point out that failure to grasp the implications of this fact result largely if not entirely from the widespread and long-standing confusion, in learned circles no less than in popular culture, between *language*, which is a matter of an Innenwelt or modeling system that is not wholly tied to biological constitution, and *communication*, which is a universal phenomenon that in and of itself has nothing whatever to do with language, although when language in the human modeling system is *exapted* to communicate something modeled, the result is "linguistic communication", "language" in the vulgar sense.

Thus zoösemiotics studies the communication systems of animals, both those that are species-specific to each animal form and those that overlap two or more forms, including

---

[19] E.g., Sebeok 1984a, b; 1986a; 1987; 1987a.

communicative modalities shared between human animals and other animal species. But language is not first of all a communication system. Language is first of all a way of modeling the world according to possibilities envisioned as alternative to what is given in sensation *or* experienced in perception. When such a modeling system is exapted for the purpose of communicating to another something modeled, the attempt succeeds, if at all, only when the other to whom one attempts to communicate such a praeter-biological content is a conspecific (that is, only when the prospective receiver likewise has an Innenwelt which is not wholly tied *omni ex parte* to biological constitution); and the result of the communication (when and to the extent it succeeds) is the establishment precisely of a *linguistic code*, which will correlate with but in no way reduce to elements accessible through one or another sensory modality of the organism. The intersubjective establishment of such a code, then, is the establishment of a new, species-specific channel of communication, to wit, *linguistic communication*, commonly miscalled and thoroughly confused with language itself. That is why, for a communication to be linguistic, it matters not a whit whether it be spoken, written, or gestured: all that matters is the type of Innenwelt underlying the communication which makes immediate, non-reductive interpretation of the linguistic code possible in the first place. That is why the "meaningful world" in which the human animal lives involves postlinguistic structures[20] accessible in what is proper to them only by a linguistic animal, whereas all the other animals, even when they employ symbolic means of communication (as is in fact fairly common), are restricted to the order of prelinguistic, sense-perceptible object domains (including postlinguistic structures only in their sense-perceptible aspects of embodiment).

---

[20] Deely 1980, 1982.

So the concept of Umwelt applies fully to the human animal insofar as humans are animals, but the invisible bubble within which the individual human being lives as a member of a biological species is permeable to things in a way that the Umwelt of no animal without language is: for the human Umwelt is not restricted to a semiotic web based only on biology. In ancient and medieval philosophy this species-specifically distinctive openness or "permeability" of the human lifeworld was expressed in two related maxims. The first said that *primum in intellectu cadit ens*, "an awareness of being marks the original distinction of understanding as species-specifically human". The second maxim expressed the consequent of this distinctive awareness: *anima est quodammodo omnia*, "the human mind in a certain way is all things", namely, in the extent of its possible knowledge. In fact, that is the reason for the very possibility of semiotics (as distinct from semiosis) in the first place. For *if*, as we saw, signs consist essentially in triadic relations which, as relations, are always suprasubjective and only sometimes intersubjective as well (insofar as semiotic relations incorporate physical relations within objectivity, as always happens), but are never themselves directly sensible even when all three of the terms they happen to unite in a signification may be sensible, *then* only an animal whose awareness is not wholly tied to biological constitution (and so to the sensory appearances of things) will be able to realize that there are signs, in contrast to merely using them, as Maritain pointed out as the case with nonlinguistic animals.

The Postmodern Definition of Human Being

In this way we arrive at a new definition of the human being, no longer the "rational animal", as in ancient Greek and medieval Latin philosophy, nor even the "thinking thing" of modern philosophy, but rather the "semiotic animal", the animal that not only uses signs but knows that there are signs, because as linguistic the human animal is capable of modeling that fundamental reality of all experience which never appears to the eyes and ears or any other biological channel of sense: relations as such in contrast to the objects or things that are related; relations as such as the fundamental reality which makes possible the experience of objects in the first place; relations as such which make possible the difference between objects and things; relations as such which, in their peculiar being (namely, existing suprasubjectively) and (in the case of the relations which constitute signs as such) irreducibly triadic form, are that which every object presupposes; relations, those invisible irreducible, suprasubjective strands of the semiotic web which constitute the Umwelt or objective world in its contrast with and difference from the physical environment as such prior and in some measure common to every life form.

In other words, the human Umwelt is so modified from within by the exaptation of language to communicate that, without ceasing to be an Umwelt, it becomes yet so different from an Umwelt based on an Innenwelt without language that some further term to characterize it becomes imperative. I have proposed that the term *Lebenswelt* should be adopted to express an Umwelt which is species-specifically human, retaining Umwelt to express the generic idea of an objective world which is in every case species-specific consequent upon biological constitution. Whether this suggestion will catch on remains to be seen, and I have rested my case mainly on the three hundred and eleven paragraphs constituting my account titled *The Human Use of Signs*. But while the question of whether my argument on this crucial point will prevail by becoming an accepted usage remains open, the question of whether Sebeok's argument is sound in asserting that the

[21] Deely 1994.

concept of Umwelt is central to semiotics may be considered decisively closed in the affirmative.

The success of Sebeok's argument by itself justifies his ranking of Jakob von Uexküll as "one of the greatest cryptosemioticians of this period" in which we have been privileged to see semiotics pass from the status of abstract proposal to successful intellectual movement, perhaps the most international and important intellectual movement since the taking 17th century taking root of science in the modern sense. Against that very background, indeed, semiotics appears as the antidote to the overspecialization of modern knowledge, and a postmodern revival of the tradition of learning in "liberal arts"[22] which equip the mind to move above and between disciplines in the transcendence proper to the human spirit where it seeks to become "quodammodo omnia", the being of all things.

---

[22] See the *Four Ages* (Deely 2001: 183–86), esp. the diagram on p. 184.

Chapter 4

How Semiotics Restores
Tradition to Philosophy

Well, we have seen the decisive break semiotics makes
with modernity in replacing the epistemological paradigm of
the way of ideas with a paradigm proper to itself (one, moreover, that is far from exclusively epistemological[1]), one which
marks out and constitutes a postmodern trail, a new beginning as radical in its own way as was the break of modern philosophy with the Latin Age in the 17th century and, before
that, of the Latin Age with ancient Greek thought through the
fifth century ad introduction of the concept of sign as a general mode of being respecting which natural and conventional signs alike are but species, specific types or varieties.

---

[1] See "Semiotica utramque comprehendit" in Chap. 6, p. 100ff. below.
See further, in the *Four Ages*, p. 261n28.

But to appreciate the full import of this break for our understanding of philosophy we need to take into account the single most astonishing fact that semiotic research of the 20th century has uncovered, namely, the fact unearthed by Umberto Eco and his team of intellectual archeologists at the University of Bologna[2] that, before the work of Augustine at the very end of the 4th century AD, we find no trace of a general notion of sign in Greek philosophy. The fact is hard to believe. I remember the incredulity I felt on first hearing this report,[3] and the years it took to realize the impact such an anomaly must have on our reading of philosophy as a whole in its historical development. What Eco and his colleagues claimed to demonstrate was that, despite our fondness in philosophy for tracing Greek origins of main concepts, in the case of the sign, the key concept of a general mode of being superior to the division between nature and culture was owing to the Greeks not at all but to one ignorant of Greek, Augustine of Hippo. After Augustine, there will be both natural and cultural signs; but before Augustine, the Greeks had thought of the sign mainly, almost exclusively, in natural terms. The σημεῖον of the Greeks was not at all what we would today call "sign in general" but rather "natural sign in particular". The notion of sign in general was, precisely, signum, Augustine's Latin term proposed just as the 4th century closed to express the idea that the universe of human

---

[2] See the "descriptive note" on Eco, Lambertini, Marmo, and Tabarroni 1986 in Deely, Williams, and Kruse 1986: xix.

[3] That was in 1983, in the course Eco and I taught together in the summer institute held that year on the Bloomington campus of Indiana University. Much later, in researching the *Four Ages*, I noted that even Markus (1972: 66), who establishes the fact in question quite independently of Eco and his group, found it hard to believe that none before Augustine thought of language as a system of signs.

experience is perfused with signs, not only through our contact with the natural being of our physical surroundings in the signs of medicine, health and weather, but also through our contact with our conspecifics in discourse and trade, even in our contact with the divine through sacrament and scripture.

There was no turning back. The Latin Age was born in the perspective of the sign as the pervasive instrument of understanding. It would take almost twelve centuries for the consequences of that fact to be worked through to their speculative ground in the *Treatise on Signs* of John Poinsot, contemporary of Galileo and Descartes, to be sure, but a man as decisively of the Latin past as Galileo and Descartes were Jekyll and Hyde (respectively) to the modern future. Otto Bird was the first to point out[4] that taking account of this development from Augustine to Poinsot leads inevitably to "a new determination of the middle ages"[5] as a period in the history of philosophy. But to appreciate the slow course of the Latin semiotic development, I think, we need to remind ourselves that human beings are *animals first of all*, and animals first of all experience the universe of nature not as things but as objects to be sought and avoided or ignored. Animals make use of signs without knowing that there are signs, let alone without realizing that signs are in the objective world of experience an instrument as universal as is motion in the world of physical being.[6]

In their absorption in the world of objects, the sign

---

[4] In a manuscript evaluation report dated 27 August 1997 that he authored for the University of Toronto Press.

[5] Bird's expression becomes the title for my "Foreword" (Deely 2001c) to Doyle 2001.

[6] The most interesting formulation of this point by far among contemporary writers is to be found in Jacques Maritain 1937–1938: 1; 1938: 299; 1956: 59; 1957: 86. Comprehensive discussion in Deely 1986a.

appeared to the Latins, even to Augustine in making his general proposal, not in its pure and proper being as a triadic relation (indifferent, like all relations, to the surrounding circumstances which make it physically real as well as objectively so, or only objective; and invisible, like all relations, to the eye through which perception sees only related things), but rather in its sensible manifestation as a connection between objects experienced whereby some one object, on being perceived, manifests also another besides itself, perhaps even one absent from the immediate perceptual surroundings, an object only remembered, longed for, or imagined. That objects in order to be experienced at all presuppose signs already at work in the activity of understanding never occurred to the Latins, though that was a clear consequence[7] of the realization that the being proper to signs is not at all that of something sensible as such but that of relation as irreducible to whatever aspects of subjectivity the relation happens to depend upon (as "representamen") for its existence in these or those concrete circumstances.

The privilege of the Latins was first to propose and then to vindicate the general notion of sign. After that came modernity, a new way of approaching the understanding of objects as such still prior to the further realization that objects presuppose signs, and indeed, a way initially developed in a manner contrary to what such a realization would entail.[8] Insofar as this new approach to objects led to the thematic and institutional establishment of ideoscopic knowledge as the new enterprise of human understanding heretofore only

---

[7]   Clear, that is, after the manner of all consequences, which is to say: once it is *further* realized.

[8]   See the details of the case as presented in Deely 1994a, along with the comments of Santaella-Braga 1994.

cenoscopically established,[9] modernity was a triumph. Yet insofar as modernity mistook the new science for the old natural philosophy and metaphysics simply done in a new way ("at last rightly"), modernity introduced a misunderstanding of epic proportions, a misunderstanding which it falls mainly to semiotics to overcome.[10] Finally came the dawn of postmodernity, the recovery of signum in the work of the first American philosopher worthy to be named in the company of Aristotle and Aquinas, Charles Sanders "Santiago" Peirce. He was among the last of the moderns, to be sure; but, more importantly, he was the first of the postmoderns, because he was the first after Descartes (with the partial exception of Hegel) to show and to thematize the inclusion within the world of objects something also of the physical being of nature in its own right — Secondness, just as it is in its prejacency to and insouciant independence of systems of human belief and speculation.

The Latins had uncovered and identified the being proper to signs as the base of our experience of objects. But action follows upon being. The next step perforce would be to thematize the action of signs precisely in order to understand in

[9]   An important way of understanding the trial of Galileo is to see in it philosophers and theologians illegitimately extending cenoscopic conclusions to claim resolution of questions concerning matters that depend upon ideoscopic means to be brought into the orbit of human understanding. In this regard, Stillman Drake (1983: 158) is correct to note that "overconfidence of philosophers in areas they had not studied . . . was what Galileo was really up against."

[10]   Imported into the postmodern context of semiotics (Sebeok 1976: x), together with Peirce's appropriation of Bentham's cenoscopic/ideoscopic distinction (Chap. 2 above, p. 19, text and note 16), the medieval Latin *scientia/doctrina* distinction (Deely 1976, 1977, 1978, 1982a, 1986b, 2001: Chap. 11) marks a good beginning toward the needed renovation. See note 13 following, in this chapter, p. 57.

detail what the being proper to sign entails. And this is precisely the step Peirce took after first learning most, though not all, of what the Latins had discovered of the sign in its proper being. He even gave to this action a name, *semiosis*, as the subject matter whose study results in a distinctive form of philosophical and even scientific knowledge, semiotics, just as biology is a body of knowledge that develops out of the study of living things, and geology out of the study of the earth. The Latins too had demonstrated the necessity of three terms involved in every sign, but their living tradition ended before any had thought to name that third term. This too fell to Peirce, who called it the *interpretant*, and who further saw (without quite ever succeeding to explain[11]) that the interpretant need not involve finite consciousness.

The bare proposal for semiotics that Locke had contradicted his own Essay by making,[12] of course, came near the beginning of modern thought; but it had no influence on the modern development. Nor did it embody any awareness of the Latin past in this matter, save perhaps the bare echo (in the English expression "doctrine of signs" which Locke used to translate his malformed nouveau Greek term σημιω) of the Latin *doctrina signorum* expression actually used by Poinsot in explaining the content and plan of his *Treatise on Signs*. Had the proposal been influential in its time, we would not now be speaking of *postmodernity*, for the mainstream modern development

---

[11] See "The Grand Vision" (Deely 1989). It is the problem we discussed in the opening pages of Chapter 1 above, the "open question" of how far semiosis reaches into the being of things.

[12] Here I can only allude to Locke's coinage of what has proved to be, as it were, the "logically proper name" for the doctrine of signs in its postmodern incarnation. But I have discussed it many times and from many angles (Deely 1985a, 1986, 1993, 1995a, 2001a), as well as in the *Four Ages*, Chap. 14.

of philosophy (as distinct from science[13]) would have been aborted thereby, or itself transformed into what we now see emerging as semiotics. But the proposal was not influential; and Mr. Hyde had many years to live and to grow into the monstrosity of idealism, the doctrine that whatever the mind knows in whatever the mind knows of it the mind itself creates, a doctrine which the late modern philosopher Jacques Maritain, in exasperation, at last proposed[14] should be denied the very name of philosophy in favor of something like "ideosophy" instead.[15]

As early as Locke's 1690 proposal for semiotics, the achievement of the Latin Age in first proposing (Augustine 397AD) and finally explaining (Poinsot 1632a) the being proper

---

[13] Our books respectively downplaying (Sebeok 2001: 8; but see the qualifying note 5, p. 185) and emphasizing (Deely 2001) the import for semiotics of the distinction between philosophy as *doctrina* and modern science as *scientia* passed like ships in the night; but since the full justification of this distinction as a thesis concerning the history of philosophy as a whole over its development before, during, and after the modern period is to be found only in (and over the course of) the *Four Ages* (Deely 2001), I have reason to believe that Sebeok's interest in the point would have been renewed had not death intervened. Most useful in this connection, as I have tried to suggest in this present work, is Peirce's appropriation and application of Bentham's terminology in distinguishing between knowledge derived from instrument-based experimentation, or "idioscopic knowledge", and knowledge analytically based on common experience, "cenoscopic knowledge", as mentioned above (both in Chap. 2, p. 19 n. 16, and in n. 10 of this Chap.), and as I was forced to realize in the course of constructing the Index for the *Four Ages*.

[14] Maritain 1968: esp. 102.

[15] But, except for the astonishing writings on this point of Peter Redpath (1997, 1997a, 1998), Maritain's suggestion so far has fallen on deaf ears, I think for the reason given in the *Four Ages*, pp. 511–12 n. 1, concluding paragraph.

to sign as a general mode of being had already crossed the social line separating contemporary concerns from the cultural unconscious, that limbo for the achievements of previous generations of human animals which have slipped outside the focus of the consciousness of a yet living generation of human animals. So let me try to show how, in refocusing on the sign, postmodern thought has as part of its destiny to recover the whole of the Latin Age unified in an unexpected way by the theme of the sign, a theme which, we will see, reprises all the familiar issues covered in the heretofore "standard presentation" of medieval philosophy from Augustine to Ockham, but reprises them as subordinate themes to that of the sign, which is the one theme which unifies the age as an organic whole. Such an approach goes beyond the "standard coverage", for it requires us to take account of that series of thinkers *after* Ockham which provide the links to the *Treatise on Signs* of Poinsot culminating the semiotic line of Latin development, and not only that series of thinkers *before* Ockham that begins with Augustine.

The Language of Semiotics

The Latin contribution to the heritage today of semiotics is massive — original, foundational, pervasive, yet, at least temporarily, inconscient in the greater part of those intrigued with signs. The situation is hardly static, but it remains true that as we enter the third millennium of the common era, the Latin contribution to semiotics exists mainly as a current or layer within the cultural unconscious, although one which little by little has begun to be brought into the light of conscious awareness beginning especially, as I have said, with the work of Umberto Eco for the world at large; but also, within the Hispanic world, by the publications of Mauricio Beuchot. The contemporary development of semiotics, we are beginning to see, owes far more to the Latin Age than it does either to modern or even to ancient times, which is not at all to deny the singular importance for semiotics of the ancient Greek medical heritage so forcefully brought out by Sebeok[16] and Manetti.[17] Nevertheless, the Latin Age has, in the matter of the sign, a historical mass in our cultural heritage that perhaps manifests its inertia in the improbable reversal of fortunes of the two terms under which contemporary study of signs has organized itself, namely, "semiology" (first and everywhere in the first six or seven decades of the 20th century), then "semiotics" (here and there in the 60s, and now become dominant over the waning band of those who, more and more wistfully, label themselves "semiologists"[18]). There is after all a weight of language, a "housing of Being", an inconscient capacity of words subtly to shade the tint of even the most present experience with the perspective and understanding of generations past, as if the ghosts of those generations were whispering memories into the mind's ear as each new generation learns to speak the words of its day.

Nor are my dates of demarcation, the end of the 4th and the beginning of the 17th century, arbitrary. For if we look at the Latin history in philosophy in the light cast by sign as a theme, we discover something astonishing: instead of a chaotic age going off in many directions, one only gradually achieving a center of gravity in the so-called "high medieval" period and afterward dissolving into nominalism and the exuberance

---

[16] See esp. Sebeok 1975, 1984, 1984b, and 1996, all reprised in Sebeok 2001.

[17] Manetti 1993, 1996, 1997a, 2002.

[18] See the survey of usage in Sebeok 1971; then further "Rectificando los términos 'semiótica' y 'semiología'", in Deely 1996: 300–17; and "Ferdinand de Saussure and Semiotics" in Tasca 1995: 75–85 (also Deely 1995: 71–83). See, finally, "Sebeok's Century", my thematic preface (Deely 2001d) to the Proceedings of the 26th Annual Meeting of the Semiotic Society of America.

of the Renaissance recovery of Plato and the remaining Greek classics, we find a distinctive age of philosophy organically unified from beginning to end above all by its first speculative initiative made in philosophy without precedent or anticipation in the world of ancient Greek philosophy.

A veritable thread of Ariadne! The sign, it turns out, was not only the original Latin initiative in philosophy, as Eco (after Markus[19]) discovered, but (to judge from their bibliographies), what seems never to have occurred to Eco's circle, the sign provides the theme that shows a true unity of that age in moving from the simple positing of the fundamental notion to its complex justification as no *flatus vocis* but rather the nexus of human experience as transcending nature in the direction of mind and back again from mind in the direction of nature .

In speaking thus we take up a theme from a German philosopher who dominated the 20th century with his cryptic pronouncement that "Language is the house of Being".[20] For "language" here did not signify at all what, say, the everyday American or Italian refers to by the vocable "language". On the contrary, Heidegger meant something much more profound, what our American *paterfamilias*[21] Thomas Sebeok explains rather[22] as the product of our Innenwelt or "modeling

---

[19] Markus 1972, for whom, however, the discovery created about the same puzzlement as did fossils in the ponderings of Albert the Great, achieving the status of a pure anomaly which surely (as Markus himself expostulated, p. 66) could not really be as it seemed to be.

[20] Heidegger 1947.

[21] Yet hardly an everyday American, he, but rather, as I have explained elsewhere (in Deely 1995a: 17–26), and as many in my circle of acquaintances independently and easily understand, a putative Martian and (what comes to the same), like Vilmos Voigt, a Hungarian.

[22] Sebeok 1984a and elsewhere.

system", that species-specifically human capacity which results in an Umwelt, an objective world, as we saw above, an arrangement of objects classified as desirable, contemptible, or beneath notice (+, –, 0) insofar as that typically animal arrangement of experience is further permeated and transformed by the human awareness of an interpretive horizon for these objects as specifically consisting of more than their relation to the one perceiving them, and thus carrying a history which imports into the individual consciousness, for the most part unknowingly but nonetheless in fact, a structure of awareness and experience which links the individual with the understanding of the world worked out and adhered to by forebears long dead whose codifications of understanding are embodied in the words we speak, those linguistic vessels which, all but entirely, preceded our individual births and will continue at play in linguistic communication long after we have died.

So the "being" which language houses is above all a historical reality, the preservation in human community of the affective and cognitive links which have their roots in times long past but which define through their presence in the psychology of living individuals the contours of what we call a natural language community, with all the vagueness and inevitable overlappings that result in that notion as a consequence of the fact that the human modeling system, alone among the animal modeling systems on this planet, is not restricted in its communicative elements and terms to sign-vehicles objectively accessible as such to sense perception.

It is from this *point d'appui* that I am here addressing, with an eye to our Latin past, the present development and immediate future of semiotics, in its bearing on philosophy in particular. For if language is, to speak in the accents properly Heidegger's own, a *seinsgeschichtliches Wesen*, "an essence freighted with being", then it is surely there, indeed, in the vocable itself "semiotics"(something that Heidegger himself never considered, even as he was typically ignorant of almost every one of the late Latin thinkers who were key to the semiotic denouement of their age in philosophy), that our heritage lies at once concealed and manifestly present in its permeation of and influence over thinkers wherever the semiotic community has taken root in our nascent contemporary "global culture". Even more so is this the case with the simple vocable "sign". So let us reflect on the Latin dimension of our heritage as it is carried within two simple English words: first "sign", and then "semiotics". What, even inconsciently, do these two simple expressions import into our present experience of the world from the predominantly Latin phase of the European development?

From Latin Signum to English Sign

The ontological weight of Latin history at play in the shaping of our contemporary use of "sign" is conveyed through a derivation directly and immediately Latin: signum. There is a conjecture that this Latin term carries over a Sanskrit sense of "to cling to or adhere", which is probable, but not probable enough to pursue for present purposes. For, so far as it is a question of the concept and destiny of sign that furnishes the foundations for what we have come to call semiotics, namely, the body of living knowledge developed out of the thematic observation and analysis of the action unique and proper to signs (both as such and in their various kinds), we are dealing with a coinage that, as a matter of fact, does not go beyond a rather late stage of the Latin language itself, it being a posit, as has been discovered, put into play just three years before the end of the fourth century of the Christian or "common" (if you prefer) era.

Well, by coincidence, this was the very time when the

move of the capital of the Roman Empire from Rome to the Byzantine region had just been consolidated. This was the time when the peoples who would form Europe were adopting the original Latin tongue of the old empire, while the rulers themselves were abandoning Latin in favor of the Greek language. This was the time, in short, when we witness in hindsight the astonishing split of a single political entity, the Roman Empire, into two halves soon to share virtually no common linguistic tie.

It is common wisdom that the term "semiotics" comes from the root of the Greek word σημεῖον, standardly translated as "sign". As is all too often true of common wisdom, so in this case "common wisdom" forms a dangerous alliance with ignorance by concealing more than it reveals while giving no overt hint of what is hidden.[23] The alliance is dangerous in this case because what the common wisdom conceals is of far greater import for any deep understanding of a European heritage in the matter of the study of signs than what it would lead the first-time comer to that study to believe. For the truth is, the astonishing truth, with which semiotic reflection needs most to begin, is that there is no general concept of sign to be found in Greek philosophy, and the term standardly mistranslated to conceal that fact is σημεῖον, a word which means, in Greek, not at all "sign" in any general sense but only very specific forms of sign, particularly ones associated with divination, both in the invidious sense of prophetic and religious divination and in the more positive scientific sense of prognostications in matters of medicine and meteorology.[24]

---

[23] We shall have to confront this pernicious alliance again in Section 4 of this chapter, pp. 84–85 below.

[24] Manetti 1993; 1996; 1997: 879, 887–88; 1997a.

Σημεία, in other words, are from outside the human realm, are from nature, either in the manifestations of the gods or in the manifestations of the physical surroundings, including our own bodies. Within the human realm are found not signs but symbols (σύμβολα) and, what is after all but a subclass of symbols, names (ονόματα), the elements in general of linguistic communication.

All this will change after Augustine (354–430AD). Too busy in his youth for one set of reasons to learn the Greek language in use all around him, too busy in later years for another set of reasons to learn the Greek language visibly losing ground in the Western regions of the Roman empire but yet dominating the realm of theological and religious discussion, and, in any event, disinclined by temperament to study Greek in any season,[25] Augustine it was who, in the bliss of ignorance, began to speak of sign in general, sign in the sense of a general notion to which cultural as well as natural phenomena alike relate as instances or "species". Not knowing Greek, he knew not the originality of his notion. That he was proposing a speculative novelty never crossed his mind, and, his principal readers being similarly ignorant, the fact is not known to have occurred to any one in his large and growing audience. What was obvious to the Latins was the intuitive clarity of the notion and its organizing power. Look around you. What do you see? Nothing or almost nothing at all that does not further suggest something besides itself, something that almost normally is not itself part of the physical surroundings immediately given when you "look around". There is a tombstone, my childhood friend's grave; there is a tree, the one planted for the occasion of the burial; there is a pot of flowers now

[25] Augustine 397: i, 14.

dead, placed here a month ago to honor the memory of this friend. And so on.

Nothing at all is all that it appears. Everything is surrounded by the mists of significations which carry the mind in many directions, all according to knowledge, interest, and level of awareness brought to bear at any given moment when we happen to "take a look around". Of course, all these perceptions involve signs, the gravestone no less than the cloud. And the fact that the one signified comes from human artifice and the other from nature makes no difference to the fact that both alike signify, that both alike, in Augustine's words, "praeter species quas ingerit sensibus aliquid aliud facit in cognitionem venire" ("over and above the sense impressions, make something besides themselves come into awareness").

So little were Augustine and the Latins after him aware of the novelty of their general notion of sign, indeed, that the novelty would appear never to have come to light before researchers of our own time turned the tools and light of scholarship to uncovering the historical origins of semiotics, of the knowledge that there are signs (or rather, of the knowledge that results from that realization). To my knowledge at least, as I have several times indicated, it was the team of researchers who have worked the fields of ancient thought from a semiotic point of view under the guidance and tutelage of the celebrated Italian scholar and Bologna professor, our friend Umberto Eco, who best brought to light and whose students subsequently established more fully[26] Augustine's incognizant originality in this particular.[27] Whatever be or not

---

[26]   Especially Manetti, in the references cited in note 24, p. 63, above.

[27]   The discovery entered our semiotic literature of today as an anomaly, a curious fact that, like Albert the Great's fossils in the 1260s, puzzled the mind without suggesting any grand hypotheses. Ironically, when

be the Sanskrit overtones, the English word "sign" comes directly and immediately from the root of the Latin term *signum*; and this term, with the familiar general sense it has for semiotics (of providing a subject matter that merits investigation into natural and cultural phenomena alike), was a novelty in the maturity of Augustine.

So there is the earliest and second most definitive[28] landmark in the Latin heritage of postmodern semiotics: the very notion of sign in the general sense was introduced at the dawn of the 5th century ad to draw attention to and mark the fact that all our objects of sense perception are experienced within a web of relations that much later thinkers – Thomas Sebeok in particular, developing a suggestion in the work of Jakob von Uexküll – aptly designate a *semiotic web*. The very word "sign" is itself a sign self-reflexively not only of the Latin but indeed of the European heritage in this area, the

an abduction was finally made and formally presented full-scale in the work of Manetti just cited, the guess missed and, for want of a familiarity with the key texts of later Latin times, as we will have occasion to mention, proffered the wild hypothesis that it was the Latins themselves, and not the late modern structuralists and deconstructionists heir to Saussure, who began the development that culminated in the semiological thesis that there are only conventional signs. See Chapter 16 in the *Four Ages of Understanding*. Nonetheless, the asymmetry of ancient Greek and modern national language philosophy on this point is worthy of note: as the ancients recognized only *natural* signs, so the moderns came in the end to recognize only *conventional* signs. The Latins, by contrast, like Peircean postmoderns, are distinguished by the theoretical means of recognizing both.

[28] The most definitive landmark, of course, would by rights be the theoretical demonstration that the general notion of sign was a *warranted* notion. But "rights" in these matters are, from the standpoint of popular culture, matters of some amusement, when they are recognized at all; were it otherwise, Poinsot would have been from the start, and not merely as a matter of future tenancy, as well known among semioticians as Augustine (or, indeed, Peirce).

very concrete fact that "Europe" was the gradual creation of the heirs and interlopers to the original Western lands of the Roman Empire who took over also its original language. This mélanges of peoples inherited and transformed the original language of that Empire through an indigenous philosophical development that began roughly in the 4th century and continued thereafter until the 17th century, the time of the decisive break of modernity from the Latin Age both in the establishment of science in the modern sense (as an intellectual enterprise distinct no less from philosophy than from theology and religious thought) and in the establishment of the developing national languages in place of Latin as the principal vehicle henceforward for the sustenance of European intellectual culture.

For since semiotics is the body of knowledge that develops through the study of the action of signs, as biology is the systematic knowledge that is developed from the study of behavior of living things, etc., semiotics may be said to have actually arisen only at that moment when the general notion of sign as a unified object of possible investigation was introduced. The mere fact that, prior to such a conception, there were signs at work throughout the living world (and, both beyond and before that, perhaps, in the wide world of physical nature itself, as Peirce first proposed[29] and as has more recently been analyzed under the rubric of "physiosemiosis", as noted in our opening pages), does not mean that there was semiotics in the universe prior to the Latin Age – except, of course, as a possibility, in the sense of having a place "marked out in advance", as Saussure is recorded so well to have put it.[30] Semiosis, Peirce's name for the action of signs taken from – or, rather, forged on the basis of – remarks in the Epicurean

[29] His "grand vision", I have called it (Deely 1989).
[30] Saussure 1916: 16.

papyrus written by Philodemus in the last century preceding the common era,[31] precedes semiotics, just as living things precede biology and rocks precede geology. But biology as a science presupposes that the world of living things be conceived as a thematically unified subject of possible systematic inquiry. Similarly, a doctrine of signs presupposes that the action of signs be conceived as a thematically unified subject matter of possible systematic investigation. And just as the first to give us a notion of sign which raises the question of this presupposed feat was Augustine, so the first systematically to demonstrate the unity underlying that possible inquiry was Poinsot.

Of course, there were investigations of various kinds based on the action of signs long before Augustine. Indeed, we now realize that every investigation is based on the action of signs. Every investigation has a semiotic component or dimension that can be brought out and highlighted theoretically. But that is not the point. Just as any predator stalking its prey relies on knowledge acquired from a study of signs, yet not every predator is a semiotician; so every semiotician owes his or her profession to the fact that someone, in fact, Augustine of Hippo, first introduced into intellectual culture

---

[31] Philodemus i.54–40BC. Manetti comments (2002: 282) that "Philodemus's *On Signs* even attracted the attention of Charles Sanders Peirce, the American philosopher who, beginning with his first Lecture of February-March of 1865, evolved a general science of signs understood as a science of formal logic. It was a reading of *On Signs* that suggested to him the idea of an autonomous science of signs, semiotics, as well as a name for inference specifically by signs, semiosis. This took place in 1879–80, when Peirce was supervising the doctoral thesis of his student Alan Marquand on 'The Logic of the Epicureans', including a translation of Philodemus's treatise". See Fisch 1978: 40–41, for earlier discussion of Peirce's derivation and coinage.

the notion of sign in general, under which notion the particular investigations we call semiotics are brought together objectively in the conception of a unified subject matter of possible investigation demonstrated in principle by Poinsot. There are not only signs as tokens; there is also sign as type, the type defining and distinguishing those investigations properly called "semiotic" in contrast to "chemical", "astronomical", "biological", and so forth, even though we can also say, from the standpoint of semiotic consciousness, that every other subject matter physical or cultural necessarily involves and develops by semiotic means.

Sign itself, the general notion or type (the "general mode of being", Peirce liked to say) of which all particular signs are instances or tokens, then, is the first and foundational element of the semiotic heritage. For it is that presupposed notion which first makes the development of a doctrine of signs possible in the first place. It marks, as we may say, the initial awakening of semiotic consciousness; and it occurs more or less at the very beginning of the Latin Age in the history both of the formations that lead to modern Europe and of that part of intellectual culture traditionally called philosophy. Semiotic consciousness owes its initial awakening, if not its name, to the introduction at the beginning of the Latin Age of the general notion of sign in the work of Augustine.[32]

But what after Augustine? Does the Latin Age contribute nothing more to semiotic consciousness than its foundational and organizing notion of sign? In fact, what the Latin Age began with proposing it also ended with disposing: the turn of the 5th century work of Augustine began the Latin Age proposing that there existed a mode of being capable of transcending the division of nature and culture by reason of

---

[32] See Augustine i.397–426 in particular.

descending into both sides of the divide; and the work of Poinsot ended that age by warranting in the 17th century (with many stages in between, in a development almost derailed, even in its day, by "nominalism") the possibility of just such a being by virtue of the uniqueness among the modes of *ens reale* of *relatio realis*, which was not (in contrast to every other mode of *ens reale*, substantially or inherently accidentally) intrinsically tied to being mind-independent in its proper possibility (i.e., as *relatio*), but indifferent to *just that* being (as, for example, a bone of a dinosaur in its osseity – itself an instance of substantiality rather than inherent accidentality – achieves indifference to whether the dinosaur as a substance be alive or dead).

As a matter of fact, Augustine's original and constitutive contribution in this regard, precisely by reason of its lack of warrant, risked in advance the disaster of that infection of speculative thought which blinds the mind to the dependence in understanding of everything the senses yield upon general modes of being insensible as such, yet as independent or more independent of human whim as anything on the order of rocks or stars.[33] For it is not enough to *propose* the general notion of sign as a mode of being. The proposal needs to be theoretically justified as well. *How is it possible* for there to be such a thing as a general mode of being that transcends the division of objective being into what exists prior to and independently of cognition and what exists posterior to and dependently upon cognition or mind?

This question never occurs to Augustine. For him, as for the next seven centuries of Latin thinkers, the general idea of sign seems so intuitively valid that we find it employed

[33] So I respond to Gilson's difficulty in defining Nominalism: Gilson 1944: 657, discussed in Deely 2001: 386ff.

throughout the theological and philosophical writings without the appearance of a second thought. Of course, the seven centuries in question are not exactly luminous with speculative developments within philosophy. In fact, they are precisely what first the renaissance humanists and many modern historians after them refer to derisively as "the dark ages", the centuries marked more by the collapse than by the rise of centers of serious learning. This was a function of the condition of civilization itself in the early indigenous Latin centuries. But by the time in the 11th and 12th centuries when we see the universities, that greatest of all the contributions to present civilization surviving from the polities of the Latin Age, begin to form at Bologna (in ad1088) and at Paris shortly thereafter, then all across what will become Europe, spreading even to China by 1900, the "constantly alive, burning and inevitable problem"[34] Augustine had bequeathed to his Latin posterity makes its way to the fore. *Signum*: general mode of being or empty nominalism, *flatus vocis*?

The burning question bursts into flame at least as early as the writings of Aquinas (c.1225–1274) and Roger Bacon (c.1214–1292). The first turn the controversy takes toward a generally theoretical development of Augustine's posit hanging in thin air (for what is to prevent the vocable signum from being a sound signifying nothing, like "phlogiston" or "aether" or "immutable crystalline spheres" or any of the countless other words posited across the centuries which turn out to be names for objects created by confusions in thought, objects that, when clarified, like witches or phlogiston, disappear from serious consideration – at least in the modern "scientific" sense outside social, psychological, or historical science) fastens not on the general notion itself but on the question

---

[34] Beuchot 1986: 26.

of whether only a sensible object can function in the capacity of a sign, whether being a sensible material structure was rightly included in the general definition in the first place. For Augustine's posit had two aspects: the general notion of sign as verified in whatever makes present for awareness something besides itself, and a proposed definition that ties this functioning to impressions made upon sense.

It was over the formulation of Augustine's definition of sign that the problem of semiotics first broke into open flames. Beginning with Aquinas[35] and Bacon,[36] then developing after them in the writings of Duns Scotus (c.1266–1308), William of Ockham (c.1285–1349), Pierre d'Ailly (1350–1420), Dominic Soto (1495–1569), Pedro da Fonseca (1528–1599), the Conimbricenses (1606, 1607), Francisco Araújo (1580–1664), and culminating in the work of John Poinsot (1589–1644), this first aspect of the problem received an all but unanimous

---

[35] Especially with Aquinas, for even though he never focused thematically on sign as a question of systematic pursuit, his work is so vast, and problems central to the eventual formation of such a systematically pursued theme recur tangentially to issues he does systematically pursue, that he leaves a trail of tantalizing suggestions to be pursued over the entire *corpus* of his writings: c.1254–1256: the *Commentary on the Sentences of Peter Lombard*, Book IV, dist. 1, q. 1, quaestiunc. 2; c.1256–1259: the *Disputed Questions on Truth*, q. 4. art. 1 ad 7, q. 9. art. 4 ad 4 and ad 5; c.1269–1272: the *Questions at Random*, q. 4 art. 17; c.1266–1273/4: the *Summa theologiae* III, q. 60, art. 4 ad 1. Indeed, just this trail is what Poinsot will follow in bringing to publication three-hundred-fifty-eight years after Aquinas' death the first systematic demonstration of a being common to all signs as such, and hence the first *demonstration* (in contrast to *posit*) of the existence of a unified subject matter for semiotic inquiry. It will be exactly three-hundred-fifty-three more years before this effort of Poinsot will surface as an independent whole outside of the Latin language — such is the slow rhythm of semiotic development.

[36] See esp. Bacon c.1267.

resolution among the Latins: not only sensible objects as sensible, but also those interpretive structures of the mind (called today "ideas and images" but in those times "species expressae") on the basis of which sensible objects are presented in experience as this or that kind of thing, fulfill the function essential to being a sign. A common terminology even evolved, after d'Ailly (or perhaps before, for this terminological point has not quite been pinned down as yet historically), to mark the point linguistically. Sensible objects as such which make present in cognition something besides themselves the Latins agreed to call "instrumental signs", while those interpretive structures of thought as such, those *psychological states of the knower*, as we would say (and not only ideas, but feelings as well, the "passions of the soul" in their full amplitude), which serve to found the relations which make sensible objects present at their terminus as this or that kind of individual, they called by contrast "formal signs".[37]

But this agreement on terminology proved to be but a verbal agreement, which is perhaps why it has proved to have little enduring power beyond the time of those who forged it. In fact, the comity among the differing Latin schools on this verbal point served to mask a much deeper disagreement that became apparent to the cognoscenti as soon as the question of Augustine's defining formula was realized to involve the more profound problem of the very being proper to signs, of the type manifested in the tokens – of the being, that is to say, enabling signs, any and every sign as such, whether in nature or in culture or at their intersecting, to function as a sign in the first place.

---

[37] The fullest historical discussion of this first phase of the later Latin development, apart from the *Four Ages*, is presented in Meier-Oeser 1997: "Die Unterscheidung von *signum formale* - und *signum instrumentale*", pp. 238–51.

Augustine's original proposal of a general definition may have been too narrow, as all came to agree, but at least it had the merit of applying to particular things. Now Ockham and his followers increasingly distinguished themselves by insisting that only particular things are real. Ideas of the mind may not be sensible characteristics of individuals, but they are subjective characteristics of individuals no less than is the color of one's skin or the shape of one's nose. *My* idea is as much a part of my subjectivity as is my shape or size or color. Hence the nominalists could distinguish formal and instrumental signs as, respectively, inaccessible and accessible to direct sense perception, without admitting that there is any type or general mode of being verified equally in the differing tokens or instances of sign.[38] For be it a sound or mark, an idea or a

---

[38] This second and decisive aspect of the late Latin development of semiotic consciousness has so far not been discussed in the literature, and Meier-Oeser, in his work splendid as far as it goes, appallingly misapprehends this aspect of the problem. I can refer the reader only to Chapters 8–10 of the *Four Ages of Understanding* (Deely 2001; see the "promissory note" in Deely 1996a), which traces the complete history of philosophy from Thales to Eco in terms of the bearing that history has on the current and prospective development of semiotics as the positive essence of what can only be called (in philosophy at least, where "modernity" is defined by the epistemological paradigm according to which the human mind is capable of knowing only the products of its own operations) a *postmodern* development. The opening of the new historical epoch, in fact, may be dated specifically to May 14, 1867, when Peirce presented his "New List of Categories". For the list in question, as we have seen, contrasts *both* with Aristotle's original list of c.360BC (by including specifically the objective products of mind as well as the knowable elements of physical nature), *and also* with Kant's list of 1781 (by including specifically objective, i.e., directly and immediately known, elements of physical nature *as well as* phenomena owing their whole being to the mind's own operations).

For the creation, in Peirce's "New List", of an "intersection of

feeling, the former as "instrumental" no less than the latter as "formal" remains a *particular*, not a general, mode of being. The mind in knowing may make comparisons among objects of which it is aware, and from these comparisons relations do indeed result. But the relations themselves, the relations as such, do not precede the knowing: they are constituted by it. Prior to the knowing, prior to the comparison and independent of it, there remain only the particulars, the subjectivities: that is all.

The Scotists and the Thomists accepted the terminology for distinguishing between signs whose foundation was and signs whose foundation was not directly sense-perceptible (instrumental vs. formal signs, respectively), but they also insisted together, against the nominalists, on a more fundamental point: when a particular object or an idea is said to be a "sign", what makes the appellation true is not the particularity of the feature in question but the fact that it serves to ground a relation to something other than itself. *This relation*, not the individual characteristic upon which the "other-representation" relation is based,[39] they insisted, is what constitutes the being proper to the sign as such. Thus the Latin authors

nature and culture" (Sebeok 1975a; cf. also Sebeok 1979) set the problematic of the sign squarely beyond the modern quarrels between idealism and realism, in conformity exactly with the terms originally set by John Poinsot for beginning a systematic development of the doctrine of signs (1632a: 117/24ff.): "the sign in general ... includes equally the natural and the social sign", that is to say, "even the signs which are mental artifacts". And if there is anything which philosophy cannot account for and remain within the constraints of the Descartes-Locke equation of ideas with the objects of direct experience, it is the possibility of a knowledge of structures of the physical environment according to a being proper to them.

[39] I.e., the relation constitutive of the representamen according to its defining position within the triadic relation constitutive of the being proper to sign: cf. Chap. 1 above, p. 6.

eschewing nominalism insisted not only that Augustine was wrong to propose a definition tying signs to sense-perceptible objects as such, but also that the *reason why* he was wrong was not merely that ideas as well as words (and rocks as well as feelings) serve as vehicles of signification. The reason is much more profound, namely, that the relations actually and properly constituting signs as signs (and in function of which the vehicles of signs are constituted as sign-vehicles or *repraesentamina*) are always as such and in every case without exception knowable in their proper being only to understanding in its distinction from the perception of sense – exactly what we assert today when we recognize that linguistic communication arises from a species-specifically distinct modeling system, and that it is this modeling system as such,[40] not the linguistic communication exapted from its distinctive function, that constitutes "language" in the species-specifically human root sense – a capacity more obscurely designated (from a semiotic point of view) "nous" among the Greeks, "intellect" among the Latins, and "understanding" among the later moderns.

Here, unnoticed by any currently established historian of philosophy, the theoretical divide between the nominalists and their Latin opponents widens to a chasm. For the nominalists, relations exist only as mind-dependent elements of awareness through and through, as comparisons made in thought by the mind itself. They exist wholly within and function as no more than a distinguishing part of subjectivity itself actively cognizing – subjectivity: that total complex of characteristics and functions whereby one individual in nature exists unto itself as distinct from the rest of the universe. For those opposing nominalists in the matter of resolving the "burning

[40] See esp. Sebeok 1987; Deely 2002.

and inevitable problem" bequeathed from Augustine, relations are as much a part of nature as are individuals, and in fact are a part of nature apart from which individuals could not so much as exist as distinct individuals.[41] For while indeed in the Latin notion of "substance" there is embodied the affirmation of natural individuals, beings existing "in themselves and not in another as in a subject of existence", the nominalist interpretation of that notion (the only interpretation, it would appear, familiar to the classical authors from whose works sprang the distinctively modern mainstream of philosophy) is completely at loggerheads with the notion as we find it in Aquinas and Scotus or their followers among the Latins, or as we find the notion of substance before them in the Greek texts of Aristotle.

For the opponents of nominalism among the Latins, substance itself is a relative notion; for the individual, "absolute" insofar as its being is one, is yet only relatively distinct from the surrounding universe. The individual maintains its actual existence as relatively distinct only through and on the basis of an unremitting series of interactions which provenate and sustain a network of actual relations, relations mind-independent and physical and essential to the continuance of subjectivity even though not themselves subjective, which link the individual to what it itself is not but upon which it depends even in being what it is. So we find distinguished subjectivity and intersubjectivity: substance, as a relative notion of what exists in itself dependently upon other things besides itself (*subjectivity*), distinguished from *intersubjectivity* or rather *suprasubjectivity*, pure relations as such which actually link the individual to whatever it is that the individual depends upon in its existence (real or not) in whatever way

[41] See Deely 1994: *passim.*

without being that other thing. Suprasubjectivity in this pure sense thus *characterizes* the individual but does not reduce to the subjectivity of the individual. Individual characteristics are thus *both* some of them (like quantities and qualities) subjective *and* others of them (relations as such and only relations, relations *"secundum esse"* in Boethius's coinage) intersubjective; and the actual existence of the individual as relatively distinct from and within its physical surroundings *depends upon* both types of characteristics.

The nominalists denied that these intersubjective characteristics had any reality outside of thought, any reality over and above subjectivity itself. For over and above subjectivity, the being of particulars, some of which happen to include cognition as part of their particularity, the nominalists hold, there is nothing at all "in the nature of things". All relations, Ockham asserted, and all the nominalists after him agreed (including Hobbes, Locke, Berkeley, and Hume; Descartes, Spinoza, Leibniz and Kant[42]), are constituted only in and by thought itself whenever and only insofar as the mind makes comparisons between objects and aspects of objects.

Comparisons the mind makes do indeed give rise to relations within thought, countered the later followers of Scotus and Aquinas. But what makes these relations unique is not the

---

[42] Such a spectrum of authors agreeing on so basic a point is worth documenting, and the first one to have done so in a brief and systematic compass, I believe, was Weinberg 1965 – although Peirce himself, as early as 1898 (CP 4.1), to cite a specific mention of a point that runs throughout his writings, had full taken note that not only is every modern philosopher from Descartes to Hegel a nominalist, but further that "as soon as you have once mounted the vantage-ground of the logic of relatives . . . you find that you command the whole citadel of nominalism, which must thereupon fall almost without another blow".

fact that thought forms them so much as the fact that they are suprasubjective without needing to be in fact intersubjective. Indeed, thought is able to form comparative relations only because the understanding has already recognized *in actu exercito* intersubjectivity as a feature of the reality of the physical world, the order of things in the experience of the physical aspects of our surroundings. On the basis of our experience of such features the mind can go on to make comparisons of its own. These further comparisons, like relations in nature, will be "between" objects as linking one to the other, but with this difference: relations between individuals in the physical environment cannot exist *except* as intersubjective, whereas relations fashioned by thought, always interobjective, yet may or may not be intersubjective in fact, inasmuch as one or the other term of such a relation either may not exist at all, or may not exist in the manner that thought presents it to exist. I may be mistaken about who my father is, even though there is no question that in fact I have a father. That is the whole and only difference between mind-dependent and mind-independent relations insofar as they are relations, but a difference that reveals a distinctive feature of pure relations as such that will prove crucial for understanding how signs are possible.[43] While every pure relation exists as such over and above whatever subjectivity the relation depends upon in order to actually exist here and now, only some relations are in fact *intersubjective*. Therefore the feature essential to and constitutive of the purely relative as such is not intersubjectivity in fact but *suprasubjectivity* in principle.

If that is so, and every sign consists in a relation as such,

---

[43] Perhaps it is not too much to say that grasping the semiotic bearing of this point is what constitutes the originality of Poinsot's *Tractatus* of 1632a.

then every sign as such serves to link an individual to something that is other than itself, *whether or not this other signified actually exists in any physical sense as a subjectivity in its own right*. The implications of this point are not only enormous, they are decisive for semiotics. The point enables us to see, in the first place, how signs can be used indifferently to lie, to blunder, or to express some truth and achieve some victory: the situation depends upon factors wholly external to the sign relation as such, just as my being or not being an uncle is quite independent of anything I do. But perhaps the most interesting theoretical implication of this last point developed among the Latins, tentatively with the Conimbricenses and Araújo, definitively with Poinsot and, after him and independently, with Peirce, is the implication that the relations in which signs consist according to their proper being as signs differ from physical relations in nature in having of necessity (or "in principle") three terms united rather than only two. In other words, it suffices for intersubjective instances of relation to be dyadic, whereas the suprasubjective instantiations of relations as signs (which realize the indifference in the nature of relation to provenance from physical being as such) must always be triadic. A car can hit a tree only if there is a tree there to be hit; but a sign can warn a bridge is out whether or not the bridge is out, or, for that matter, whether or not there is even a bridge there at all where the sign "leads us to believe" there is a defective one!

Semiotic consciousness, thus, had its beginning in the time of Augustine, at the turn of the 5th century; but its principal development as a theoretical theme did not occur until much later, beginning with Aquinas and Roger Bacon in the 13th century and continuing thereafter right down to the time of Galileo and Descartes, when it found its theoretical vindication in the early 17th century work of John Poinsot. This main period of theoretical development occurred in two phases, both of which have been identified only in the most recent times, and both of which in consequence have only begun to be explored in depth.

The first stage occurs between Aquinas and Ockham, or perhaps rather d'Ailly, when it comes clearly to be recognized that the being proper to signs need not be directly perceptible to sense, a recognition that culminates in the linguistic marker of the "formal/instrumental sign" distinction. The second stage occurs between Soto and Poinsot, when it comes clearly to be recognized that the being proper to signs not only need not but *cannot* be directly perceived by sense, for the reason that this being is constituted not by any subjective characteristic as such upon which a relation happens to depend existentially (such as the shape of an object perceived or the timbre of a sound heard) but by the very relation itself which, as suprasubjective – as over and above its mayhap sense-perceptible occasion of existing o mayhap not (its "foundation" in the Latin sense[44]) – is *never* itself sense-perceptible, and need not even be intersubjective. It follows from this that sign relations, that is to say, the relations in which the being proper to signs as such consists (or, simply, in which signs most formally and properly speaking consist), must also be triadic and never merely dyadic; and this remains true even when the sign happens to relate actually existing physical subjectivities, for actuality in that sense depends upon factors wholly extrinsic to the sign-relation as such.

---

[44] This sense needs to be specified, for "foundation" and "ground" are fairly enough often taken synonymously; but "ground" in the sense Peirce gives it conveys the diverse conception the Latins termed rather "formal object", and clarity on this difference in sense is essential to avoid seriously misleading confusions in the development of the doctrine of signs today. See the Index entries for these various terms in the *Four Ages* (Deely 2001).

It further follows that signs are never mere individual things but exist only insofar as individual beings are involved with things other than themselves, and this with "others" both actually existing and only possibly existing or once having existed (as in the case of dead parents) or only thought mistakenly to exist or have existed (as in the case of inquisitors charged with the detection of witches). The sign, it turns out, is not merely an object linking another object in thought, but that upon which every object depends in order to be in thought at all, whether truly or falsely. And the understanding of all of this depends initially on the doctrine of relation which the Latins inherited from Aristotle's discussion of categories of physical being. But the Latins expanded upon Aristotle's terse text enormously,[45] especially under the pressure of seeking to come to terms with "the burning and inevitable problem" (or rather nest of problems) which Augustine, in his ignorance of Greek, had so casually handed them with his naive, innocent proposal of sign as a genus to which culture no less than nature contributes species.

In this way we find that, as it belongs to the cultural heritage of the species anthropos, semiotic consciousness is an originally and indigenously Latin development, first made possible thematically at the outset of the Latin Age by

---

[45] This can be seen most readily in their subsumption of Aristotle's categorical relation, the *relatio praedicamentalis seu realis*, together with the thought-constituted relation, *relatio rationis*, under the more general rubric of *relatio secundum esse*, together with their setting of this general mode of being in contrast with the order of subjectivity *tout court* subsumed under the rubric of *relatio transcendentalis seu secundum dici*, which latter expression conveyed the requirement both for discourse and for physical existence that substances (subjectivities or "absolute" beings) be always in interactions and pure relations with their surroundings either to be or to be understood. See esp. the "Second Preamble" of Poinsot's 1632a *Tractatus*.

Augustine's naive posit, but first reduced systematically to its theoretical ground in the being proper to relation by John Poinsot's *Treatise on Signs*, a work brought to print as the Latin Age is nearing its end, and thereafter lost for more than three centuries in the language that bid fair to become its tomb.

How recent is this discovery of the crucial role of the Latin past for semiotics as a postmodern development, and how far we have to go to achieve something like a general appreciation of that crucial role, may be garnered obliquely from the fact that, even as the 20th century ended, distinguished figures in the nascent field of semiotics who name their ancestry appear routinely ignorant of more than half of the Latin names brought up in this discussion, including most glaringly that of John Poinsot, who stands easily without peer in uncovering the foundations in being itself of the semiotic consciousness which Augustine may have introduced thematically but which proves on sufficient further investigation to be the consciousness most distinctive of the human animal. It is not as "rational" that the human being finds its distinctive flourishing nearly so much as it is as signifying. This is why, in our last chapter, we went so far as to say that semiotics as an essentially postmodern development carries within it the implication of a new definition of the human being. Even as Descartes introduced modernity by replacing the ancient definition of human being as *animal rationale* with the modern formula, *res cogitans*, so the advent of semiotics at once transcends modernity in the direction of the past even as it surpasses modernity in the direction of a future in which the "thinking thing" becomes rather once again an animal, the animal *semeioticum*. I turn to my second terminological point, my second "essence freighted with being".

Where Is the Latin in the English Word "Semiotics"?
Here I will not repeat even in substance the several times,

nearing a baker's dozen,[46] inspired by the seminal essay of Romeo,[47] that I have explored in detail Locke's introduction of the vocable σημιωτική, an only apparently Greek word, mis-spelled at that, as it turns out, into the concluding English paragraphs (so brief is his final chapter[48]) of his *Essay concerning Humane Understanding* of 1690, which propounds in its body an epistemological theory that is anything but hospitable to or compatible with this alternative development he concludes by suggesting[49] – namely, the "way of signs", as I think it should be called.

Let us cut to the chase, and reach our main conclusions.

We have seen that if we take the English word "sign" and ask where it comes from, the answer is that it comes from the *signum* of Augustine of Hippo, the first thinker of record to forge a general notion of sign as a genus (we might even say "genius") to which natural and cultural phenomena alike are species.

But "semiotics" as an English word is more problematic. Surely its derivation is Greek, as at least learned common sense can divine from its very alphabetic formation.[50] But here common sense, as is usual even with learned common wisdom, relies on a secret covenant with ignorance. What investigation of the matter shows is that the linguistic formation in question comes about from a kind of bastard Greek coinage

---

[46] Deely 1977; 1978; 1982; 1985a; 1986; 1990a; 1993; 1994a: 109–143; 1994b; 2001: 590–607; and 2002a forthcoming.

[47] Romeo 1977.

[48] The whole of Locke's chapter from the original edition of his *Essay* is photographically reproduced in Deely 1994a: 112, and again at the opening of Deely 1993.

[49] I would refer the reader to the Allen–Deely exchange in *The American Journal of Semiotics* 11.3/4 (Allen 1994: 23–31; Deely 1994c: 33–37).

[50] See the remarks on this point by the "would-be realist" in Part III of this book, p. 164 below; and see above, p. 63f.

actually made by the Englishman John Locke when he pro-
poses Σημιωτική as a one-word equivalent of the English
expression, "doctrine of signs" – itself an expression not merely redolent of but exactly translating, almost to a point of
proving an exception to Hill's dictum on the non-existence of
perfect synonyms, the older and well-established Latin formula central to the work of Poinsot and his Latin forebears:
doctrina signorum. Locke's term may have come only indirectly, as Romeo persuasively urges,[51] from a Greek medical dictionary. Be that as it may, it remains that the term as it appears
in Locke is malformed. By the applicable requirements of
Greek orthography, it should have had an epsilon separating
the mu from the iota, which it did not. Nor can this malformation be dismissed as a printer's error; for, in every subsequent edition of the *Essay* prepared by Locke prior to his
being overtaken by the boundary of time and made a definitively *past* author, the original malformation is meticulously
maintained.[52]

Now it is curious that *"semiotics" is not a straight transliteration of Locke's Greek malformation.* What is a straight transliteration of the Greek malformation Locke introduced, however,
is the Latin term *"semiotica"*, which no Latin author ever used.
So the term, a Greek malformation in Locke's Essay, is in effect
a neologism in Latin transliteration. But the term means in
English "the doctrine of signs", according to the only definition Locke provided in his original introduction of and comment upon the would-be Greek term.

The reason that this detour through the nonexistent Latin

---

[51] Romeo 1977: 43 and *passim.*

[52] I have actually verified this through combined holdings of the
Library of Congress and the libraries of the Smithsonian Institution,
both in Washington, DC: see the detailed discussion in Deely 2002a,
forthcoming.

transliteration of Locke's Greek malformation is interesting is because "semiotica" as Latin neologism would be a neuter plural name that could only be translated into English as "semiotics". Professional linguists have been careful to point out that there is in English a class of "-ics" words which do not conform to the usual rule that an English noun is made plural by adding an "s" to its ending.[53] By this reckoning, "semiotics" is not the plural form of "semiotic". Nonetheless, "semiotics" is the direct English transliteration of the Latin "semiotica", which in turn is the direct transliteration of the Greek malformation Locke introduced into the closing chapter of his Essay, and *would* be a true English plural if taken from the Latin.

So a Latin, rather than a Greek, background proves etymologically decisive for sign and semiotics alike as terms expressing postmodern notions, despite Locke's conscious choice of the Greek root (*sem-*) for the notion of "natural sign" (*semeion*) in his one-word summation or name (*semiotike*) for the doctrine of signs.

Of course, the Greek philosophical contribution to what would eventually take form in contemporary culture as an explicit attempt to develop the doctrine of signs can hardly be underestimated, particularly in Aristotle's doctrine of categories – for example, with his sharp development of the contrast between subjective being in the doctrine of substance (what Poinsot clarified long-standing Latin usage by terming *transcendental relation*,[54] which is not really relation at all but

---

[53] "At least a part of the confusion which learners experience in handling the -ics words ... is caused by the fact that no dictionary makes clear that the final -s in these words, no matter what its origin, is not identical with the familiar plural morpheme of nouns which happens to be homonymous with it" (Hill 1948).

[54] Actually *relatio transcendentalis seu relatio secundum dici*, since in fact we know of no case where Poinsot spoke or wrote a word of English.

subjective being itself viewed in terms of its existential and ontological dependencies upon the surroundings), and supra-subjective being in the doctrine of relation (which Poinsot followed Aquinas in terming *ontological relation*[55]). But it remains that it is first in the late 4th century Latin of Augustine that the general notion of sign appears, and that it is first in the early 17th century Latin of Poinsot that this general notion is decisively fully vindicated as more than a nominalism. Contemporaneously, the Latin Age itself recedes into the shadows of times past as modern philosophers with their nominalistic doctrine of ideas as the self-representing objects of direct experience take control of European intellectual development in philosophy.

Peirce's Privileged Purchase

By the time Charles Peirce passed from the status of future, that is, not yet living, to the status of present contributor to philosophical discussion, the richness of the Latin notion of *signum*, its origin, development, and vindication over the 1200 or so years of the Latin Age had passed into oblivion, forgotten to all present contributors to the discussion of philosophy. Peirce in this matter, fortunately for us all, proved not to be a typical modern. He did not contemn the past of philosophy, in particular its Latin past. He undertook instead to explore it.[56] And, though his exploration did not reach as

---

[55] Again actually: *relatio secundum esse*, the expression Boethius originally introduced to express *relatio realis* in the restrictively categorial sense proposed by Aristotle, now expanded to cover equally all *relationes* in the being proper to them as *relationes*, be it from nature or from thought (*"sive naturae sive cognitionis"*).

[56] The matter has been documented in Beuchot and Deely 1995. And I suggest that one of the most telling results of Peirce's forays into the late Latin jungle was his singular "ethics of terminology": see Peirce 1903; Deely 1998a, or 2001: 662–67.

far as the work of Poinsot, they did bring him as far as Poinsot's principal teachers and immediate predecessors in the matter of the doctrine of signs, Thomas Aquinas, Duns Scotus, and the Conimbricenses.

As a result, Peirce was able to recover the Latin notion of *signum* very nearly at the point where the Latins had left it, that is to say, at the point where it had been realized and definitively explained that signs strictly speaking are not their sensible or psychological vehicles ("representamina"), but that such a vehicle, loosely called a "sign" (especially in the case where it is a sensible object), is but the subjective foundation or ground[57] (the vehicle, we might say) for an irreducibly triadic relation which, in its proper being, is not subjective but suprasubjective in linking its subject term to a terminus or object signified as represented to some observer or interpretant, prospective or actual in its subjective being; and which, as a relation, is indifferent to passing back and forth between psychological and material vehicles of conveyance as well as between nature and culture, in the spiral of infinite or quasi-infinite semiosis, as we will see.[58] Thus, while both the sign vehicle and the observer when actual are subjective beings, the sign itself is always and irreducibly suprasubjective. And the "object signified", or (simply) significate of the sign, is itself always and irreducibly sustained as the direct terminus of a triadic relation regardless of whether it has any subjective being at all as an immediate part of its objective being (its "objectivity", or status as signified).

If the most important development for the immediate future of philosophy (and perhaps for intellectual culture as a whole) is to be, as I believe, the realization of the centrality of the doctrine of signs to the understanding of being and

---

[57] With the caveat entered in n. 44, p. 81 above.
[58] In Part III, p. 164 diagram, below.

experience for human animals, the realization of the presupposed character of signs and the action of signs to the very objects, structure, and texture of experience as containing and manifesting to us equally *entia realia* and *entia rationis* intertwined, then Peirce's recovery of the notion of signum from the Latins may be said to have marked the beginning of a new age in philosophy. By overcoming the forgottenness of *signum*, the veritable *Zeichensvergessenheit* of modernity (as including Heidegger in this particular), Peirce also destroyed the common foundation upon which the mainstream modern philosophers (from Descartes and Locke to Kant in the classical phase, continuing to Husserl and Wittgenstein, the analytic philosophers and phenomenologists in our own day) had constantly built. There are some today, it is true, who embrace modern philosophy's culminating doctrine that only the mind's own constructions are properly said to be known, ones whose followers have yet tried to coin and appropriate the phrase "postmodern" to advertise their stance. But the vain appropriation cannot conceal the stipulation which guarantees that these would-be postmoderns are nothing more than remnant survivors of a dying age, not even the last of the moderns, but rather the "ultramoderns".

The future, in philosophy and in intellectual culture more broadly conceived, belongs nonetheless to semiotics, the clearest positive marker we have of the frontier which makes modernity be to the postmodern epoch what Latinity was to philosophy's modern future in the time of Galileo and Descartes – though this time, as the joint work of Williams and Pencak[59] has notably shown, we will hardly be able to repeat Descartes' mistake of counting history as nothing.

---

[59] See Williams and Pencak 1991; Williams 1983, 1984, 1985, 1985a, 1985b, 1990, 1990a, 1991; and Pencak 1993.

Chapter 5

Classical Antiquity and Semiotics

W hat about the Greek world before the coming of *signum*? Is Eco's discovery really credible? Of course, we can not pretend in this small compass to resume in detail the whole of the Greek world of antiquity and philosophy's birth, such as Manetti accomplished or even as was essayed in Part I of the *Four Ages*. Suffice to say here that, glancingly in Plato and thematically in Aristotle's discussion of relation among the categories, we find the beginnings of the solution of the mystery of how there can be a being as at home in fiction as in fact, in nature as in culture, in psychological states as in physical structures.

It remains that, when we look back from the present to those two ancient ages of understanding when the development of philosophy was carried first by the Greek language and then by the Latin, the general notion of sign amounts to the first Latin initiative in philosophy. Even as the age of modernity began in the early 17th century, the Latin Age as an organic whole ended in speculatively justifying the general notion of sign with the promulgation of which that age had begun, the general notion of sign we today take for granted as the badge of postmodernity, the birthright of semiotics.

In the ancient world, as might be considered indirectly indicated from a survey of its more prominent philosophical features, the notion of "sign" was neither a central notion nor even the general notion that has become central to establishing the contrast of postmodern with modern thought.[1] The

---

[1] The 1846 first American ed. of Liddell & Scott's *Greek-English Lexicon* enters three fields or ranges of usage under the entry for Σημεῖον (p. 1341). First: a mark by which something is known; a sign from the gods, an omen; a signal to do a thing; a standard; a device or badge; a signal, watchword or war cry. Second: a sign or proof. Third: a point. The 9th English ed. of the same lexicon (p. 1593) expands upon these three ranges as follows. First: mark by which a thing is known; sign from the gods, omen; sign or signal made by flags to do a thing; standard or flag; landmark, boundary, limit; device upon a shield or figure-head upon ships; signet on a ring; watch-word, war-cry; a birthmark or distinguishing feature. Second: sign, token, indication of anything that is or is to be; in reasoning a sign or proof, an instance or example; a probable argument in the logic of Aristotle, an observable basis of inference to the unobserved in Stoic and Epicurean philosophy; in medicine symptom; shorthand symbols; critical mark. Third: a mathematical point, instant, unit of time.

In this threefold range, notice first the absence of any usage that pertains to a general theoretical discussion of sign. Notice further that the few examples of usage designating cultural phenomena as signs are examples of cultural items that function indexically, the way that medical symptoms function. Notice finally that the examples adduced from theoretical contexts of discussion are just those I emphasized in (in the *Four Ages*) in Aristotelian, Stoic, and Epicurean logic.

In ancient Greek usage, thus, a sign appears at most as a type of phenomenon among and contrasting with other types, never in the theoretical guise of a general mode of being ranging across and into

notion of sign whereby Peirce, borrowing from the Latins, is able to mark the initiation of yet a fourth age of human understanding, one as discontinuous with modernity in its epistemological thrust as modernity was from Latin times, is nowhere to be found in the original Greek florescence of philosophy. We have made this point using the authority of the celebrated Liddell and Scott *Greek-English Lexicon* in the last footnote, but the point is perhaps even better illustrated by consulting the work of Cicero,[2] who, after all, created the main original Latin version of the ancient Greek philosophical vocabulary four centuries before Augustine will take up his pen. Cicero's use of the term *signum* in his Latin writings and translations from Greek reflects the same practical, naturalistic, and divinatory particular usages mirrored so many centuries later from ancient Greek writings in the Liddell and Scott *Lexicon*.

Among the Greeks, we may close with the reminder that, when we look to usage in theoretical texts, the sign belonged all but exclusively to the natural world, and was regarded as belonging above all to the province of medicine and the forecasting of weather (or of science in the modern sense, we

which all other types of phenomena enter, as Augustine will be the first to suggest and Poinsot the first finally to explain sign to be for the medieval Latin usage. Postmodern times begin only when the Latin conception is not merely recovered but its consequences first developed and explored theoretically in the pioneering studies of Peirce. "From sign as an object among other objects to that which every object presupposes" is a fair summary of the semiotic trajectory along which philosophy traverses the centuries of speculation from ancient to postmodern times, the trajectory according to which we plot the "one long argument" which is the work titled *Four Ages of Understanding*.

[2] Compare the Liddell and Scott σημεῖον entry with the entry "Signum" in Merguet's *Lexikon zu den Philosophischen Schriften Cicero's*, Vol. III, pp. 534–36.

could say, had the Greeks clearly conceived of science in that sense), whence, even though a notion of sign played a major role in the epistemological positions debated between the Stoics and Epicureans,[3] the sign as conceived in and central to that debate was not "sign in general", as verified alike in cultural and natural phenomena, but only "sign in particular", as instantiated in the class of natural, sensible phenomena. Whence, too, even that specific notion of sign crucial to the epistemological development of late Greek antiquity played no major part in the traditional modern histories of ancient philosophy.

The Greek term normally translated as "sign", σημεῖον ("semeîon"), is therefore inevitably misunderstood unless the reader of the translation is clued to the fact that this so-called "sign" is more like what we would call a *symptom* of disease, for example, or what the Latins would call a "natural sign", *signum naturale*, such as the "red sky in the morning from which sailors take warning", or the presence of milk in a woman's breast signifying childbirth.

To our much later consciousness it may seem odd, but the Greek philosophers never conceived of the phenomena of culture as such (excepting only very specific, indexical instances or types of cultural creations, such as insignia and standards), including the species-specifically human exaptation of language to communicate (an exaptation itself commonly mislabeled as "language"), in terms of signification or the action of signs. The sign was viewed in the perspective of Greek philosophy and science principally, all but exclusively, as it manifested itself on the "nature" side of the "nature-nurture" dichotomy.

In this original perspective of understanding, the σημεῖον or "sign" pertains to human discourse only insofar as that dis-

---

[3] See "The Stoic vs. Epicurean Polemic over Signs and Inference" in the *Four Ages* (Deely 2001: 108–12); further Manetti 2002.

course attains to an understanding of nature or speculative truth, in the *lekton* of Stoic logic or in the *proposition*, the *dicisign*, of Aristotle. Thus, whether in the medical tradition from Hippocrates (c.460–377BC) to Galen (129–c.199AD)[4] or in the logical traditions that develop after Aristotle first and later also Chrysippus (the Stoic line) and others,[5] the sign in ancient times is thought of as encountered in the Umwelt only in sensible nature and, derivatively therefrom, at that singular juncture of human discourse where the understanding attains an object under the guise of being adjudicable as "true" or "false".[6] That such an attainment was species-specifically human was a firm opinion among the ancients; yet the ground of this attainment, as I have elsewhere exhibited, began to be thematically considered in its own right only in some of the more neglected aspects of the writings of Aquinas,[7] and in a development traceable from his contemporary, Roger Bacon (c.1214–1294).[8]

In passing from "natural sign" or σημεῖον to "sign in general" or *signum*, we may say, we first cross the frontier separating the Latin Age from the original Greek florescence of philosophy. Similarly, we have seen that in the later forgetfulness of *signum* the thinkers of what will become the classical

[4]   On this, see especially the work of Sebeok 1984b and 1996.

[5]   On this, see especially the work of Deledalle 1987.

[6]   See, for example, in Aristotle c.348/7: Ch. 27 closing his *Prior Analytics*, 70a3–b38, where σημεῖον as a term recurs no less than eighteen times. I am grateful to Professor Deledalle who marked for me and sent to me this text in the Greek in a correspondence dated 15 October 1996.

[7]   See Chapter 7 in the *Four Ages* (Deely 2001), esp. the section on "The Problem of Being as First Known", p. 341ff. I have also taken this matter up in a separate monograph, not historical but directly speculative, under the title *What Distinguishes Human Understanding?* (Deely 2002).

[8]   Ibid.: Chaps. 8 and 9.

modern mainstream will establish a principal boundary separating modern times from the later Latin Age. And, later still, we find that in the Peircean recovery of *signum* semiotics establishes yet another line of demarcation, a new frontier separating authentic postmodern thought from the various idealistic pretensions to surpass modernity, pretensions the hollowness of which is betrayed by their preservation of the epistemological and metaphysical essence of modern philosophy in conceiving of the sign as a vehicle exclusively arbitrary or linguistic in its construction.

No doubt there will be a "fifth age" (let us not make Hegel's mistake of presenting a Prussian state as the end of history), and beyond that yet other ages as new themes sufficiently vast emerge in awareness to define and govern new epochs in the development of human understanding over the next two thousand years. But, if the past history and gait of philosophical development are reliable indicators, that "Fifth Age" will not even begin to take form before the 22nd century at the very earliest, more likely the 25th. By then, the notion of an "action of signs" and of the dependency of objectivity on that action and the systems of signs it generates while interweaving the natural and the cultural, the speculative and the practical, will be so well established and so prominent at the forefront of popular consciousness that the time when "semiosis" was a strange new word will seem a time positively neanderthal. Such is the pattern according to which the presuppositions that guide each age in its development are first formed and then taken for granted as the new generations of semiotic animals get on with the business of their life: for among intellectual beings, understanding is what distinguishes their life,[9] even as to perceive and act accordingly is the life distinctive of animals, or to take nourishment is the life distinctive of plants.

[9]   "Intelligere in intelligentibus est esse", as Aquinas might have said.

Chapter 6

Prospective

So what shall we say is to be the impact of semiotics upon philosophy?

History as Laboratory and Landscape

We see right off that semiotics revises the outline of the standard history of philosophy dramatically. *Instead of* seeing the Latin Age as a dark period of superstition wherein only gradually are the threads of Greek speculation taken up anew to culminate in the mighty Aquinas and thereafter descend to the Nominalism of Ockham which, taken up in the 17th century, becomes modern philosophy on one side and modern science on the other, but in between nothing; we see rather, from its first proposal in Augustine to its vindication in Poinsot, a tropical landscape of signs with an organic unity in the ontologically relative being proper to sign as transcending the divide between nature and culture, inner and outer, passing back and forth in its ground, like a shuttlecock, weaving the fabric of experience according to changing circumstances of realization, all the while feeding and sustaining the growth of awareness and habits in individuals which, suprasubjectively shared, constitute the reality behind and within what we otherwise call "history".

Modern science, far from being itself any child of nominalism, appears rather as a continuation of the realism which animated ancient Greek and medieval Latin thought alike,[1] but now become aware of its requirements as ideoscopic, not cenoscopic,[2] that is to say, aware of its difference from knowledge adequately derived from and based upon what has become the common stock of human understanding in any given age, a difference grounded in an aiming at further horizons of understanding which cannot be brought into view without recourse to experiments and instruments and often formulations in mathematical symbolisms which may presuppose but do not adequately reduce to the symbolic structures of natural language.

Modern philosophy, in sharp contrast, appears rather as nominalism indeed, as at odds with the health of scientific understanding as Mr. Hyde was to the health of Dr. Jekyll. Modernity stands out starkly as an interval wherein the natural development of the doctrine of signs was suspended within philosophy in favor of the more immediate tasks of developing and institutionalizing modern science and bringing restraint to religious authority in political and civil life – about which there is much of the utmost importance to be said, not

---

[1] Deely 1984: 265–66.

[2] On this terminology (originally derived from Peirce through Bentham) and its variant spellings, I refer the reader to the earlier mentions in Chap. 2 (p. 19 n. 16) and Chap. 4 (p. 55 n. 10, and p. 57 n. 13), and to the "dialogue between a semiotician and would-be realist" in Part III below.

only in the matter of religious reformation but in the matter of inquisition and Pierre Bayle's attempt (the first thematic such[3]) to refute Augustine's warranting of the use of police powers of the state to regiment religious orthodoxy among individual thinkers.

Nor is the interest "purely historical", in the sense that analytic philosophers today chimerically dismiss as "history" in contrast to really "doing philosophy". A vain pretense, this distinction, when it is used to avoid dealing with the fact that deductive logic applied to ideas clearly in mind is hardly the sufficient instrument of philosophy. For history viewed philosophically (which cannot be done when ignorance and narrowness of purview is cultivated in the name of philosophy) proves the very laboratory of philosophical ideas, the one place where long-range consequences of philosophical proposals become unmistakable, as Gilson liked to point out.

"If the question were simply what we do mean by a sign," Peirce noted,[4] "it might soon be resolved." But we are rather in the situation of the zoölogist who wants to know what is sign such that it can function in the way that it impresses us as doing, revealing nature, stitching together culture and nature, real and unreal relations, in weaving the fabric of experience, and leading us down blind alleys and cul-de-sacs as well as broad avenues of being in the forests of human belief. By any standard, the displacement – or thorough remaking at least – of what passes for epistemological theory in philosophy is directly at stake, the "midmost target" of semiotic development, as Sebeok put it,[5] beyond which lies the ultimate goal of mediating reality and illusion.

As early as the 1st century BC, we know from

---

[3]   Bayle 1686/8; cf. Powell 2000.

[4]   Peirce 1904: 8.332.

[5]   Sebeok 1991: 2.

I.6: Prospective

Philodemus,[6] "the most complete and best preserved work which has reached us from antiquity on the subject of sign-inference",[7] that the notion of natural sign, the σημεῖον, was an epicenter of dispute over the nature of inference between Stoics and Epicureans, and was even before that seen as focal to Aristotle's notion of propositional content.[8] Augustine expanded the horizon considerably when he brought also language under the rubric of *signum* as transcending the divide between nature and culture. Aquinas, Scotus, Ockham, and the later Latins d'Ailly, Soto, Fonseca, Conimbricenses, Araújo, Poinsot, Mastrius, expanded the horizon further still by bringing psychological states under the same rubric, transcending now the distinction between the inner and outer universe, so that already the Conimbricenses could say,[9] as Peirce would repeat, that all thought is through signs.

But still, whether we speak of psychological states ("ideas and feelings") or sense perceptible phenomena ("natural and conventional occurrences") as "signs", the realization that the sign strictly speaking, in the being proper to and constituting itself as such, consists not in any particular thing – natural or cultural, inner or outer – as vehicle but in the very relation itself triadic and imperceptible (in contrast to the related things) uniting three particulars (two of which need not even exist outside of the in-principle-public sphere of objectivity),

---

6   Philodemus i.54/40BC.

7   Manetti 2002: 296; see further Manetti 1993, and the *Four Ages* (Deely 2001).

8   Aristotle c.348/7BC: *Prior Analytics* (see Chapter 6, note 6, p. 55, above).

9   Conimbricenses 1607: q. 2. art. 3. sect. 3 (Doyle ed. p. 86/87): "Initio illud statuimus nihil ducere in cognitionem alterius, quod in aliquam speciem signi non reducatur" – "At the outset we are stating that there is nothing which leads to the knowledge of something else which may not be reduced to some species of sign".

as Poinsot demonstrated,[10] was a decisive moment for the theory of knowledge. This realization of the invisible being proper to sign as such, its "soul", so to speak, in contrast to the elements of its embodiment, vindicated (not indeed for the first time, but in an especially inescapable fashion[11]) a long suspicion harbored over the whole history of philosophy that there is a distinction in principle between sense perception, as restricted to grasping related things ("using signs without knowing that there are signs", as Maritain put it), and understanding, the biologically underdetermined modeling system of "language", able to think relations as such in their difference from related terms.

This realization also reveals as a blind alley the many attempts to isolate "signs" as some class or subclass of objects among other objects that can be seen and pointed to. For signs prove to be rather strictly invisible networks of relations which every object presupposes in order to *be* as an object (in order to be, that is to say, as something experienced and apprehended). Far from being reducible to any subjectivity, whether physical or psychological, signs belong rather to the suprasubjectivity whereby subjectivity itself is objectified and made public in communication (intersubjectivity achieved, wherever it occurs) and, in principle if not always in fact, in human understanding.

"Semiotica Utramque Comprehendit"[12]

Plato and Aristotle were the first clearly to show that speculative understanding is what most distinguishes the life of the human animal. For such understanding is the only understanding that takes rise from a grasp of the difference between

---

[10] Poinsot 1632a: Book I, esp. qq. 1 and 3.
[11] Deely 1982; 2001 throughout.
[12] Cf. Aquinas 1266: *Summa theologiae Prima Pars*, q. 1, art. 4c.

objects, whatever is known precisely in its relation to us the knowers, and things, whatever is known insofar as it involves a being transcendent to whatever relations it may have to us or whatever impressions we have of it. Speculative understanding, Aristotle went on to say, is distinguished by its aiming at knowing what is independently of human thought, feeling, and action; while practical understanding, by contrast, is aimed precisely at what we can do about the things that are, at human control over being so far as such control can be attained by means of human thought and action.

It might seem at first glance that, in this case, animal knowledge as such in contrast to human understanding is entirely practical, but so to think is to fail to grasp the real point of Aristotle's distinction. For just as human understanding consists in an ability to think relations in contrast to related things while perception consists in the construction and grasp of related objects, so knowledge restricted to the grasp of related objects is neither practical strictly speaking nor speculative but simply perceptual. There is not yet so much as a question of a grasp of how things are in themselves, but wholly and solely a question of how things are so far as the perceiving organism is concerned. Such an awareness, zoösemiosis occurring outside of (or within) anthroposemiosis, is *more like* a practical anthroposemiosis than theoretical understanding, but is yet prior to the very distinction between practical and speculative knowledge. For the distinction arises from modeling the difference, real or imagined, between things as they are in our experience and things as they are or might be independently of or prior to such experience; and only in the light of this difference conceived can we subsequently speak of a difference between knowledge aimed straight at determining "what is the case" and knowledge aimed rather at "what should be done about things". Zoösemiosic awareness begins and ends in the latter concern, whereas anthroposemiosic awareness, beginning indeed in zoösemiosis, awakens at its own level to the *difference* between what is and what should be done, *and thematizes that difference.* Only afterward can we speak about "speculative concerns" as distinctive of anthropos as human, of "understanding" in its difference from perception.

Of course it has near-always been known that what we can and cannot do something about changes over time, such that what is one time purely speculative knowledge becomes at a later time practical. Superficially this awareness has led many to discount or deny the speculative/practical distinction as purely relative to the condition of human knowledge at a given period of time. But at least as early as Aquinas the error of this way of thinking had been pointed out, from the consideration that however much knowledge may grow, and with it the extension of human control over nature, there remain at the limit matters over which human action can never gain control and such are the matters, at root, that define the speculative realm in its contrast with the practical.[13]

[13] Maritain's remarks (1921: 19), beyond the polemical context of their time, still bear consideration: "Practical activity, prudence, the moral virtues, ... leave man – where they find him – in human life." By contrast, the activity of "the speculative intellectual virtues . . . transports him into – all but merges him in – the object and thus bears him above the level of human life". We can see in this why, as Sommers (2001) has recently shown for the context of the medieval anti-mendicant controversies, Aquinas saw the highest fulfillment of the human vocation not in the opposition of speculative to practical life but rather in the overflowing of contemplative understanding toward the transformation of the human Lebenswelt in the direction of securing the goods of human flourishing for an ever-increasing many (cf. Rasmussen and Den Uyl 1991). Understanding prescissively considered is speculative *or* practical, but cognitive life fully as human perforce embraces both, *"utramque comprehendit"*. And just this truth is what semiotics brings to the fore within the sciences, both cenoscopic

I.6: Prospective

For example, the existence of God: it matters not our opinion in this matter, in that we are correct if we think God does not exist if and only if God does not exist, just as we are correct if we think God exists if and only if God exists (always presupposing the details of this or that conception of "God"). For example, the immortality of the human soul: it matters not our opinion in this matter, in that we are correct in thinking that the soul is capable of surviving the body if and only if the soul as the substantial principle of life has an activity not directly dependent upon and exercised through a bodily organ. It matters not how long we can extend life through medical and technological advances. If the human soul, like the plant soul, is drawn wholly from the potentiality of matter, then, like last year's snow, back into the potentiality of matter it goes when the body corrupts sufficiently no longer to sustain the principle by which it exists as living. For example, it mattered not a whit that Aristotle and the best minds after him thought that the sun revolved about the earth, nor did it matter a whit more that the Inquisition as chosen instrument of an infallible teaching authority endorsed Aristotle's opinion as heaven-sent in the Bible: the fact remained that over all those thousands of years of counter opinions the earth revolved rather around the sun than the sun around the earth.

There is the plan today in NASA as to how we might move the orbit of the earth a little farther from the sun than presently in order to counter global warming, making what was once a matter of speculative knowledge (the size of earth's orbit) a possibility of practical control. Yet this does not change the basic distinction: for, to borrow Aquinas's trenchant formula, "the speculative intellect becomes practical by

(such as philosophy and theology) and ideoscopic (science in the modern sense).

extension". That is to say, practical action is well founded only to the extent it is based on a grasp of how things are. An illustration should make the point. Since the beginning of the human species, human beings have been sexual animals. Sex is not as old as life, and human beings are not as old as sex, but there have been no human beings, male, female, or hermaphrodite, who were not sexual. Now every human being through the twentieth century at least came into existence through the fertilization of some woman's egg by some man's sperm. At that moment of conception, a genotype was established which (yes, had first to implant, then develop through embryonic stages to birth, childhood and adolescence in order to reach human adulthood, but which) itself remained constant, the underlying biological constant in the life of the human organism until death. Only in the twentieth century, however, did we *come to know* of the reality of genotypes, and only late in the century did we come to know *enough* to envision the possibility of intervening in a genotype to replace or repair such individual genes as we could see would cause phenotypic problems in the organism's development. So the genotype, an object of speculative knowledge, became by extension of that knowledge a matter of practical concern, something about which something might be done. Speculative understanding, by extending itself far enough in the case, had become veritably practical.

So speculative and practical as forms of knowledge are polar opposites, but within human understanding they differ first by the aim understanding takes, as it were (at being – seeing what is; or at doing – seeing what can be accomplished); and within human understanding, though the line dividing the two can never be wholly erased (the point of Aristotle's original distinction), neither can the line between them be wholly fixed in time (the point of Aquinas' maxim) but depends on the state of human understanding in its grasp of the real, particularly insofar as that grasp is sustained and extended, as Peirce put it, not by the individual consciousness but by the individual consciousness insofar as it has become "scientific", that is to say, embedded in a community of inquirers not limited to individuals now living but collaborating across the generations.

In relation to this ancient distinction of practical from speculative within the orbit of distinctively human understanding, semiotics occupies a unique place in the universe of human knowledge; for semiotics provides the only standpoint whence can be seen exactly how and why the boundary in time between the speculative and the practical shifts (even though not the poles themselves, or ultimate terms, of the distinction) from time to time and place to place. In the original awakening of reason from the animal Umwelt where objects are the sole and whole reality to a first realization of being in (so to say) its hard-core sense of something which is what it is supremely indifferent to human beliefs, desires, and opinions, the idea of "reality" was born, the first offspring of the difference between objects and things as given in the course of human experience. This was the central node of the First Age of Understanding, the birth of speculative thought, the awakening of the human animal as human. The Second Age, the age of the sign, the first naissance of semiotic consciousness, had its own epiphany, not in the awareness of being as such so much as in the awareness that human reason cannot escape its own responsibility to account for experience on its own grounds by abdicating that responsibility in favor of a "leap of faith" of whatever confessional color. This was the point Aquinas made in distinguishing *theology*, the confessional use of reason, from *philosophy* (which he did not yet foresee as needing the further fundamental division into and institutionalization

as ideoscopic science in its difference from cenoscopic doc-
trines) as a relatively autonomous sphere both speculative
and practical.

The advantage Thomas saw in the new theology was
twofold. First, of course, that, according to the times, it drew
on God's own understanding of the world (insofar as that
might be divined from the texts taken to be revealed, the
sacred scriptures), and even from the traditions of human
beings insofar as those traditions were true expressions of a
right understanding of the divine will for humankind – a
tricky business, to say the least. Second, and consequent on
this, the new theology, distancing itself from the imperialism
of patristic and Augustinian thought by distinguishing and
freeing reason from exclusive subservience to and entangle-
ment with authoritarian interpretations of "sacred texts" in
order to allow its development in its own line, both in the
speculative order and in the practical order of ethics, politics,
and art (exactly what would result, in four more centuries of
growth, in the offshoot of ideoscopic knowledge from the
cenoscopic trunk of philosophical understanding), could yet
claim for itself the highest place in the organization of human
knowledge ("queen of the sciences") by virtue of transcending the distinction between speculative and practical knowledge. For in knowing God as its proper object, theology, albeit
confessionally advantaged or disadvantaged by its presuppositions concerning revelation, still attained in the knowing of
God a knowledge of all that He makes as God, i.e., as Creator
upon whom the totality of finite beings in the particularity of
their individualities depends at each moment, the Source of
existence of the totality, Ipsum Esse Subsistens, in the formula no less metaphysical than theological by which Aquinas
interpreted at once the experience of Moses as recorded in
Exodus and the experience of every human being that the
world of experience is a world of changeable being where

what a thing is remains ever at risk of becoming detached, as it were, from the world of actual fact. It was the high point of the Second Age, wherein "the highest grade of reality was reached by signs" from within human experience.[14]

Thus Thomas saw in theology an essential superiority over the highest of the philosophical disciplines so far as philosophy had developed to his day. For the highest of the philosophical sciences – what Aristotle had called simply "first philosophy" or "theology" (natural theology, a knowledge of the universe in relation to the source of its actuality achieved by reason itself through the analysis of the experience of changing being), but what was already called in Aquinas' day by its later name of "metaphysics"– remained a purely speculative science, in contrast with the new theology, which was speculative in its ground but included the practical order as well within its distinctive province.[15]

After that came a new awakening of reason, an awakening from within philosophy itself of its difference from quite another and new possibility of human understanding, relatively autonomous not only from the dictates of religious or ecclesiastical authority but also from the dictates of the "common sense" upon which knowledge as cenoscopic centrally and necessarily depends in its development and conveyance. It was the main point or achievement of that Third Age of Understanding, modernity. For who, merely by thinking about it, could have established through discourse alone that

---

[14] E.g., Aquinas c.1266: *Summa theologiae* I. 3. 4. ad 2.

[15] *Ibid.* I.1.4c: "licet in scientiis philosophicis alia sit speculativa, et alia practica, sacra tamen doctrina comprehendit utramque; sicut et Deus eadem scientia se cognoscit, et ea quae facit" (although human disciplines of knowledge are either speculative or practical, yet theology embraces both the speculative and the practical; just as God knows by one and the same knowledge himself and the things which he makes"). See the parallel constructed in n. 21, p. 111 following.

massive bodies fall at the same rate as ethereal ones, or that pressure if applied to an enclosed fluid will be transmitted equally in all directions, or that planetary orbits are rather elliptical than circular, and[16] "other propositions, which are not less remarkable, and which capture the understanding, so to speak, against its own will"?

For a few centuries, the rooting of science in the ideoscopic sense seemed to contemporaries to have replaced entirely the need for cenoscopic disciplines, such as had been the traditional sciences in the ancient and medieval sense of speculative philosophy (subdivided into physics, mathematics, and metaphysics) contrasted with the art, politics, and ethics of practical thought. Indeed, at the dawn of modernity, Galileo and Descartes deemed themselves brothers in the common enterprise of interpreting nature directly without regard for the traditional texts of the philosophers commenting on Aristotle or other ancients. Yet today, no one looking back with today's eyes sees in Galileo the future of philosophy, or in Descartes the future of science. Just the opposite. We see in Galileo precisely the beginning of science in the modern sense, leading to Newton, then to Einstein, and beyond; and in Descartes we see the beginning of classically modern philosophy, eschewing in the end the knowability of anything in direct experience beyond the mind's own workings,[17] the "placing under erasure" of *ens reale* in the Kantian critiques.

In the meantime, while the distinction between philosophical reason as cenoscopic and scientific reason as ideoscopic was taking root, and before its growth became sufficiently clear as to be admitted on all hands, reason took its

---

[16] To apply to propositions of ideoscopic science words of Kant (1747: 8) which, taken in their own context, are rather misapplied. See the *Four Ages* (Deely 2001: 555 n. 17).

[17] See, in the *Four Ages*, "The Strange Case of Dr. Jekyll and Mr. Hyde" (Deely 2001: 540ff.).

autonomy from authoritative texts (in just the sense Aquinas had identified in separating theological reason from reason *tout court*) more and more seriously, not only to establish ideoscopic knowledge – science in the modern sense – more and more fully in its own right but, at the same time, to establish the structures of civil life, the "life of nations" as more and more properly outgrowths of human understanding than imagined as impositions from above of an order of everyday life "divinely revealed" as the will of God, whether according to clerics charged with the mission of mediating the eternal salvation of mortal souls, or according to kings whose legitimacy was asserted to be a matter of "divine right".

As the modern societies came increasingly to depend on the ideoscopic fruits of modern science, the ancient distinction between speculative and practical came less and less well to be understood. The extension of speculative reason wherein it becomes practical came more and more to the fore, as in Francis Bacon's early modern prognostication that "knowledge is power". Philosophers as late as James and Russell in the twentieth century came to believe that science consists in the answers to the questions the philosophers raise, so that a question remains a philosophical question only to the extent that its answer eludes us. As soon as its answer comes into view we pass out of philosophy into the realm of science. This naive view,[18] the

---

[18] This "dream of reason", so quaintly 'rediscovered' by Gottlieb (2001) after the fashion of Lyotard's proposed meaning for postmodernity (see Part II, Section 2, n. 3, p. 120 below), ironically mirrors on the part of secular philosophers an older religious view that theology provides the answers to questions philosophy raises. The view is no less fatuous for being secularized. Unfortunately, perhaps, but nonetheless, it is not by returning to its origins that late modernity gives way to postmodernity. It is by coming up against its limits at a time when the understanding finds a way (in the present case, the way of signs) to transcend those limits those very limits theretofore deemed unsurpassable.

quintessence of the Enlightenment in speculative thought, perhaps (if not in the practical order which saw a glorious freeing of human life and intelligence in the direction of realizing the possibilities of individual understanding and individual responsibility), itself now appears incredible, as it becomes unmistakable that, just as philosophy cannot answer the questions central to theology or science, nor theology those central to science or philosophy, so neither can science answer the questions central to either philosophy or theology.[19]

Yet knowledge is not the same as power, however much power accrues from the constant ideoscopic extensions of human understanding; and the speculative requirements upon human understanding in its distinctiveness cannot be made to go away. So it is fitting that just as a Fourth Age of Understanding dawns in Peirce's proposal[20] of a New List of Categories able to accommodate the interweaving of the workings of nature and mind in the fabric of experience, so also should develop a new "science" – a renewal of philosophy itself, more exactly – able to accommodate within the order of human understanding on its own ground and in its own right the inter-relation of speculative and practical thought through the action of signs. For semiotics, like the confessional notion of theology distinguished from philosophy in the time of Aquinas, extends equally to the speculative and practical orders, inasmuch as all thought, whether speculative or practical, is in signs. So the doctrine of signs, analogous to the dogmatic theology achieved after the thirteenth century, is not restricted to the speculative or practical orders

---

[19] See the sections "Questions only Humans Ask" and "Reasonable Questions Philosophy Cannot Answer" in the *Four Ages* (Deely 2001: 487–91).

[20] Peirce 1867: CP 1.545–67; see commentary in the *Four Ages* (Deely 2001: 637ff.).

but extends to both, *utramque includit,* yet for a very different reason: not because it supposes the illumination of a light superior to human understanding, a revelation authored as such by God, but because it provides the means whereby speculative and practical understanding alike are achieved. Semiotics provides, in this way – but this time from within the very order of human understanding as human – a distinction which unites the speculative and practical orders within one inter- or trans-disciplinary perspective provided by the awareness and study of semiosis.[21]

Interdisciplinary studies, the need for which became felt increasingly as the ideoscopic demands of scientific specialization increased over the modern centuries, suddenly finds its natural home in semiotic as the doctrine of signs. For semiotic takes its thematic orientation from the instrument of all knowledge, cenoscopic or ideoscopic, confessional or experimental, the sign, which weaves its web of triadic relations no less across than within the specialized areas of human experience constructed by the sciences, by the different religious traditions, by the different cultural traditions of the various groups of human animals.

---

[21] To paraphrase the text of Aquinas (above, p. 107n15) manifesting how sacred theology transcends the terms of the speculative/practical distinction, we may say that semiotics achieves transcendence of those same terms as follows: Licet in scientiis philosophicis alia sit speculativa, et alia practica, signorum tamen doctrina comprehendit utramque; sicut et anthropos eadem actione signorum seu «semiosis» se cognoscit et ea quae facit, ea facitur natura et ea facitur cultura. (Although human disciplines of knowledge are either speculative or practical, yet the doctrine of signs embraces both the speculative and the practical; just as the human being by one and the same action of signs or 'semiosis' knows both the self and what the self does, the things made by nature and things made by culture.) Cf. the *Four Ages* (Deely 2001: 606).

The sign embraces the realms both of nature and culture, underlying their unification in human experience, and opening the way to those sound extensions of our knowledge of what is whereby that knowledge becomes practical in new areas. The way of signs, in this fashion, opens beyond modern philosophy, which came to see itself as confined to the order of mind-dependent being (*ens rationis*), but beyond as well the central preoccupation of ancient and medieval philosophy with the objects of speculative knowledge as such (*ens reale*), to the world of human experience in its totality which includes "common sense" at the core of cenoscopic knowledge no less than that distinctively modern development of ideoscopic knowledge which alone we had come to call "science" by the postmodern dawn. "The unifying function of semiotics", as Petrilli and Ponzio put it,[22] "concerns proposals and practical orientations for human life in its wholeness (human life considered in all its biological and socio-cultural aspects)", no less than in revealing the foundations for human understanding in what is distinctive of it as achieving a grasp in the first place of the speculative order precisely in those foundational aspects which can never be brought under the control of any finite being.

Vale

These are matters of importance and of the greatest interest philosophically: providing a view of history as not merely the landscape but veritably the laboratory of ideas insofar as knowledge develops cenoscopically, enlarging the very scope of "common sense" in history; while at the same time exposing the unity in semiosis of the whole reach of human understanding whereby semiotics becomes a knowledge that in

---

[22] Petrilli and Ponzio 2001: 34.

principle embraces both the ideoscopic and the cenoscopic orders, even while remaining primarily cenoscopic ("philosophical", if you like) in its distinctive character. *Speculativa et practica utramque comprehendit semiotica* – semiotics as a distinctively postmodern development embraces practical understanding no less than speculative. If at least this much has been conveyed, this small book shall have served a purpose.

I hope that the suggestion of a new overall outline of philosophy in its history, a redrawing of the map of philosophy as it provides any guidance at all into future developments of understanding (the understanding of understanding in particular), is sufficient for the present purpose. For, as Peirce best noted, the meaning of what we say in our present cannot be fully determined here and now, but ever depends in part on discourse yet to come; or, to speak rather in the accents of Aristotle before him, time is a good partner in filling in what has once been well-outlined, while progress in the pertinent arts and sciences tends to a standstill in the absence of such an outline. It is time, after a century of traveling in logical circles, for some genuine progress in philosophy.

Part II.
The Quasi-Error of the External World

Section 1

Betwixt and Between

There is a story according to which Professor Sebeok was on a panel of distinguished speakers who received from the audience a challenge to show cause why the basic ideas of semiotics, such as that of Umwelt, were not simply one more version of solipsistic idealism. Each of the speakers in turn addressed the matter, each beginning with a protestation (outdoing in earnestness the previous speaker) to the effect that, "Of course, I am not a solipsist". Finally, Tom's turn arrived. He shrugged, and said simply: "I'm a solipsist". It was one of those seminal moments, of which Tom created so many, like the time in Toronto where he mentioned in passing in his main remarks that "Everyone thinks of language in terms of communication. But language has nothing to do with communication." In the question period, the very first questioner challenged him on the point. "You said that language has nothing to do with communication", the audience member reminded him. "Why did you say that?" "Because it doesn't", Tom answered pointedly,[1] and proceeded to call on the next questioner.

---

[1]   Later Sebeok would say (1995: 91, or 2001: 70), in the form of a summary maxim, as from a medicine man to the tribal elders, "Resist the temptation to jumble three incommensurate semiosic practices and their corresponding appellations: *communication*, *language*, and *speech*."

Section 2

The Egg of Postmodernity

It was fascinating, to borrow Tom's own description of a former instance of the type of event in question,[1] "to note a clue *in nuce*, lurking" in these calculated rhetorical outrages; but even more fascinating was it to watch these clues unfold into full-blown theoretical insights over the following months and years, floating like water lilies on seas of detail.

Now Tom Sebeok was a man of details. Even though he never assumed for himself the mantle of philosopher, as the twenty-first century advances, it will prove difficult, if not impossible, for professors and students of philosophy to maintain ignorance of his name. Mayhap no single man of the

---

[1] Sebeok 2000: 143. He was referring to the 1969 oral presentation of Langer 1971, in which he saw a glimmer of his later distinction between language as component of the species-specifically human modeling system and its exaptation to create linguistic communication. It is perhaps beginning to be "in the air": cf. Ashley 1985: 40.

twentieth century, save perhaps Peirce himself (though in quite a different and less collegial fashion!), had as shaping an influence on the intellectual culture and climate of what is destined, in my opinion, to be called with a positive sense the "postmodern era".

For "postmodern" has a very different meaning as it bears on philosophy than has heretofore generally been suspected. For example, Karol Wojtyla noted that the term "postmodernity", as it began to find currency in the late twentieth century, was first used with reference to aesthetic, social and technological phenomena. The term was then transposed into the philosophical field, "but has remained somewhat ambiguous", mainly because "there is as yet no consensus on the delicate question of the demarcation of the different historical periods."[2] Interesting pretensions to the contrary notwithstanding,[3] in the end, the consequence that "postmodern" supersedes "modern" is unavoidable.

[2]   Wojtyla 1998: ¶91: "A quibusdam subtilioribus auctoribus aetas nostra uti tempus «post-modernum» est designata. Vocabulum istud, saepius quidem adhibitum de rebus inter se dissidentibus, indicat emergentem quandam elementorum novorum summam quae sua amplitudine et efficacitate graves manentesque perficere potuerunt mutationes. Ita verbum idem primum omnium adhibitum est de notionibus ordinis aesthetici et socialis et technologici. In provinciam deinde philosophiae est translatum, at certa semper ambiguitate signatum, tum quia iudicium de iis quae uti «post-moderna» appellantur nunc affirmans nunc negans esse potest, tum quia nulla est consensio in perdifficili quaestione de variarum aetatum historicarum terminis. Verumtamen unum illud extra omnem dubitationem invenitur: rationes et cogitationes quae ad spatium post-modernum referuntur congruam merentur ponderationem."

[3]   Lyotard 1984: 79: "A work can become modern only if it is first postmodern. Postmodernism thus understood is not modernism at its end but in the nascent state, and this state is constant." How nice to realize that modernity, after all, is an eternal condition. Cf. Part I, Chapter 6, p. 109, text and n. 18, above

II.2: The Egg of Postmodernity

Well, "the delicate question of the demarcation of the different historical periods", I make bold to say, has been recently addressed at length. Modernity, in philosophy, means that period, beginning with the *Meditations* of Descartes, which came to assume in its mainstream development that the products of the mind's own workings provide alone the direct objects of experience on the side of consciousness.[4] Locke shared this supposition with Descartes, and Kant did not challenge it, even though he introduced into the notion of consciousness a structure of relationality which considerably distanced him from his modern forebears, but nonetheless without overturning the essential tenet of idealism: what the mind knows the mind makes.

Now there is hardly room for doubt at this juncture of history about a social construction of reality, that human consciousness structures human experience of objects, and perhaps even that the main contours of what we experience is a product more of our thinking and socio-cultural conventions than of any input from a "nature" recognized as such that is operative within our experience as well as prior to, and independently of, that experience. "Reality" for the traveler today, is less a matter of undiscovered lands and seas than a matter of correct papers of identification and negotiation of officials at travel and custom points along the various frontiers. These boundaries, moreover, themselves depend upon diverse traditions, so that the boundaries of nations today are not those of a thousand years ago, nor of a thousand years hence. Even the Pope of Roman Catholicism, an icon of a spiritual reality transcending humanity, for many centuries now, is chosen by election among "Cardinals". Yet no one doubts that cardinals are wholly a creation of human tradition within that Church, no different as objective realities than the Electors in the

---

[4]   See Deely 2001: Chapters 11–14.

Electoral College of the United States, or the former Electors of the erstwhile "Holy Roman Empire".

So the objective world of human experience is at best a mixture of nature and culture, but a mixture in which the predominant formal patterns come more from culture than from nature. These formal patterns from culture underlie the presentation to us of objects directly experienced. The situation in this regard in fact was no different for the ancients or medievals; but they had not awakened to the fact. Who are our relatives? It depends on what kinship system is regnant in the culture in which we are raised. What is our religion? Allowing for individual exceptions, again the answer depends mainly on the historical circumstances into which we are born and raised.

The moderns, awakening to all this, had good reason to see in the objects experienced creations of the mind's own workings. Even science might be reduced to the same: such was the Kantian experiment, undertaken from the impetus of Hume's discourses maintaining nothing more to experience than customary associations among objects. If all thoughts reflect mere habits, and all objects cannot be known to be anything other or more than mental self-representations, whatever suspicions we may have on "common sense" grounds that there is a world independent of us, skepticism is the final warrant of all knowledge. That, to Kant, was unacceptable. He could swallow everything else his modern mainstream forebears taught him, but not skepticism. Their mistake, as he saw it, was in reducing knowledge to subjectivity – that is to say, their mistake was in identifying ideas in the individual mind with the objects of direct experience. They have failed to grasp that knowledge is essentially relational in structure, and that relations are over and above the subject. So, ideas in the individual give rise to or "found" cognitive relations to objects. But the *objects* are that at which the relations terminate, not that upon which the relations are founded and whence they provenate. And the manner in which these relations are generated in giving form to objects is according to a pattern inbuilt, a-priori to, the human mind, not a mere matter of habits of association.

Now, when it comes to the objects of specifically scientific knowledge, according to Kant, we are dealing with a universality and necessity which comes from the mind itself, not some mere habit pattern and customary generalization. Even though the external world remains unknowable in its proper being, still we know *that* it is there; and our manner of thinking it intellectually is not capricious or culturally relative but universal and necessary, the same for all humans. Even though we know only what our representations give us to know, and the representations are wholly of our mind's own making, still they are made into objects not by association but a-priori, independently of the vagaries of custom and individual experience; and their cognized content is not subjective but objective, that is to say, given at the terminus of relations which our representations only found. The scientific core of human experience, contrary to the animating conviction of scientists themselves, mind you,[5] but according to the modern philosopher Kant, is prospectively the same for all because the sensory mechanism generating the representations involved in it and the conceptual mechanism organizing relations arising from these representations is the same in all: similar causes result always in similar effects. Such was Kant's version of the medieval adage, *agens facit simile sibi.*

By this simple expedient Kant thought to have settled the objectivity of knowledge and put skepticism at bay. The scandal of not being able to prove that there is a world external to

---

[5] We will have further occasion to expand on this point: see Section 4 below, p. 131; and cf. Sokal and Bricmont 1998.

the human mind had been removed by the proof that indeed there is an unknowable realm to which knowledge cannot extend, and this realm is precisely the external world, known of a certainty to exist as stimulating our representations (in sense intuition) and unknowable in itself (through concepts, which yield knowledge only in correlation with the representations of sensory intuitions but result in yet another realm of unknowables, the noumena, if we try to extend them beyond the boundary of what is represented in intuitions of sense).

Later variants on this Kantian theme would concentrate on the phenomena in our experience of objects, after Husserl. Yet others would concentrate on the language itself in which human representations are mainly systematized, after Frege, Russell, and Wittgenstein. Russell, indeed, emphasized the role of relations in language and (hence) in knowledge. But Kant had already done this;[6] and Russell confessed in the end that he, too, was unable to transcend solipsism:[7]

> My own belief is that the distinction between what is mental and what is physical does not lie in any intrinsic character of either, but in the way in which we acquire knowledge of them. . . . I should regard all events as physical, but I should regard as *only* physical those which no one knows except by inference.

We are linked to other minds in exactly the same manner by which we are linked to any reality external to ourselves: by inference. Directly we experience only what is in ourselves. Such was modernity when Sebeok came along. Such was modernity when he left it.

[6] See the analysis in Deely 2001: 561–63.

[7] B. Russell 1959: 254.

Section 3

The Egg Hatches

This conundrum, this Gordian knot of "external reality", with which modernity had paralyzed the philosophers, was precisely what Sebeok cut. Faced with the dilemma of the modern implication of a maze of the mind's own workings, he found the way out:[1]

> What is one to make of all this? It seems to me that, at the very least for us, workers in a zoösemiotic context, there is only one way to get through this thicket, and that is to adhere strictly to Jakob von Uexküll's comprehensive theses about signs.

Of course, Sebeok is speaking here about *Umweltstheorie*, nothing less, to which nothing is more central than Sebeok's own distinction between language in the root sense (that

---

[1]   Sebeok 2001: 78, and 193 n. 6.

aspect of the human modeling system or *Innenwelt* that is underdetermined biologically and as such species-specific to us) and the exaptation of language to communicate (resulting in linguistic communication as, again, a species-specifically human *moyen*). The mistake of the cultural relativists of whatever stripe, and of the moderns in general, from Sebeok's point of view, was to treat of language as an autonomous system all-encompassing, instead of to realize its zoösemiotic context.[2] In this context "the uniqueness of man" stands out only insofar as it is sustained by and depends upon commonalities of signifying that define and constitute the larger realm of living things within which human beings are perforce incorporated and bound up by a thousand million lines of relationships which the very understanding of human life must ultimately bring to some conscious incorporation. In other words, Sebeok's final contribution, from within modernity, was to realize that there was a way beyond modernity, the Way of Signs.

The question in this form never interested him, but in the wake of his work it is worth asking: what would postmodernity have to be? It could only be a view of the world which somehow managed to restore what is external to ourselves as knowable in its own or proper being without letting go of or denying the modern realization that much if not most of what we directly know reduces to our own customs and conventions according to which objects are structured and inferences made. Now Sebeok may indeed have been thoroughly modern. But no one did more than he to ensure that the modern era, at least in intellectual culture and in the philosophy of which he never claimed to assume the mantle, was over. Sebeok became, in spite of himself, postmodern to the core.

I say "in spite of himself", for I know he had an aversion

---

[2]   Deely 1980.

II.3: The Egg Hatches

to the designation "postmodern", for a very good reason. The greater part of Sebeok's professional life had been devoted to exposing and overcoming what has come to be known as the "*pars pro toto* fallacy",[3] according to which the doctrine of sign finds its adequate foundation on a linguistic, not to say verbal, paradigm. Such was the thesis, well known by the twentieth century's end, of Saussure's proposal for "semiology". By contrast, Sebeok promoted from the first that the doctrine of signs must be rooted directly in a general study of the action of signs, the distinctive manner in which signs work, for which action he accepted from Peirce the name "semiosis". But if the doctrine of signs concerns first of all the action revelative of the distinctive being of signs, then the proper proposal for its development is not the term "semiology" but rather the term "semiotics", which expresses the ideal of a paradigm not language-bound and refers to the action of signs as larger than, surrounding, and indeed presupposed to any action of signs as verbal. "Semiosis", Sebeok said early on,[4] "is a pervasive fact of nature as well as of culture." Semiology he always saw as having a legitimate place within semiotics – the glottocentric part of the larger enterprise, as he put it, but impossible to be the whole.[5]

You can see that Sebeok from the first, without at all thinking of the matter in these terms, set the semiotic enterprise beyond the philosophical boundaries of modernity. His was a postmodern enterprise, from the philosophical point of view,

---

[3]   "Pars Pro Toto", Preface to Deely, Williams, and Kruse 1986: viii–xvii; also in Deely 1986c.

[4]   Sebeok 1977a: 183.

[5]   E.g., see the "Introduction" to Sebeok 2001: esp. xix–xxiii. It was always an irritant to Sebeok that Greimas, a glottocentrician if ever there was one, claimed for his portentously-named "Paris School" the designation "semiotics" rather than the far more apt title of a school of "semiology".

right from the start, however gradually has this fact come into the light. Two things conspired to make it difficult for him (as for us around him) to recognize this. The first was that, by his own profession (what turned out to be to his great advantage), he had not made his forte philosophy. The boundary of modernity as a philosophical epoch had not yet been clearly drawn in the days when Sebeok set out along the Way of Signs, even though Sebeok's own works within linguistics, anthropology, and folklore, as well as later in semiotics, were pushing intellectual culture in the direction of a becoming conscious of just that boundary, as well as of a way across it. The second, much more immediate reason was that, within the larger orbit of semiotics, a group of thinkers vaguely semiological, certainly glottocentric, with Jacques Derrida at their center,[6] had clustered in the consciousness of popular culture around the label "postmodern". The general intellectual thrust of this group, besides being "abjectly based on the *pars pro toto* fallacy", was, to Sebeok's intellectual sensibilities (not to put too fine a face on it), abhorrent. Viewing this development within semiotics and popular culture more generally, Sebeok once confided to me that he deemed the appellation 'postmodern' as "so hopeless as better never to be used".[7]

Yet the term has a logic of its own. Since that which every object as experienced ("real" as the sun or "unreal" as the witches of Salem) presupposes is the action of signs, the way

---

[6] Outside the orbit of Continental semiology, the late-modern "pragmatism" of Richard Rorty performed on the American scene the same function of extending the modern twilight even into the postmodern dawn.

[7] Conversation c.1984. He was not so far removed on this point from the devastating remarks of Sokal and Bricmont 1998, who, however, made the same mistake: to wit, to accept at face-value ("nominalistically", as it were) the claim that thinkers styled "postmodern" have ipso facto just claim to the label.

out of the closet of modernity's solipsism is not by going back to a simple ancient or medieval realism but rather by going forward into a brave new world. *Faute de mieux* the new world will be, and not only for philosophy but for intellectual cultural in its trajectory overall, *postmodern*. Sebeok's objection to those already identified with the label "postmodern" in end-of-the-twentieth-century popular intellectual culture was their abject manipulation of the glottocentric model, their wholesale debasement of the possibilities proper to semiology as a normal part within the larger doctrine of signs. It did not occur naturally to Sebeok that this situation was not by any means "postmodern" in any philosophical sense. In a philosophical sense, the situation in question was rather *ultramodern*, the simple carrying to the extreme of the modern proposition that the mind knows only what the mind makes. The "postmoderns falsely so called" were not postmodern at all: they were philosophical modernity extended to the extreme that Kant had essayed to forestall: swamping science itself in a linguistic tangle of terminally clever solipsistic relativism.

If modern philosophy depends upon an epistemological paradigm which knows no path beyond the representative contents of consciousness, while epistemology constitutes for semiotics no more than its "midmost target",[8] the reason is that study of the action of signs finds precisely a path[9] beyond the representative contents of consciousness. These contents are not self-representations (objects) but, precisely, themselves signs (other-representations)[10] rooted in the being of relations which transcend the division between nature and culture,

---

[8] Sebeok 1991: 2.

[9] "Renvoi", as has been said (after Jakobson 1974): Deely 1993a, and Part III below, p. 183ff.

[10] The point is fundamental: cf. Poinsot 1632a: 117/12–17. Cf. the statement of the position of the representamen above, p. 5.

inner and outer, and so cannot be confined to either side of any such divide, real or imagined. The "central preoccupation" of semiotics may be, à la modernity, "an illimitable array of concordant illusions", Sebeok reported to the Semiotic Society of America in his Presidential Address of 1984,[11] but "its main mission" is "to mediate between reality and illusion." Petrilli and Ponzio, in their recent study of Sebeok's work (which had something of his endorsement),[12] capture the postmodern essence of the way of signs as Sebeok envisioned it exactly: "there is no doubt that the inner human world, with great effort and serious study, may reach an understanding of non-human worlds and of its connection with them."

[11] Sebeok 1984: 77–78.
[12] Petrilli and Ponzio 2001: 20.

Section 4

Skirmishes on the Boundary

When the postmoderns falsely so called entered the fray from the fringes of semiology, just when semiotics was promising to come into its own, Sebeok could not but be dismayed. For Sebeok, insofar as he was modern, belonged to the scientific, not the philosophical, side of modernity. So it needs also to be noted, as mentioned above in passing,[1] that modern intellectual culture became frankly and unreservedly idealistic only on its philosophical side, and this even in spite of itself. Neither Galileo nor Descartes set out to make the external world problematic, still less unknowable. These were rather the consequences ineluctably radiating from the modern starting point which only the philosophers wholeheartedly embraced, to wit, the premiss that we directly know nothing but self-representations fashioned by the mind under the

---

[1] See Section 2 above, p. 123 n. 5.

provocation of stimuli directly unknown. A realistic spirit never wholly died, neither within the popular culture as a residual "common sense", nor within the scientific enterprise with which modernity thought to replace cenoscopic knowledge with a wholly ideoscopic edifice (the "Enlightenment" project), even if only to learn ruefully that, after all, cenoscopy has its irreducible place in the realm of knowledge alongside and in some ways naturally prior to ideoscopy.[2] Modern science took its origin not from a repudiation of but in continuity with the ancient and medieval concern with exposing in knowledge the very structures and modalities proper to *ens reale*, the order of things-in-themselves.[3] Galileo's social problems arose not from proposing hypotheses about what might be but from proposing a hypothesis about *the way things are*, in the spirit and with the conviction that such was knowable, even if it required new instruments and different means than were developed by or available to the medieval "natural philosophers" and early modern (or any other) religious authorities.

So the modernity upon the scene of which Sebeok entered and of which he was one of the most noble heirs of its high intellectual culture had a schizophrenic, not to say psychotic, side, for the purpose of understanding which I have proposed we might usefully exapt the story of Dr. Jekyll and Mr. Hyde.[4] Fortunately for all of us, Sebeok was a man of thoroughly

---

[2] See Deely 2001: Chapter 11, esp. pp. 489–92; cf. Heidegger 1927: 10–11, on how "ontological inquiry", provided it does not remain "naïve and opaque" in its researches after the manner of Galileo's critics and judges at the time, "is indeed more primordial, as over against the ontical inquiry of the sciences".

[3] I would direct the reader's attention to remarks I made on this subject at one of the many conferences organized by Sebeok: Deely 1984: 265–66.

[4] Deely 2001: Chapter 13.

scientific temper, and while he had respect for philosophy and its conundrums, and even while the sciences in which he immersed himself concerned objects which could be in nowise reduced to the *ens reale* at the heart of the original enterprises of philosophy and science alike, neither was he about to be taken in by a central thesis that served to define little more than philosophy's distinctively modern mainstream. He was never one for abjectly mistaking some part for the whole, or for respecting the claims of those who transparently did so, such as the ultramoderns, "the postmoderns falsely so called".

"For us, workers in a zoösemiotic context, there is only one way to get through this thicket."[5] Realism is not enough. The Way of Things has been tried and found wanting, even if not so completely so as the Way of Ideas proved wanting. For along the Way of Signs, we find that realism, "scholastic realism", as Peirce insisted ("or a close approximation to that"[6]), if insufficient, yet pertains to the essence of the enterprise. The only way to realism in the minimalist sense required (the sense of "scholastic realism", that is, as Peirce correctly termed it) is by a warranting within experience of a distinction not only between signs and objects (the former as presupposed to the latter's possibility), but further between objects and things. Here "things" refers to a dimension within the experience of the objective world which not merely does not reduce to our experience of it but is further knowable as such within objectivity through the discrimination in particular

---

5   Sebeok 2001: 78, and 193 n. 6.

6   Peirce 1905: CP 5.423. By *scholastic realism* Peirce intends in general a sense of realism sufficiently strong and clear as to prove incompatible with all variants of Nominalism as the denial of relations sometimes obtaining in their proper being as relations independently of the workings of finite mind.

cases of what marks the difference between *ens reale* and *ens rationis* in the being of objects experienced. In this way (and for this reason),[7] the "minimal but sufficient module of distinctive features of +, −, or 0, variously multiplied in advanced zoösemiotic systems" which yet remain wholly perceptual in nature, "is a far cry from the exceedingly complex cosmic models Newton or Einstein in due course bestowed upon humanity."

And the only way to a difference between things experienced as objects through their relation to us and things understood, actually or prospectively, as things in themselves prior to or independent of any such cognitive relation is through a modeling system capable of proposing within some object of experience a difference between aspects of the object given in experience and those same aspects giveable apart from the particular experience. In Sebeok's trenchant terms, the distinction between objects and things depends upon a modeling system, an *Innenwelt*, which has among its biologically determined components a component which is biologically underdetermined, the component Sebeok labels "language". Thanks to language we can model the difference between "appearances" in the objective sense and "reality" in the scholastic sense, and propose experiments to test the model, leading to its extension, refinement, or abandonment, depending upon the particulars of the case.

An Umwelt species-specifically human is not needed in order for the mind to be in contact with reality in this scholastic sense.[8] For reality in the scholastic sense need not be envisioned

---

[7] Sebeok 1995: 87, or Sebeok 2001: 68.

[8] What Peirce calls "scholastic realism", in view of its medieval provenance in the explicit recognition of the contrast between *ens reale* and *ens rationis*, I call "hardcore realism", in view of the continuity of the medieval notion of *ens reale* with the ov of which Aristotle spoke as

in order to be objectively encountered. The *idea* of reality, we will shortly see, is no less than a representative component of an Innenwelt species-specifically human. But the *objective content* of that idea (not, indeed, formally prescissed as such, but, indeed, "materially" in the scholastic sense) is part of the Umwelt of every animal.[9] Sebeok liked to quote Jacob on the point:

> No matter how an organism investigates its environment, the perception it gets must necessarily reflect so-

scholasticism's grandfather. Thus, hardcore realism means that there is a dimension to the universe of being which is indifferent to human thought, belief, and desire, such that, for example, if I believe that the soul survives the destruction of my body and I am wrong, when my body goes so does my soul – or, conversely, if I believe that the death of the body is also the end of my mind or soul and I am wrong, when my body disintegrates my soul lives on, and I will have to take stock accordingly. Or, to give a more historical example, from the time of Aristotle to at least that of Copernicus, all the best evidence, arguments, and opinions of every stripe held that the sun moves relative to the earth, while in hardcore reality, all along, supremely indifferent to these stripes of opinion, it was the earth that moved relative to the sun, and the sun also moved, but not relative to the earth.

[9] Cf. Poinsot 1632a: "First Preamble on Mind-Dependent Being", Article 3, 66/47–72/17: "The internal senses do not form mind-dependent beings formally speaking, although materially they are able to represent that on whose pattern some fictive entity is formed, which is to form mind-dependent beings materially.

"We say that the internal senses 'formally speaking' do not form mind-dependent beings, that is, they do not form them by discriminating between mind-dependent being and physical being, and by conceiving that which is not a being after the pattern of physical being. Materially, however, to cognize a mind-dependent being is to attain the very appearance of a being physically real, but not to discriminate between that which is of the mind and that which is of the physical world. For example, the imaginative power can form a gold mountain, and similarly it can construct an animal composed of a

called 'reality' and, more specifically, those aspects of reality which are directly related to its own behavior. If

she-goat, a lion, and a serpent, which is the Chimera [of Greek mythology]. But in these constructions the imagination itself attains only that which is sensible or representable to sense. Yet internal sense does not attain the fact that objects so known have a condition relative to non-being, and from this relative condition are said to be constructed, fictive, mind-dependent, or purely objective – which is formally to discriminate between being and non-being.

"The reason seems clear: internal sense cannot refer to anything except under a sensible rationale; but the fact that that which is represented to it as sensible happens to be opposed to physical being, does not pertain to internal sense to judge, because internal sense does not conceive of being under the rationale of being. The fact, however, of anything's being regarded as a constructed or fictive being formally consists in this, that it is known to have nothing of entitative reality in the physical world, and yet is attained or grasped on the pattern of a physical entity; otherwise, no discrimination is made between mind-independent being and purely objective, constructed or fictive being, but only that is attained on whose pattern a mind-dependent being is formed. When this object is something sensible, there is no reason why it cannot be known by sense. But sense attains only that which is sensible in an object, whereas the condition relative to the non-being in whose place the object is surrogated and whence it fictively has being, does not pertain to sense. For this reason, sense does not differentiate an objective or constructed being, under the formal rationale of being a construct, from a true being.

"But that sense is able to know fictive being materially is manifestly the case. Not, indeed, from the fact that even external sense can, for example, cognize a fictive color or appearance, because this color, even though it is the color [of a given object] only apparently, is nevertheless not a fictive being, but one true and physical, that is to say, it is something resulting from light. But that sense grasps mind-dependent beings is proved by this fact, that internal sense synthesizes many things which outside itself in no way are or can be. Sense therefore knows something which is in itself a constructed or purely objective being, although the fiction itself sense does not apprehend, but only that which, in the fictive being, offers itself as sensible. . . .

the image that a bird gets of the insects it needs to feed
its progeny does not reflect at least some aspects of reality,

". . . The understanding needs some comparative act in order that
mind-dependent beings might be formed and be said to exist formally and not only fundamentally.

"This conclusion is taken from St. Thomas's . . . *Disputed Questions
on the Power of God*, q. 7, art. 11, [when] he says that the objective relations that the understanding invents and attributes to the things
understood are one thing, but the objective relations that result from
the mode of understanding are quite another, although the understanding does not devise that mode, but proceeds in conformity with
it. And relations of the first sort the mind indeed brings about by considering the ordering of that which is in the understanding to the
things which are independent thereof, or also by considering the
ordering of the things understood [as such] among themselves; but
the other relations result from the fact that the understanding understands one thing in an order to another. Therefore St. Thomas thinks
that all [mind-dependent] intentions are formed by some act of comparing or relating. . . .

"By the phrase 'a comparative act', however, we understand not
only a compositive, in the sense of a judicative, comparison (which
pertains to the second operation of the mind), but any cognition
whatever that conceives [its object] with a connotation of and an
ordering to another something that can also occur outside of the second operation of the mind, as, for example, when we apprehend a
relation through the order to a terminus. A mind-dependent being
can also come about as the result of a compositive or of a discursive
comparison. Indeed, because the understanding affirms that there is
such a thing as blindness, the Philosopher, in his *Metaphysics*, Book V,
and St. Thomas in his *Commentary* thereon (reading 9, n. 896), as well
as in numerous other places, proves that blindness is a mind-dependent being. Through that enunciation, therefore, whereby something is
affirmed of a non-being, non-being is conceived positively as if it
were a being, specifically, through the connotation of the verb 'is'.

"And I have said in this third conclusion that the understanding
requires a comparative act 'in order that mind-dependent beings
might be said to exist formally and not just fundamentally'. For the fundament of an objective relation does not require this comparison. . . .

"From this you can gather that, in the case of mind-dependent

then there are no more progeny. If the representation that
a monkey builds of the branch it wants to leap to has

relations, there comes about a denomination even before the relation
itself is known in act through a comparison, owing solely to this: that
the fundament is posited. For example, . . . the letters in a closed book
are a sign, even if the relation of the sign, which is mind-dependent,
is not actually considered; . . . In this, mind-dependent or mental relations differ from mind-independent or physical relations, because
mind-independent relations do not denominate unless they exist. . . .
The reason for this difference is that in the case of mind-dependent
relations, their actual existence consists in actually being cognized
objectively, which is something that does not take its origin from the
fundament and terminus, but from the understanding. Whence many
things could be said of a subject by reason of a fundament without
the resultance of a relation, because this does not follow upon the
fundament itself and the terminus, but upon cognition. But in the
case of physical relations, since the relation naturally results from the
fundament and the terminus, nothing belongs in an order to a terminus by virtue of a fundament, except by the medium of a relation. We
understand, however, that this denomination arises from the proxi-
mate fundament absolutely speaking, but not in every way, because
not under that formality by which it is denominated by the relation
as known and existing. . . . This is something that does not occur in
cases of physical relations, because when the relations do not exist,
their fundaments in no way denominate in an order to a terminus.

". . . The cognition forming a mind-dependent being is not a reflexive cognition respecting that being as a thing cognized as the object
which [is known]. . . .

"The reason for this conclusion is clear: such a cognition, whereby
a mind-dependent being itself is denominated cognized reflexively
and as the 'object which', supposes the [already] formed mind-
dependent being, since indeed the cognition is borne upon that being
as upon the terminus cognized. Therefore such a reflexive cognition
does not initially form that mind-dependent being, but supposes its
having been formed and, as it were, examines that objective construct. Whence a [subjective] denomination in the one cognizing does
not come about from the intentions thus reflexively cognized . . .
when anyone understands these intentions by examining their nature
. . . then the very intentions examined are not formed, but upon them

nothing to do with reality, then there is no more monkey. And if this point did not apply to ourselves, we would not be here to discuss this point.[10]

others are founded, inasmuch as they are cognized in general or by way of predication, etc. And so . . . a mental construct or being is effected precisely when the understanding attempts to apprehend something that is not, and for this reason constructs that non-being as if it were a being. . . . What formally and essentially forms initially mind-dependent being is not, therefore, the reflexive cognition whereby precisely a mind-dependent being is denominated cognized as being mind-dependent, but the cognition whereby that which is not is denominated cognized on the pattern of that which is."

Ibid., 74/27–48: "Simple apprehension does not compare one thing to another by affirming or denying, but it does indeed compare by differentiating one thing from another and by attaining the order of one thing to another, just as it knows things that are relative and attains the definition of a thing, the congruity of terms, and the distinction of categories. Whence in discussing the categories, according to the Philosopher, one treats of simple apprehension, as St. Thomas says in his *Commentary* on the first Book of Aristotle's treatise *On Interpretation*, reading 1. Simple apprehension, therefore, has enough comparison for forming a mind-dependent being. Moreover, we do not deny to internal sense the formation of a mind-dependent being on the grounds of the absence of comparison, but on the grounds of the absence of a knowing of universality, because sense does not cognize the more universal rationales by discriminating between true being and constructed or fictive being, which is something that simple apprehension does do; for simple apprehension discriminates between categorial things and those things that are not in a category of mind-independent being."

[10] Jacob 1982: 56.

Section 5

Reality too Is a Word

So a *grasp* of reality is not the issue. The issue is much deeper, and surely begins with the realization concerning which Sebeok was fond of citing Niels Bohr:[1] "'Reality' is also a word, a word which we must learn to use correctly." Now, as a word, "reality" has a history, one which, in philosophy at least, leads to the notion of something existing regardless of its status as known. But of course this raises at once the problem: please give an example of something unknown? Well, it is not impossible. What will completely defeat the AIDS virus: that is something just now unknown.[2] The belief that *there is* something, simple or complex, that meets this description is what drives scientific research in the area. When and if it is

---

[1]   From French and Kennedy Eds. 1985: 302.

[2]   Actually, just now it is not even known that there actually is such a virus to be defeated.

found the belief will be vindicated, but at that moment this currently "unknown x" will become itself an "object x identified that is not merely an object". So we can say that *if* something believed in is a part of reality in the hardcore or scholastic sense, then that something has the possibility of passing from unknown to known. At that moment, the only difference will be an extrinsic one: a relation to some knower whereby the thing existing in its own right comes now to exist also as an object, as part of a larger objective world, an item, mayhap, or process therein.

We see thus exactly that and why "such questions as how concepts are related to reality"[3] are "ultimately sterile." Reality, for the animal, *is* simply the objective world, the Umwelt. Later on, but only for the human animal, experience will give rise to the *further* consideration that there seems to be more to objects, a dimension within the objective world, that does not reduce to our experience of objects. How to name this irreducible dimension globally, "generically" – that is to say, without having (or being by any means able!) to specify in detail its specific contents (which is a much more difficult task)? Such is the origin of the *idea* of reality within the human Innenwelt, an idea the medievals termed more expansively "being as first known".[4] This idea is a sign, a representation of something other than itself that is largely unknown but

---

[3] Sebeok 1991b: 143.

[4] Poinsot 1633a: 24b18–25a31, italics added: "quando dicimus ens esse primum cognitum ly ens non sumitur pro abstracto in statu universitalitatis et separationis ab omni inferiori, sed sumitur ens ut concretum et imbibitum in aliqua re determinata, quae tunc occurrit cognitioni, quasi praedicatum quodam ipsius, ita quod in ipso obiecto sic occurrente non discernuntur determinatae rationes, sed solum accipitur seu concipitur secundum quandam indeterminationem, in qua quidquid ad tale obiectum pertinet, confunditur *et fere est idem quod cognoscere rem quoad an est*. Atque ita idem est dicere, quod in aliquo

determinable and to be determined within experience, something that *distinguishes* the way objects exist in relation to me and my perceptual categories of the "to be sought" (+), "to be avoided" (–), and "the safely ignored" (0) *from* what might be true of those objects apart from such classification ("fere est idem quod cognoscere rem quoad an est" – "it amounts to recognizing that an object does not reduce to my experience of it", as Poinsot says). Thus Sebeok sees the fact that "we can approach the 'real' richness of the universe only by entertaining multiply contending, mutually complementary visions" as but the "quotidian implication" of Niels Bohr's celebrated

obiecto, ut totum actuale est, incipimus a cognitione entis, id est a cognitione praedicati ita confusi, quod non discernantur praedicata in eo inventa et determinatae rationes, sed praecise cognoscatur id, in quo nulla est discretio nec segregatio, scilicet ipsum esse; hoc enim est maxime confusum, quia maxime indistinctum..

"Unde nec D. Thomas nec Caietanus negant rem ipsam, quae primo occurrit intellectui tamquam id, quod cognoscitur, ut obiectum *quod* esse aliquam quidditatem sensibilem et speciem specialissimam, sed dicunt, quod in hoc concreto et in hoc toto et in hac specie, quae occurrit, primum quod offertur intellectui tamquam ratio *quae,* est illa confusio entis et quasi cognitio quoad an est, non quia attingatur actu suprema illa universalitatis, sed quia de ipso obiecto seu natura primum, quod attingitur, est ratio maxime indiscreta et confusa. Et quia tanto aliquid est confusius, quanto pauciores rationes discernuntur, ita quod earum propriae differentiae seu praedicata non distinguantur, illud erit maxime confusum, in quo nec ipsi supremi gradus et communiora praedicata, v. g. substantia et accidens discernuntur. Et hoc vocamus ens concretum seu applicatum quidditati sensibili, id est in natura aliqua sensibili inventum, non ut subest statui abstractionis et universalitatis secundum habitudinem et respectum ad inferiora, ad quae potentialiter se habet, sed ut actualiter intrat ipsam compositionem rei, et ut cognoscitur secundum se; siquidem modo loquimur de cognitione confusa totius actualis, non totius potentialis."

adage[5] that "physics concerns what we can say about nature". I see this quotidian implication as an upshot of the fact that we are inevitably workers in a zoösemiotic context rather than disembodied minds. Bohr[6] is simply wrong, as Sebeok should have been the first to point out, further to conclude *without qualification* that "to think that the task of physics is to find out how nature is" is "wrong". The qualification needed, of course, is the fallibilist one that we can never find out exhaustively "how nature is" – quite another matter than not finding out at all, and Sebeok's real point[7] in citing Bohr's statement in the first place.

"Reality" (in the scholastic, or "hardcore", sense), thus, is a representation of objectivity that transcends biological heritage, for it is only indirectly tied to my biological type as an organism within a determinate species. Every animal lives in a species-specific objective world, determined from the ground up by its biology. "What is commonly called the 'external world'," in this context, we may be forgiven for considering[8] as "the brain's formal structure (*logos*)" under the stimulus the senses convey from the physical surroundings, as this collusion gives rise to the objective world or Umwelt in which the animal lives and moves and has its being, "models of purlieus frequented by and appropriate to the survival of each organism and its species".[9] This is true also of the human animal, but the uniformity of the objective world is, so to say, partially ruined at the level of culture by the incorporation of diverse specifications of "reality" generically considered, as

---

5   According to Pais 1991: 427.

6   Ibid.

7   Sebeok 1992a: 339.

8   As Sebeok put it, 1992: 57.

9   Sebeok 1995: 87 (or 2001: 67–68), referencing J. von Uexküll 1920.

we see in the different customs of marriage, family, and religion (particularly in the matter of which texts – if any, the
skeptics will say – have "God himself" or "Allah" or
"Jahweh", etc., as their "true author"), not to mention the
astronomical controversies which led to the bootless break
between medieval cenoscopy and modern ideoscopy. God
and the physical environment, thus, are but the polar
extremes under the idea of *ens reale* according to which the
species-specifically human objective world diversifies itself
internally through language exapted in communication.

In other words, the notion of reality is a species-specifically human achievement based on the species-specifically
human component of the generically animal modeling system
or Innenwelt thanks to which, as Sebeok puts it, we are and
cannot but be "workers in a zoösemiotic context"; for we are,
even as anthropos, animals from the outset and to the end of
our days. We awaken not to a physical environment of pure
ens reale but to an objective world which, like that of every animal,[10] is a mixture of *ens rationis* and *ens reale* in the presentation and maintenance of objects, the objects we need in order
to survive, grow, and flourish. Within these objects what is
important is precisely their relation to us, not the "relation to
themselves" (itself, note, this "self-relation", an *ens rationis*
without which the notion of "hardcore reality" no less than
that of "thing" could not arise[11]) which an altruist or, mayhap,
a scientifically minded inquirer, might want to pursue.

---

[10] See again the text of Poinsot 1632a: Second Preamble, cited in Section
4, note 9, p. 135, above. See also Deely 2001f, or 2002: 126–43, on
Umwelt (resumed in Part I, Chap. 3, pp. 31–48 above).

[11] Guagliardo 1993; Deely 1994: Part IV.

Section 6

A Modeling System Biologically Underdetermined

Here Sebeok would typically reveal his modern side by missing a point which his postmodern "better self" was about to make. "It was Niels Bohr who first emphasized the doctrine that scientists have no concern with 'reality'; their job has to do with model building."[1] How ironic a point to miss, since the very notion of reality itself results from a modeling within the species-specifically human Umwelt; and further such modeling, both cenoscopic and ideoscopic, aims precisely to clarify the generic intuition in specific ways and circumstances. For, as we have just seen, "reality", in its philosophical notion as "hardcore" reality, is precisely an achievement, species-specifically human, of modeling, exapted to

---

[1] Sebeok 1987a: 72.

communicate in the linguistic expression "reality", concern with which – either preclusively (a largely chimerical goal) or as something to be correlatively distinguished within the objective world from the factors of *ens rationis* and identified as such – is equally at the cenoscopic 7th/6th century BC origins of philosophy and the 16th/17th century AD ideoscopic origins of modern science. The concern of scientists, Sebeok aimed at saying, is with the building and testing of models concerned with distinguishing in verifiable ways what in our experience belongs to the order of *ens reale* and what to the order of *ens rationis*, which would not be a problem were it not for the fact that, within human experience, the elements of both orders, however different "in themselves" as connected with subjectivity, are equally objective strands within the semiotic web that we call culture.

So we come by a devious route to what Sebeok called "the ultimate enigma":[2] the union of nature and culture within human experience, and the dilemma of disentangling the strands of experience within which this unity is given (first as Umwelt, then, in the wake of the awakening to the idea of "reality", as Lebenswelt, that species-specifically human variant of the generically animal Umwelt insofar as the Umwelt is transformed or modified from within by the components and considerations introduced into the objective horizon of experience by the representative elements formed by language within the Innenwelt and exapted into objective structures of linguistic communication transmogrifying Umwelt to Lebenswelt – all without for a moment suppressing or obviating the "animal roots" of every individual's world as objective, that is to say, experienced and "known" in the context of society as well as individually).

[2] Sebeok 1981a: 199.

Section 7

Blickwendung
A Glance in the Rear-View Mirror

In my private semiosis, these public considerations carry me
back to my youth as a student of philosophy in the school my
Dominican professors maintained in River Forest Illinois.[1] My
first suspicion of the external world as a quasi-error came not
from Sebeok, who gave me the expression, but from Kant,
who seemed to me to have imposed on understanding the
requirements distinctive rather of sense. I remember visiting
the room of one of my professors, Ralph Austin Powell, to
inquire whether what Kant had to say of "reason" with its a-
priori forms was not a fundamental confusion of what could

---

[1] The school originally was a Pontifical Faculty, but by my time had
also acquired the standard secular accreditation from the North
Central agency.

only be true of perception insofar as sense is wholly determined biologically by the type of body we happen to have.

"That's a very interesting idea, Brother", Powell replied.
"Why don't you write it up as a paper?" The suggestion may
have been a device to get me out of his room, but in any event
it was a good suggestion. It primed me years later to appreciate one of history's greatest ironies in the arena of philosophy.
Von Uexküll, by his own attestation, was influenced above all
by Kant in arriving at and formulating his *Umweltstheorie*.
Kant distinguished only between percepts and concepts, the
former arising from sense, the latter from understanding. In
fact, this conflation of sensation with perception in the pro-
duction of representations was a fundamental blunder, for no
analysis of knowledge can do without the distinction between
sensation prescissively considered as such, wherein mental
imagery is superfluously assumed, and perception likewise
considered, wherein imagery (or "ideas": *species expressae*, as
the Latins generically said[2]), proves essential. But on any such
distinction, it becomes quickly apparent that concepts belong
to perception before they belong to understanding, and do not
belong at all to sensation. Thus the proper question in distinguishing understanding from sense concerns not the difference between sensory "percepts" and rational "concepts", but
rather the difference between the concepts proper to understanding and the concepts proper to perception in its difference from sensation.

This last difference is precisely that between concepts of
objects classified as to be sought, to be avoided, or to be
ignored, and concepts of objects classified as belonging primarily to *ens reale* or *ens rationis*. The relation of an object to
itself, which underlies, in the species-specifically human

---

[2] See the summary in Poinsot 1632a: Book II, Question 2, text and
notes; and the discussion in the *Four Ages* (Deely 2001: 345–47).

originary grasp of being,[3] the recognition of the difference between objects which are only objects and objects which are also things, is itself already an *ens rationis*, but one consisting in a representation which is not wholly biologically determined, one which therefore belongs to that aspect of the modeling system which Sebeok labels "language" and which is species-specifically human. Communication, but not language, is alone needed for the concepts of perception, and these concepts alone pertain to von Uexküll's "functional cycle", even as the concepts of understanding alone pertain to scientific as distinguished from the ideas of artistic understanding.

In arriving at his concept of the Umwelt, von Uexküll was already employing his animal modeling system in its species-specifically human dimension, which would not have been possible were the Kantian dyadic contrast between "sense" and "reason" the contrast obtaining "in reality". This is why I have said[4] that, in a wholly logical world, the study of the purely perceptual intelligence of animals would have been rather the inspiration for the jettisoning of Kantianism in the philosophy of intellectual mind.

---

[3] *Ens primum cognitum*, which divides from within, over the course of experience, between *ens reale* and *ens rationis*.

[4] See Part I above, Chapter 2, n. 11, p. 16f.

Section 8

Updating the File

The realization that human experience, being animal experience first of all, does not begin simply with *ens reale* but with a world of objects which are normally (at least in historic, if not prehistoric, times) predominantly constituted by *entia rationis* (and include *entia realia* formally recognized as such only as a virtual dimension and indistinctly as to particulars) is not unprecedented in the history of philosophy.[1] But the full thematization of this realization *is* unprecedented,[2] and may be said to constitute the essence of postmodernity insofar as we are to conceive of it as a distinct philosophical epoch in the wake of the mainstream philosophical development which

---

[1] Aquinas, notably (e.g., c.1268/72: *Commentary on Aristotle's Metaphysics*, IV. 6), called it *ens primum cognitum* under which experience leads us to distinguish *reale* from *rationis*: see Deely 2001: 350–57.

[2] Guagliardo 1994 is one of the very few who have troubled to unearth some precedents in this move toward thematization.

II.

runs from Descartes in the seventeenth century to Wittgenstein and Husserl in the twentieth century. Heidegger pointed to the need for such a thematization under the classical rubric of "being", but he only got as far as the posing of the question to which semiotics begins the answer.[3] Why is it, he asked, in terms with an intersemioticity resonant of von Uexküll, that humans experience beings as present-at-hand, rather than ready-to-hand, which is "closer" to us and indeed the way beings are given proximally and for the most part? The answer lies in the difference of an Umwelt experienced on the basis of an Innenwelt having language as a component in its forming of representations.[4]

---

[3] Heidegger 1927: 487. The question was part of the transition to the never completed final sections of this great work.

[4] The distinction between the ready-to-hand and the present-at-hand is a distinction that does not arise for any animal except an animal with a modeling system capable of representing objects (as such necessarily related to us) according to a being or features not necessarily related to us but obtaining subjectively and/or intersubjectively in the objects themselves (mistakenly or not, according to the particular case) – an animal, in short, capable of *wondering* about things-in-themselves and conducting itself accordingly. Now, since a modeling system so capacitated is, according to Sebeok, what is meant by language in the root sense, whereas the exaptation of such a modeling in action gives rise not to language but to linguistic communication, and since 'language' in this derivative sense of linguistic communication is the species-specifically distinctive and dominant modality of communication among humans, we have a difficulty inverse to that of the nonlinguistic animals, although we, unlike they, can overcome the difficulty.

Our difficulty – the source of the quasi-error of the external world, if I may say so – is that, within an Umwelt, objects *are* reality so far as the organism is concerned. But without language, the animals have no way to go beyond the objective world as such to inquire into the physical environment in its difference from the objective world. Within a Lebenswelt, by contrast, that is to say, within an Umwelt

The external world is a species specifically human representation. The quasi-error arises from the routine mistaking of objects simply for "things", leading to the confusion of "external reality" (as became the custom within philosophy) with the more fundamental notion of *ens reale*, which is neither identical with "the external world" nor the starting point as such of species-specifically human knowledge, but merely a recognizable dimension experienced within objectivity. The "external world" does not lie beneath or outside of thought and language, as the moderns tended to imagine, but is precisely given, to whatever extent it is given, within objective experience, as semiotics from the first[5] instructed us. Sebeok liked to quote while constantly reassessing Bohr's asseveration[6] that "We are suspended in language in such a way that we cannot say what is up and what is down". In my assessment this is an asseveration whose truth and best interpretation depends on the fact that we are linguistic animals and not just perceptual animals, as I have argued pointedly at some length.[7]

As linguistic animals, we can become aware not only of the difference between a thing and an object, between objective world and physical environment as but partially incorporated within objectivity, but we can further become aware of the status of language as a system of signs, and its dependence

internally transformed by language, the reality so far as the organism is concerned is confused with and mistaken for the world of things. Objects appear not as mixtures of *entia rationis* with *entia realia*, but simply as 'what is', 'real being', 'a world of things'.

[5] Using "first" here in the sense of the original treatise which established the unity of signs in the being proper to relation as indifferent to the distinction between *ens reale* and *ens rationis*, namely, the *Tractatus de Signis* of Poinsot 1632a.

[6] From French and Kennedy 1985: 302.

[7] Deely 2002.

upon yet other signs in the constitution of objects. It is these objects and their interconnections which go together to form our experience of "reality" (so far like that of any other animal); but within this sphere of objective experience, thanks to language, we can also fashion an *idea* of "reality" establishing an intelligible sense which is not simply given in perception, but is *attained* through sensation *within* perception owing to the difference of sensation from perception.[8] And with that idea thus experimentally grounded, perhaps *only* with that idea, we may say, the human animal begins to awaken to its humanness. Our species is drawn by this aboriginal abduction to set out on the long road of philosophy and science, eventually to come across – quite late in the journey, as it happens – that crossroads having the Way of Signs as one of its forks. At that juncture the human animal realizes that, while every animal and perhaps all nature is *semiosic*, the human animal alone is a *semiotic* animal; and in that moment of realization, which few or none have done more than Sebeok to inaugurate, in philosophy at least, postmodern intellectual culture begins – indeed, takes wing. The quasi-error of the external world need no longer beguile or bemuse us, for its nature and origin have been exposed by the very clearing of the opening to the Way of Signs. We see now to have uncovered a path leading "everywhere in nature, including those domains where humans have never set foot,"[9] but to an understanding of which semiotics gives us the means integrally

---

[8] Aquinas liked to say that "things are per se sensible but they have to be made intelligible": it is the perpetual task of human understanding in its difference from sensation and perception alike.

[9] Emmeche 1994: 126; staying silent for the moment on the question over which Sebeok turned conservative, the question of whether semiosis is co-terminus with the emergence of life, or whether there is not indeed a broader origin in which semiosis must be seen as coterminous with the physical universe *tout court*: see Nöth 2001.

to aspire. Call it the postmodern interpretive horizon, may-hap, the "coincidence of communication with being".[10] It is the heart of semiotics, vindicating against modernity the medieval conviction which modern science never wholly abandoned, despite the philosophers: *ens et verum convertuntur*. To be for nature is to be intelligible for the animal whose being is to understand.

[10] Petrilli and Ponzio 2001: 54.

Part III.
Dialogue between
a 'Semiotist' and a 'Realist'

A Dialogue between a Semiotician and a Would-Be Realist[1]

A Sign is *What?*

Everyone knows that some days are better than others. I was having one of those "other" days, when a colleague approached me to express interest in the forthcoming Annual Meeting – the 26th, as it happened – of the Semiotic Society of America.

"Come on", said the colleague. "Tell me something about this semiotics business."

[1] The original version of this exchange was delivered as the presidential address of the Semiotic Society of America at its twenty-sixth Annual Meeting held at Victoria College of the University of Toronto, Canada. The term 'semiotist' as a synonym for 'semiotician' as 'one who investigates the action of signs' is from Rauch 1983, the eighth presidential address. See Deely 1990: 119–20.

"What's there to say?" I said, not in the mood for this at the moment. "Semiotics is the study of the action of signs, signs and sign systems." I knew it would not help to say that semiotics is the study of semiosis. So I let it go at that. But inwardly I cringed, for I could see the question coming like an offshore tidal wave.

"Well, what do you mean by a sign?" my colleague pressed.

Who in semiotics has not gotten this question from colleagues a hundred times? In a way it is an easy question, for "everyone knows" what a sign is. How else would they know what to look for when driving to Austin? All you have to do is play on that, and turn the conversation elsewhere.

Maybe it was a change in mood. Maybe it was the fact that I liked this particular colleague. Or maybe I wanted to play *advocatus diaboli*. Whatever the reason, I decided not to take the easy way out, not to play on the "common sense" understanding of sign which, useful as it is and not exactly wrong, nonetheless obscures more than it reveals, and likely as not makes the inquirer cynical (if he or she is not such already) about this "new science" of signs.

You know the routine. Someone asks you what a sign is. You respond, "You know. Anything that draws your attention to something else. Something that represents another." And they say, "You mean like a traffic sign?" And you say "Sure. Or a word. Or a billboard. Anything." And they say, "Oh. I think I get it." And life goes on.

But this time I decided to go against the grain, and to actually say what I thought a sign was. So I looked my colleague in the eye for a few moments, and finally said, not averting my gaze in the least, "OK. I'll tell you what a sign is. A sign is what every object presupposes".

My colleague's eyes widened a bit, the face took on a

slightly taken-aback expression, and my ears detected an incredulous tone in the words of reply: "A sign is *what*?"

"What every object presupposes. Something presupposed by every object", I said again.

"What do you mean? Could you explain that?" The colleague seemed serious, and I had no pressing obligations or plans for the moment, so I said "Sure, but let's go outside." I opened my office door and indicated the stone table and bench at my disposal in the private fenced area at the end of the driveway that comes to the outer door of my office.

My colleague had no way of knowing, but in my private semiosis of that moment I could only recall the SSA Presidential Address given some seventeen years previously by Thomas A. Sebeok, wherein he compared the relations of semiotics to the idealist movement with the case of the giant rat of Sumatra,[2] "a story for which, as Sherlock Holmes announced, the world is not yet prepared."

In that memorable speech, Sebeok had taken the occasion "to indulge in personal reminiscences, comment on the institutionalization of our common cultural concerns, and then to prognosticate about the direction toward which we may be headed."[3] Now, some seventeen years later, this mantle of SSA President had fallen to me; and the institutional status of semiotics in the university world, healthy and promising as Sebeok then spoke, had in American academe become somewhat unhealthy and parlous in the succeeding years, even as the interest in and promise of the intellectual enterprise of semiotics had succeeded beyond what any of us in the eighties could have predicted in the matter of the contest as to whether the *general conception* of sign study should be conceived

[2] Sebeok 1984: 18.

[3] Ibid: 3.

on the model of Saussurean semiology or (picking up the threads and pieces in this matter left by the teachers common to Peirce and Poinsot[4]) Peircean semiotics.[5]

It is true enough that I was in a position, as an associate of Sebeok since the late sixties, and particularly as the only living SSA member who had personally attended every Executive Board meeting since the founding of the Society in 1976 (and before that in the 1975 preparatory meeting[6]), to indulge in personal reminiscences illuminating how this passage from promising to parlous had been wrought, but the exercise would only be for my expectant colleague across the stone table hugely beside the point of anything reasonably to be expected in the present discussion. Far better, I thought, to imitate the example set by Phaedrus the Myrrhinusian in responding to Eryximachus the Physician at the symposium in the House of Agathon. The present occasion called for nothing less than a furthering of the abductive assignment that our then-elected medicine man proposed as the main mission of semiotics: to mediate between reality and illusion.[7] Such was my private semiosis of the moment.

---

[4] Beuchot and Deely 1995; Deely 1994b

[5] See Petrilli and Ponzio 2001: 4–11, esp. 6 and 10. The mistaking of "a part (that is, human signs and in particular verbal signs) for the whole (that is, all possible signs, human and non-human)" that lay at the heart of this contest had already been identified as a *pars pro toto fallacy* (Deely 1986c) and made the subject of a landmark anthology of the period (Deely, Williams, and Kruse eds. 1986).

[6] The First North American Semiotics Colloquium, convened July 28–30, 1975, "at the University of South Florida for the purpose of founding a Semiotic Society of America", as the jacket of the volume memorializing the colloquium (Sebeok Ed. 1977) announces.

[7] Sebeok 1984: 21: "the central preoccupation of semiotics, I now hold, is . . . to reveal the substratal illusion underlying reality and to search for the reality that may, after all, lurk behind that illusion."

A *Sign Is* What?

I needed no further inducement. For the public semiosis of the occasion in which I found myself I decided then and there to test the interest, intelligence, and patience of my inquiring colleague, and to plunge us together at once into the "illimitable array of concordant illusions"[8] semiotics is centrally preoccupied in bringing to light.

The first illusion under which I was sure my colleague suffered, and which every standard loose answer to the question of what a sign is serves only to further, is the impression that some things are signs while others are not – in other words, that the world of experience can be adequately divided among particulars which are signs and particulars which are not signs. Right away, the situation called for an exorcist rather than a shaman. The ghost of William of Ockham is always present at the outset of these discussions, and, not to under-rate his importance or power, at the outset, at least, it is best to exorcise him. Later on, he can be recalled to further the spirit of the discussion and, indeed, will be essential therefor; but at the outset he mostly causes trouble.

"Look around you", I urged my colleague, "and, like a good phenomenologist, give me a brief inventory of the main types of object that fall under your gaze." Of course, I had already taken into account my colleague's angle of vision, and knew that it fell directly on something that I could see only by turning, something that would be a key to the course of our conversation.

"Well", the colleague noted, "of course there is this side of the building itself whence we exited with its doors and windows; and there is the portico of the driveway with its pillars, the driveway itself, this marvelous tree which gives us shade, and this fence which gives us privacy. How did you get such a setup for your office?"

---

[8] As Sebeok put it in his 1984 presidential address, p. 21.

"Stick to the point", I said, "and tell me if you see for your inventory anything which could be called a sign."

"Of course. Out there, beyond the driveway and over toward the sidewalk, is the sign that identifies this building as Monaghan House."

"Yes", I said, "there is so-located a sign. But", I counseled, "you should read it more with your eyes than with your memory, my friend. Take a closer look."

"Of course", my colleague said, hand to forehead, squinting and abashed. "The sign has been changed to say 'Sullivan Hall'."

"Indeed it has", I agreed. "Are there any other signs in your inventory?"

"No", the colleague said. "From here, that is the only sign as such that appears."

"Ah so", I said, "but in your preliminary inventory you concluded by asking how I had managed such a setup for my office. So what you saw around you, even before you misidentified the sign for the building, led you to think of something not actually present in our perception here, namely, my office."

"What do you mean? Your office is right there", said the colleague, pointing to the nearest door.

"To be sure. But for that door to appear to you as 'Deely's office door' presupposes that you know about my office; and it is that knowledge, inside your very head, I dare say, that presents to you a particular door, which could in fact lead to most anything, as leading in fact to my office. So one door at least, among those you noted in this side of the building, even though you did not inventory it as a sign, nonetheless, functioned for you as a sign of my office" (the office, after all, which cannot be perceived from here, being an object which is other than the door which indeed is here perceived).

"I see what you mean", the colleague said. "So any

particular thing which leads to thought of another may be called a sign."

"Perhaps", I said, "but not so fast. Tell me first what is the difference between that former Monaghan House sign and my office door, insofar as both of them function in your semiosis as representations of what is other than themselves?"

"Function in my semiosis?"

"Forgive my presumption in bringing in so novel a term. 'Semiosis' is a word Peirce was inspired to coin in the context of work connected with his Johns Hopkins logic seminar of 1883,[9] from his reading in particular of the 1st century BC Herculanean papyrus surviving from the hand (or at least the mind) of Philodemus the Epicurean.[10] Cognizant no doubt of the reliable scholastic adage that action is coextensive with being,[11] in the sense that a being must act in order to develop or even maintain its being, with the consequent that we are able to know any being only as and insofar as we become aware of its activity, Peirce considered that we need a term to designate the activity distinctive of the sign in its proper being as sign, and for this he suggested the coinage 'semiosis'. So whenever in your own mind one *thought* leads to another, it is proper to speak of an action of signs, that is to say, of a function of semiosis private to you, of the way signs work, the associations that occur, if you like, in 'your particular semiosis'. In fact, the whole of your experiential life can be represented as a spiral of semiosis, wherein through the action of signs you make a guess (or 'abduction'), develop its consequences ('deduction'), and test it in interactions ('retroduction'),

---

[9] Cf. Peirce Ed. 1883, and the discussion in Part I above, Chap. 4, p. 40 n. 31.

[10] Philodemus i.54–40BC.

[11] "*Agere sequitur esse*", in the original. Extended commentary in Deely 1994.

leading to further guesses, consequences, and tests, and so on, until your particular semiosis comes to an end. So" – and here I sketched for him on a scrap of paper a Semiotic Spiral representing our conscious life as animals:

The Semiotic Spiral, where **A = abduction, B = deduction, C = retroduction**

Now my colleague is remarkable in a number of ways, one of which is in possessing an excellent knowledge of Greek. So I was horrified but not surprised when my colleague expostulated: "Aha! An excellent coinage, this 'semiosis', though perhaps it should include an 'e' between 'm' and 'i'! For probably you know that the ancient Greek term for 'sign' is precisely σημεῖον."

Horrified, for I had not expected to be confronted so soon with what is surely one of the most incredible tales the contemporary development of semiotics has had to tell. It was my turn to deal with the tangled web of a private semiosis, my experience in particular on learning through my assignment to team-teach a course with Umberto Eco,[12] that there in fact was no term for a general notion of sign among the Greeks. I remember vividly my own incredulity on first hearing this claim. On the face of it, the claim is incredible, as any reader

---

[12] Eco and Deely 1983.

of translations of ancient Greek writings from the Renaissance on can testify. At the same time, the credibility of Eco as a speaker on the subject equaled or surpassed the incredibility of the claim. The evidence for the claim has since been developed considerably,[13] and I have been forced to deem it now more true than incredible. But how should such a conviction be briefly communicated to a colleague, particularly one more knowledgeable of Greek than I?

There was nothing for it. "Not exactly so. In truth the term σημεῖον in the Greek age does not translate into 'sign' as that term functions in semiotics, even though the modern translations of Greek into, say, English, obscure the point. For actually the term σημεῖον in ancient Greek names only one species of the things we would single out today as 'signs', the species of what has been called, after Augustine, *signa naturalia*, natural signs."[14]

Looking perplexed, my colleague avowed "I am not so sure that is true. Are you trying to tell me that the word 'sign' as semioticians commonly employ it has a direct etymology, philosophically speaking, that goes back only to the 4th or 5th

---

[13] At the time, the main evidence in the public record (at least within the intellectual community of semioticians) traced back to 1983, as summarized in the "Description of Contributions" for Reading 6 (Eco, Lambertini, Marmo, and Tabaroni 1986, q.v.) in Deely, Williams and Kruse 1986: xix. Since then, the substantial work of Manetti 1993–2002 has been added from within semiotics, and the earlier independent confirmation of the original point by Markus 1972 bears consultation. A survey of the point both in its evidence in the ancient Greek context and in its more general import for the Latin Age and for the understanding of semiotics today is found in Deely 2001, referred to throughout notes to this dialogue as the *Four Ages*.

[14] See the Index entries for σημεῖον and for NATURAL SIGN in the *Four Ages* (Deely 2001: 838 and 939); and see Part I, Chap. 5 above, esp. n. 1 p. 53.

century AD? And to Latin, at that, rather than to Greek? To Augustine's *signum* rather than to the σημεῖον of ancient Greece? Surely you jest?"

"The situation is worse than that", I admitted. "I am trying to tell you that the term 'sign', as it has come to signify in semiotics, strictly speaking does not refer to or designate anything of the sort that you can perceive sensibly or point out with your finger, even while saying 'There is a sign'."

Flashing me a glance in equal proportions vexed and incredulous, my colleague said: "Look. I wasn't born yesterday. We point out signs all the time, and we specifically look for them. Driving to Austin, I watch for signs that tell me I am on the right road, and what exit I should take. Surely you don't gainsay that?"

"Surely not", I sighed. "Surely not. But semioticians, following first Poinsot[15] and, more recently, Peirce,[16] are becoming accustomed to a hard distinction,[17] that between signs in the strict or technical sense and signs loosely or commonly speaking, which are not signs but elements so related to at least two other elements that the unreflecting observer can hardly help but take them as signs among other objects which, at least comparatively speaking, are not signs. Let me explain the distinction."

"Please."

The giant rat of Sumatra was veritably on the table, a problem in a culture for which rats are not considered palatable; a

---

[15] Poinsot 1632a: Book I, Questions 1 and 3. Commentary in the *Four Ages* (Deely 2001: 432–33, 433 n. 58).

[16] Cf. Peirce 1897 and after; commentary in the *Four Ages* (Deely 2001: 433n58, 639–40, 641 n. 90.

[17] See the Index entry SIGN in the *Four Ages* (Deely 2001: 993–94), esp. the subentry "strict sense of being of sign . . . distinguished from loose sense", p. 994.

problem compounded by my own situation in a subculture about as not yet prepared to entertain considerations of idealism as the world was in the time of Sherlock Holmes to consider the case of the very giant rat now sitting, beady-eyed, on the table between me and my colleague. Fortunately for me, or unfortunately for my colleague, it happened that the stare of those beady eyes was not fixed upon me, so it could not unnerve me so long as I kept control of my imagination.

Now you must consider, in order to appreciate the turn our conversation takes at this point, that the department in which I teach is affiliated with a Center for Thomistic Studies, and probably you know that the late modern followers of Thomas Aquinas prided themselves on "realism", a philosophical position that holds for the ability of the human mind to know things as they are in themselves, prior to or apart from any relation they may have to us. To refute idealism, these fellows generally deem it sufficient to affirm their own position, and let it go at that, their puzzlement being confined to understanding how anyone could think otherwise.[18]

But semiotics cannot be reduced to any such position as a traditional philosophical realism, even if Peirce be right in holding (as I think he is right[19]) that scholastic realism is essential to if not sufficient for understanding the action of signs. In other words, the conversation had come to such a pass that, in order to enable my companion to understand why every object of experience as such presupposes the sign, I had to bring him to understand the postmodern point enunciated by Heidegger to the effect that[20] "as compared with realism, idealism, no matter how contrary and untenable it

---

[18] See the *Four Ages* (Deely 2001), pp. 740–41, text and n. 9.

[19] Peirce 1905: CP 5.423, and c.1905: CP 8.208; commentary in the *Four Ages* (Deely 2001: 616–28).

[20] Heidegger 1927: 207

may be in its results, has an advantage in principle, provided that it does not misunderstand itself as 'psychological' idealism". Best, I thought, to begin at the beginning.

"You would agree, would you not" – I put forward my initial tentative – "that we can take it as reliable knowledge that the universe is older than our earth, and our earth older than the life upon it?"

"So?" my colleague reasonably inquired.

"So we need to consider that consciousness, human consciousness in particular, is not an initial datum but one that needs to be regarded as something that emerged in time, time being understood[21] simply as the measure of the motions of the interacting bodies in space that enables us to say, for example, that some fourteen billion years ago there was an initial explosion out of which came the whole of the universe as we know it, though initially bereft of life, indeed, of stars and of planets on which life could exist."

"Surely you're not just going to give me that evolution stuff? And what has that got to do with signs being something that objects presuppose, a proposition that doesn't exactly leap out at you as true, or even as particularly sensible?"

"Actually it is not evolution, but something more basic that I have in mind. I want to suggest that semiosis is more basic than evolution, and perhaps explains *better* what has heretofore been termed evolution.[22] But, I admit, that is a bit much to ask at this point. Perhaps indeed I cast my net too wide. Let me trim my sails a bit, and ask you to agree only to this much: there is a difference in principle between something that exists in our awareness and something that exists whether or not we are aware of it?"

---

[21] See the re-definition of "The Boundary of Time" and "Time and Space" in the *Four Ages* (Deely 2001: xxix–xxxiii, 70–72).

[22] Deely 1996b, *in finem*. See Part I, Chap. 1, p. 6; and below, p. 125.

A Sign Is What?

"What are you getting at?"

"A distinction between objects and things, wherein by 'object' I mean something existing as known, something existing in my awareness, and by 'thing' rather something that exists whether or not I have any awareness of it."

"But surely you do not deny that one and the same thing may be one time unknown and another time known? This is merely an accident of time, an occurrence of chance, hardly a distinction in principle."

"Ah so. But surely you do not deny that an object of experience as such necessarily involves a relation to me in experiencing it, whereas a thing in the environment of which I have no awareness lacks such a relation?"

"Well anyone can see that."

"And surely you concede that an object of experience need not be a thing in the same sense that it is an object?"

"What do you mean in saying that?"

"Consider the witches[23] of Salem."

"There were no witches at Salem."

"Then what did we burn?"

"Innocent women."

"Innocent of what?"

"Of being witches."

"But the people at Salem who burned these women[24] thought they were burning witches."

---

[23] Witches: women (usually women) who (according to the official views promulgated in medieval and renaissance church documents), in exchange for their worship, were endowed by Satan with supernatural powers. To paradigmize a huge literature: see the gloss on Kramer and Sprenger 1487 in the References.

[24] Actually, the witches at Salem were hung rather than burned, I am told, "death for witchcraft" being the result in either case. My colleague apparently was familiar, as I at the time, only with the more 'colorful' version of the Salem trials.

"They were wrong."

"So you say. But surely you see that, if the burners were wrong, something that did exist was burned because of something that did not exist? Surely you see that something public, something objective in my sense – the being of a witch – was confused with something that did exist – the being of a female human organism – and that something existing was burned precisely because it was objectively identified with something that did not exist?"

"I think I am beginning to see what you are getting at", my colleague said; "but what does this have to do with signs?"

"Every mistake involves taking something that is not for something that is", I said.

"True enough", said my colleague.

"So every mistake involves an action of signs."

"Yes", said my colleague. "I see that to see a witch you have to be mistaken; but to see a woman you only need eyes, not signs. It is the truth I am interested in. By your account, all that signs account for is the possibility of being mistaken. What about the possibility of being right? Are you a realist or aren't you?"

"If you grant me that an object necessarily, whereas a thing only contingently, involves a relation to me as cognizant, then, in order to advance my argument that every object presupposes sign, I need to ask you to consider the further distinction between sensation and perception, where by the former I understand the stimulation of my nervous system by the physical surroundings and by the latter I understand the interpretation of those stimuli according to which they present to me something to be sought (+), something to be avoided (–), or something about which I am indifferent (0)."

"I see no problem with that."

>170<

A Sign Is What?

"Then perhaps you will grant further that, whereas sensation so construed always and necessarily involves me in physical relations that are also objective in their termini, perception, by contrast, insofar as it assimilates sensation to itself, necessarily involves physical relations that are also objective, but further involves me in objective relations that may or may not be physical, especially insofar as I may be mistaken about what I perceive. In other words, sensations give me the raw material out of which perception constructs what are for me objects of experience, such that these objects have their being precisely as a network of relations only some of which are relations independently of the workings of my mind – and which relations are which is not something self-evident, but something that needs to be sorted out over the course of experience insofar as experience becomes human experience."

"Why do you say insofar as it becomes human experience?"

"Because, for reasons we can go into but which here I may perhaps ask you to assume for purposes of advancing the point under discussion, the notion of a difference between objects and things *never occurs* to any other animal except those of our own species."

"Huh?"

"Well, you're a 'realist', aren't you?"

"Of course."

"What do you mean by that?"

"Simple. That the objects we experience have a being independent of our experience of them."

"But you just admitted that we experience objects which are not things."

"Yeah, when we make mistakes."

"But not only when we make mistakes."

"How do you figure?"

"Is there a boundary between Texas and Oklahoma?"

"Is the Pope Catholic?"

"I take that to be a 'Yes'." I let pass that the Pope at the moment was Polish: *transeat majorem*.

"Of course there is a boundary between Texas and Oklahoma. I'm no Okie."

"But look at the satellite photographs. No such boundary shows up there. Would you say that the boundary exists objectively rather than physically, but nonetheless really?"

"That's a funny way of talking."

"Not as funny as thinking that social or cultural realities, whether involving error or not, exist inside your head as mere psychological states. Consider that what sensations you have depends not only on your physical surroundings but just as much upon your bodily type. Consider further that how you organize your sensations depends even more upon your biological heredity than it does upon the physical surroundings. If you see that, then you should be able to realize that the world of experience, not the physical environment as such, is what is properly called 'the objective world'; and you cannot avoid further realizing that the objective world of every species is species-specific."

"Species-specific objective worlds? I thought the objective world was the world that is the same for everybody and everything, the world of what really is."

"On the contrary, the world that is 'the same regardless of your species' is merely the physical environment, and it is, moreover, a species-specifically human hypothesis rather than anything directly perceived. Because sensation directly and necessarily puts us in contact with the surroundings in precisely something of their physical aspect of things obtaining independently of us, we can from within experience conduct experiments which enable us to distinguish within our experience between aspects of the world which exist physically as well as objectively and aspects which exist only objectively. That, my friend, is why 'realism' is a philosophical problem, not a self-evident truth. After all, 'reality' is a word, and needs to be learned like any other. You need to read something[25] of Peirce."

"You seem to be veering into idealism." My colleague frowned mightily, hardly in sign of approval.

"Not at all. I thought you liked to acknowledge what is? And certainly an objective world shot through with emotions and the possibilities of error, which is specific to humans and even subspecific to different populations of humans is the reality we experience, not just some physical environment indifferent to our feelings about it? The indifferent physical environment is a hypothetical construct, a well-founded guess, which science confirms in some particulars and disproves in others. For surely you don't think it was theology or philosophy that disproved witches, do you? Haven't you read the old papal decrees on the subject, or the theological treatises on how to discriminate between ordinary women and women who are witches?[26] It behooves you to do so if you are married or even have a girlfriend."

"But all you are talking about is mistakes we have made, psychological states disconnected from objectivity."

"On the contrary, there are no such thing as psychological states disconnected from objectivity. Objectivity precisely depends upon psychological states which give the subjective

---

[25] I had in mind the modern distinction between primary and secondary qualities of sensation, and the very different ways in which the scholastic realists of Latin times and Peirce at the end of modern times himself resolved the distinction to the common end of vindicating the transcendental equivalence of truth with being – that "communication and being coincide", as Petrilli and Ponzio (2001: 54) put it. See the Index entries QUALITIES GIVEN IN SENSATION, and TRANSCENDENTALS, in the *Four Ages* (Deely 2001: 973 and 1005–6).

[26] See Kramer and Sprenger 1486.

foundation or ground for the relations which terminate in the publicly experienced interpretations that are precisely what we call objects. The key to the whole thing is relation in its unique being as irreducible to its subjective source always terminating at something over and above the being in which the relation is grounded." I could not help but think of the two main texts in Poinsot[27] which had so long ago first directed my attention to this simple point made quasi-occult over the course of philosophy's history by the obtuse discussions of relation after Aristotle.[28]

"But I thought knowledge consisted in our assimilation of the form of things without their matter."

Now I knew for sure my colleague was indeed a closet Thomist at least, versed in the more common Neothomist version of ideogenesis, or theory of the formation of ideas through a process of abstraction.

"Well", I ventured, "in the first place, that is not a self-evident proposition, but one highly specific medieval theory of the process of abstraction; and further, absent the context of a full-blown theory of relations as suprasubjective links[29] to what is objectively other than ourselves with all our psychological states, affective as well as cognitive, such a theory is finally incoherent. For any 'form', with or without 'matter', if and insofar as it is 'in me', is part and parcel of my subjectivity, except and insofar as it mayhap give rise to a relation to something over and above my subjectivity, which is by definition what is meant by 'terminating objectively'."

---

[27] Poinsot 1632a: *Treatise on Signs*, Second Preamble, Article 2, 93/17–96/36; and Book I, Question 1, 117/18–118/18.

[28] See the summaries of the matter essayed by Grote 1872, as learned as the confusion gets. Cf. the discussion in the *Four Ages* (Deely 2001), pp. 72–78, 226–31, and 423–27.

[29] See the Index entries for SIGN and SUPRASUBJECTIVE BEING in the *Four Ages* (Deely 2001: 993–94, 1001–2).

A Sign Is What?

"Could you state clearly your meaning of 'subjectivity' here", asked my colleague.

"Indeed. Subjectivity is the sum total of everything that distinguishes me from the rest of the universe,[30] and relations are whatever ties over and above my subjectivity link me to anything other than myself, be that other physical as well as objective or merely objective."

"*Merely* objective?" my colleague queried with eyebrows raised.

"Merely objective: existing as known and insofar publicly accessible but not as such existing physically in the environment,[31] like the border of Texas with Mexico or the office of President of the United States, and so on. Subjective existence is physical existence, including the whole of one's private psychological states. Objective existence, by contrast, is public in principle, in the way that any two otherwise isolated subjectivities can yet be in relation to a common third."

"But this 'common third', as you put it, surely must be something real?"

"Not at all, if by 'real' you mean existing independently of the workings of mind, something subjective, a physical entity. It suffices that it 'exist' as the terminus opposed to the foundation or ground in subjectivity of some relation, which relation as a relation exceeds the subjectivity in which it is grounded by terminating at something over and above subjectivity as such, something 'other' than that subjectivity. This 'other' may indeed also exist independently of the cognitive or affective relation terminating thereat, in which case it will

---

[30] See the Index entry SUBJECTIVE BEING, SUBJECTIVITY in the *Four Ages* (Deely 2001: 1000–1001), in contrast with the entry for INTERSUBJECTIVE BEING, INTERSUBJECTIVITY.

[31] See the Index entry OBJECT, OBJECTIVE BEING in the *Four Ages* (Deely 2001: 944–45).

be a thing as well as an object. Subjectivity, you can see, is what defines things as things. Objectivity, by contrast, obtains only in and through relations, normally a whole network of relations, which give even the things of the physical environment their status as experienced and whatever meaning they have for the lifeform experiencing them. Since objectivity always includes (through sensation) something of the subjectivity of things in the environment, this objective meaning is normally never wholly divorced from the subjective reality of the physical world, but it is never reducible to that reality either."

"Surely you are not saying that every object is merely the terminus of some relation?"

"Exactly so – some relation or complex of relations, a 'semiotic web', as we like to say in semiotics. Except your use of 'merely' here seems hardly appropriate, when one considers that the terminus of cognitive and affective relations normally involves something of the subjectivity of things in their aspects as known, even though the terminus of every relation as terminus owes its being as correlate to the fundament to the suprasubjectivity distinctive of the being peculiar to and definitive of relation."[32]

"And where does sign come in?"

"At the foundation, my friend; but not *as* the foundation. That was the mistake the scholastics made[33] in trying to divide signs into 'formal' and 'instrumental' signs without

---

[32] Since my colleague fastened on another point, I didn't go further into this point here; but I was about to explain how this seeming technicality explains our ability to talk about nonexistent things, and not just talk around them, as Frege and Brentano essayed in the background, respectively, of analytic and phenomenological philosophy: see Deely 1975.

[33] See Chapter 8 of the *Four Ages* (Deely 2001: esp. 388–91).

realizing that our psychological states are no less particulars than are physical objects we point to when we single something out as a 'sign'."

"You are losing me."

"Go back to the σημεῖον. Consider the howl of a wolf. Would that be a σημεῖον?"

My colleague pondered, consulting within the privacy of self-semiosis a knowledge of ancient Greek. I awaited the result of this consultation.

"I am not so sure. The σημεῖα were always sensible events, to be sure, and ones deemed natural at that. But they were primarily associated, as I remember, with divination, wherein the natural event manifested a will of the gods or a destined fate, or with medicine, wherein the natural event is a symptom enabling prognosis or diagnosis of health or sickness. No, I am not so sure the howl of a wolf would fall under σημεῖον, or at least I don't see how it would."

"All right then", I suggested, "let us consider the howl of a wolf first just as a physical event in the environment, a sound or set of vibrations of a certain wavelength propagating over a finite distance from its source within the physical surroundings."

"I see no difficulty in that", my colleague allowed agreeably.

"Now let us suppose two organisms endowed with appropriate organs of what we call hearing, situated within the range of propagation of that sound. What would you suppose?"

"I would suppose they would hear the sound, if they are not asleep or too distracted."

"Let us suppose they hear the sound, the one organism being a sheep and the other another wolf. Now the sound occurring physically and subjectively in the environment independently of our organisms' hearing of it enters into a relation with each of the two organisms. The sound not only exists physically, it now exists also objectively, for it is heard, it is something of which the organisms are respectively aware. It is a kind of object, but what kind? For the sheep it is an object of repulsion (–), something inspiring fear and an urge to hide or flee. For the other wolf, a male wolf, it happens – heeding the advice of St. Thomas to use sexual examples to make something memorable – let us say that the howl reveals a female in heat. Such a sound, no different in its physical subjectivity from the vibrations reaching the frightened sheep, inspires in the male an attraction, as it were (+), what former President Carter might call 'lust in the heart'."

"What are you saying?"

"That one and the same thing occurring in the environment gives rise in awareness to quite different objects for different organisms, depending on their biological types. Sensations become incorporated into perceptions of objects not merely according to what things are in the surroundings but especially according to how the sensations are interrelated within the experience of the perceiving animal as part of its total objective world."

"So this is what you meant when you said that objective worlds are species-specific?"

"Exactly so. Every organism in its body is one subjectivity among others, a thing interacting physically with other things in the environment. But if the organism is a cognitive organism, its body has specialized parts suited to a psychological as well as a physiological response to those physical environmental aspects proportioned to the organ of sense. The psychological response in those cases is no less 'subjective', no less 'inside the organism', than the physical effects of the interaction; but the psychological effect gives rise to a cognitive relation, a relation of *awareness* of something in the environment. But what is that 'something'? The organism, according to its own nature and past experiences, attaches a value to the stimulus and relates that stimulus to its own needs and desires. In other words, the mere stimulus of sensation becomes incorporated objectively into a whole network of experience wherein it acquires a meaning."

"But that is subjectivism", my colleague blustered indignantly. "Values are real, objective, not subjective. You are making them subjective."

"Pay attention", I pleaded. "Of course the values are objective. Anything existing within awareness is objective. They are also bound up with the subjectivity of the physical environment, both in the being proper to whatever is the source of the stimulus and in the being of the cognizing organism. Insofar as the subjectivity of the physical world bespeaks a being independently of whatever I may know, feel, or believe, the values *partake* of that being. But, as values, they reveal *more* the being of the organism evaluating than the subjective nature of the stimulus in the environment. They belong as values to the species-specific objective world of the experiencing organism."

"This is troubling", my colleague alleged.

"Let me put you at ease", I offered. "In order for an organism to be aware of something outside itself, there must be inside itself a disposition or state on the basis of which it is related cognitively (and, I would add, affectively[34]) to that outside other. If the outside other has an existence of its own quite independent of the cognition of the cognizing organism, then it is a thing, indeed. But insofar as it becomes known it is an object, the terminus of a relation founded upon the psychological states inside the organism. Neither the relation nor the thing become object are inside the knower. All that is

---

[34] See the discussion below of "cathexis" and "cathecting": p. 195, n. 64; and p. 201 n. 84.

inside the knower is the disposition or state presupposed for the thing to exist as known.[35] And the relation is inside neither the knower nor the known but is over and above both of them. Compared to the subjectivity of either the knower or the known the relation as such is suprasubjective. But as related cognitively to the knower the thing known is the terminus of a relation founded in the knower's own subjectivity. As terminating the relation it is an object. That same object if and insofar as it has a subjective being of its own is not merely an object but also a thing."

"But what if the object has no subjectivity proper to it?" my colleague probed, thinking, as I suspected from his nonverbal signs, of Salem and witches.

"Then it is only an object, what the scholastic realists used to call a 'mind-dependent being'.[36] So do pay attention: every mind-dependent being is an objective reality or being, but not every objective reality is a mind-dependent being. Some objects are also things, in which case they are mind-independent beings[37] as well as objective realities."

"But I thought an *ens rationis*, what you call a mind-dependent being, was a mere mental reality, a psychological state like error or delusion."

"Hardly. Surely you recall that, according to the scholastic realists so beloved of Peirce, logical entities all are *entia rationis*? And the relations of logic are supremely public, binding upon all? Now it is true that logic reveals to us only the consequences of our beliefs, of our thinking that things are this

---

[35] See the Index entry FORMAL SIGN in the *Four Ages* (Deely 2001: 893–94).

[36] *Ens rationis*. See the Index entries ENS RATIONIS and MIND-DEPENDENT BEING in the *Four Ages* (Deely 2001: 883–84 and 934–35, respectively).

[37] *Entia realia*. See the Index entries ENS REALE and MIND-INDEPENDENT OR PHYSICAL in the *Four Ages* (Deely 2001: 884–85 and 935–37, respectively).

way or that, not necessarily how things are in their independent being. But the fact that logical relations are public realities, not private ones, that logical relations reveal *inescapable* consequences of this or that belief, not private whims, already tells you that they belong to the Umwelt, not to the Innenwelt, and to the Umwelt as species-specifically human at that."

"Umwelt? Innenwelt? Where does that come from?"

"Sorry. Umwelt is shorthand for objective world. In the case of the species-specifically human objective world it is often called rather a Lebenswelt; but please", I pleaded, "let us not get into that particular right now or we will never get to the bottom of the question you have raised as to why a sign is best defined at this stage of history as what every object presupposes."

"But", my colleague interjected, "why in the world do you speak of the definition we are seeking to plumb as best 'at this stage of history'? Surely you know that a real definition tells what something is, and is not subject to time? Are species not eternal?"

"Surely you will allow for more subtlety than that as regards definitions?" I replied hopefully. "After all, even when we try to express in words what a thing is, it is our understanding of the thing that we express, not purely and simply the thing itself? And this is true even when and to the extent that our understanding actually has some overlap, identity, or coincidence with the being of the thing – even when, that is to say, our definition partially expresses a thing objectified, a thing made object or known?"

"I see what you mean. Even a definition supposed real expresses only our best understanding of some aspect of real being, and insofar as this understanding is not exhaustive it may admit of revision or of being supplanted through subsequent advances or alterations of understanding", my colleague allowed.

"I am glad you see that", I breathed aloud, "for, in the case of the sign, there have been at least three, or even more (depending on how you parse the history) revisions of the definitory formula generally accepted,[38] and I expect more to come."

"Don't discourage me", my colleague pleaded. "Let us at least get clear for now about this new formula you deem best at 'our present historical moment'. I get your meaning of Umwelt. What about this Innenwelt business?"

"Innenwelt is merely shorthand for the complexus of psychological powers and states whereby an organism represents to itself or 'models' the environment insofar as it experiences the world. So Innenwelt is the subjective or private counterpart to the objective world of public experience comprising for any species its Umwelt."

"That helps, but I fail to see what all this new terminology and idiosyncratic way of looking at things has to do with signs, let alone with signs being presupposed to objects."

"Then let me introduce at this point the great discovery of semiotics, actually first made in the 16th century, or early in the 17th at the latest,[39] although never fully marked terminologically until Peirce resumed the Latin discussion around the dawn of the 20th century.[40] Signs are not particular things of any kind but strictly and essentially relations of a certain kind, specifically, relations irreducibly triadic in character."

"But surely you are not denying that *that*", my colleague said, pointing to the physical structure renaming the building beside us as Sullivan rather than Monaghan, "is a sign?"

"No, I am not exactly denying that; what I am denying is

---

[38] See the Index entry for DEFINITION OF SIGN in the *Four Ages* (Deely 2001: 874–75).

[39] See the Conimbricenses 1607, especially in the bilingual edition by Doyle 2001; and Deely 2001c.

[40] See the Index entry INTERPRETANT in the *Four Ages* (Deely 2001: 914–15).

that what makes what you are pointing to a sign is anything about it that you can point to and directly see with your eyes or touch with your hands. What makes it a sign is that, within your Umwelt, it stands for something other than itself; and because it *succeeds* (in your Umwelt) in so standing it is for you a sign. But *what makes it thus succeed* is the position it occupies in a triadic relation giving it its place in the spiral of your semiosis and that of this institution in determining what is what and where is where on campus; and, strictly speaking, it is *that relation as a whole* that is the being of sign, not any one element, subjective or objective, within the relation."

"I don't understand", the colleague confessed. But there was interest in the voice, not impatience or indifference. So I was encouraged to continue.

"I suppose we usually think of a relationship dyadically, as a link between two things", I ventured.

"Sure", my colleague interjected, "like the relation between a sign and what it signifies. Why don't you just accept Jakobson's famous formula for defining sign,[41] *aliquid stat pro aliquo*, one thing standing for another?"

"I am delighted you are familiar with that essay by Jakobson, which has become a classic,[42] one of the landmarks in the semiotic development of the last century", I said, pleasantly surprised again by my colleague's learning. "It took me almost nineteen years to realize a major flaw in that formula, in that the *aliquo* allows for a misunderstanding along Cartesian lines, wherein objects are reduced to ideas in the subjective or psychological sense. I made a major address to the Semiotic Society of America on this point in 1993,[43] showing,

---

[41] Jakobson 1974.

[42] See Eco 1987.

[43] Deely 1993a, the Semiotic Society of America Thomas A. Sebeok Fellowship Inaugural Lecture.

or attempting to show, that this classic formula should be revised to read rather *aliquid stat pro alio*, in order to leave no doubt that the sign, unlike an object,[44] stands never for itself but always for another than itself."

"But since you have brought up Jakobson's formula", I continued, "let me remind you that he intended the formula to express the relation distinctive or constitutive of sign, a relation Jakobson felicitously characterized as *renvoi*."

"I had forgotten that expression *renvoi*", my colleague admitted, "but I don't see how it helps us here."

"Well", I said, "I am slow, proof of humanity. Since my initial proposal for revision of Jakobson's formula nineteen years after the fact, eight more years have passed before a second revision occurred to me as necessary."

"A second revision?" queried my colleague.

"Yes. If you will recall, *renvoi* for Jakobson was not merely the relation of sign to signified, insofar dyadic, as you have suggested. *Renvoi* was a relationship wherein the so-called sign manifested its significate to or for someone or something. So the formula in fact not only needs to be so revised as to preclude the typically modern epistemological paradigm wherein signs as other-representations can be confused with objects as self-representations, as I manifested in my 1993 Sebeok Fellowship inaugural address, it needs also to be revised to include a Latin dative expressing the indirect reference to the effect wherein an action of signs achieves its distinctive outcome, its 'proper significate outcome', as Peirce put the matter."

"You raise two questions in my mind", my colleague said with some agitation. "You say that the sign manifests 'to or for someone or something'. How is 'to' equivalent with 'for'?

---

[44] Poinsot 1632a: *Tractatus de Signis*, Book I, Question 1, 116/14–117/17; Deely 1986d.

A Sign Is What?

And how is 'someone' equivalent with 'something'? But before you respond to these two queries, please," my colleague requested, "tell me how would you have the classic formula finally read."

"*Aliquid alicuique stans pro alio*, one thing representing another than itself to *yet another*", I suggested, "although the impersonal verb form *stat* would work as well as the participial *stans*. Only with a final revision like this could it be said finally, as Sebeok said (as I now see) a little prematurely,[45] that by the term *renvoi* Jakobson had 'deftly captured and transfixed each and every sign process conforming to the classic formula'; for if a relation is not triadic, it is not a sign relation. Whence the truly classic formula: *Aliquid alicuique stat pro alio*."

"Very interesting", my colleague allowed. "Now could you answer my two questions?"

"Your questions cut to the heart of the matter. Consider the bone of a dinosaur which is known as such. It functions in the awareness of the paleontologist as a sign. He recognizes it, let us say, as the bone of an Apatosaurus. Consider that same bone chanced upon by a Roman soldier in the last century BC. Whatever it signified, if anything, to the soldier, it did not signify an Apatosaurus. Agreed?"

"Agreed", my colleague allowed. "In those circumstances it was more an object than a sign, not a fossil at all, so to speak."

"And yet it *was* a fossil, waiting to be seen through the right eyes. It was not an Apatosaurus sign *to* someone there and then, in that last century BC, but it remained that it was prospectively such a sign for a future observer."

"Yes", the colleague conceded, "but that prospective signification was to *someone*, not to *something*."

---

[45] Sebeok 1984: 9.

"You raise the difficult question of whether the 'to or for which' of a sign need always be a cognitive organism or not. Let me acknowledge the difficulty of the question, but not try to answer it now. Suffice it to say, for the moment at least, that when an organism interprets something as a sign, that interpretation is required to complete the sign's signification as something actual here and now."

"I can see that. A sign requires an interpretation if it is to succeed as a sign and not just be some dumb object. But I don't see how an inorganic substance can provide an interpretation. Come on!"

"So", I continued, proposing to steer the discussion more directly to the point at hand, "pay attention: what you call a sign, which I will shortly manifest is a loose rather than a strict way of speaking, doesn't just (dyadically) relate to what it signifies, it signifies what it signifies (triadically) *to* or *for* something else. Always hidden in the sign-signified dyad is a third element, the *reason why* or *ground upon which* the 'sign', as you call it, signifies whatever it does signify and not something else." The important distinction between "ground" in the technical Peircean sense, redolent of the old *objectum formale* of scholastic realism, and "ground" in the scholastic realist sense of *fundamentum relationis* loomed here,[46] but I thought to bring it up on my own would risk shipwreck for the course of the conversation overall. Better, I thought, to follow the ancient advice of Roman sailors: *ad naufragium evitandum, merces proiecit in mare* – "better to lose the cargo than the ship". Happily, my colleague called for no clarification along this line, and this particular part of the cargo slipped unnoticed beneath the public waves of our common semiosis.

---

[46] The very point touched on in Part I above, Chap. 4, p. 47 n. 44. See the Index entry for GROUND, senses A & B, in the *Four Ages* (Deely 2001: 900–903).

Instead, my colleague called for a concrete illustration, much simpler to provide. I secretly breathed a sigh of relief.

"Give me an example", demanded the colleague.

I hastened to comply, before the absolute point so pertinent here might occur to my interlocutor (inexplicably, my friend Joe Pentony came into my mind).

"I make a noise: 'elephant'. It is not just a noise, but a word. Why, hearing the noise 'elephant' do you not think of a thin-legged, long-necked, brown-spotted animal that nibbles leaves, instead of a thick-legged, large gray animal with a prehensile proboscis?" Since my colleague fancied to be a 'realist', it was not difficult to anticipate the reply about to come. Nor was I disappointed.

"Obviously because 'elephant' means elephant and not giraffe", the colleague said, this time a touch impatiently.

"Yes, of course", I granted, "but is that not only because of the habit structures internalized in your Innenwelt which make the noise 'elephant' a linguistic element in our Lebenswelt on the basis of which we are habituated to think first, on hearing the noise, of one particular animal rather than another? So in the experience of any signification is there not only the 'sign' loosely so-called and the signified object, but also the matter of the basis upon which the sign signifies this object rather than or before some other object? You see that?"

"I do."

"Then you see that the relation making what you with your finger point out as a 'sign' to be a sign is nothing intrinsic to the so-called sign, but rather something over and above that subjective structure; to wit, a relationship, which has not one term but two terms, to wit, the signified object for one and, for the other, the reason why that rather than some other is the object signified?"

"I think I do see that. I think. But please explain further, so I can be sure." Realists like to be 'sure'. Infallibility is their ideal goal, as it were, the modern variety at least (rather more naive in this than their Latin scholastic forebears, I might add), ironically the final heirs of Descartes, who prized certainty, in the end, above 'realism'. The means defeated by the end, as it were.

"Well, here, history can be a great help. Animals, including human animals, begin with an experience of objects, and objects normally given as outside of or other than the animals themselves. In order to mature and survive, every animal has to form an interior map, an Innenwelt, which enables it sufficiently to navigate its surroundings to find food, shelter, etc. This 'sufficiently' is what we call an Umwelt, and it contrasts in principle with, even though it partially includes something of, things of the physical environment."

"I think", my colleague marveled, "I begin to understand your ironic manner whenever the subject of 'realism' in philosophy arises. Realists assume our experience begins with things as such, whereas now I see that our experience directly is only of things as subsumed within objects and the species-specific structure of an objective world! If *entia realia* and *entia rationis* are equally objective within our experience, then the sorting out of which-is-which is a problem rather than a given!"

"Exactly so", I answered, delighted at this sudden burst of light from my colleague, while thinking myself of Sebeok's description of "the substratal illusion underlying reality" and the "search for the reality that may, after all, lurk behind that illusion" that in everyday experience we deal straightforwardly with *ens reale*. "Now if only I can get you to see how object presupposes sign, perhaps we can get some lunch."

"Please do so", the colleague said, "and, now that you mention it, the quicker the better, for I am getting hungry."

"Permit me an *obiter dictum*, nonetheless", I pleaded, "for

A *Sign Is* What?

I think it will facilitate our progress to a successful outcome of the main point before us."

"By all means", the colleague allowed, drawing an apple from a bag and taking a bite.

"Even though you have heretofore deemed yourself a 'realist'," I ventured, "I have noticed from earlier conversations that you have a definite partiality to phenomenology, even though Husserl himself conceded that his position in the end proved but one more variant in the characteristically modern development of philosophy as idealism.[47]

"So notice two points. First, the phenomenological idea of the 'intentionality' of consciousness[48] reduces, within semiotics, to the theory of relations,[49] and expresses nothing more than the distinctive characteristic of psychological states of subjectivity whereby they give rise necessarily to relations triadic rather than dyadic in character. But second, and more fundamentally, recall the question with which (among others) Heidegger concluded his original publication of *Being and Time*:[50]

> Why does Being get 'conceived' 'proximally' in terms of the present-at-hand *and not* in terms of the ready-to-hand, which indeed lies *closer* to us? *Why* does this reifying always keep coming back to exercise its dominion?

Within semiotics we can now give an answer to this question."

"We can?"

"Indeed. Ready-to-hand is the manner in which objects exist within an animal Umwelt. Human beings are animals

---

[47] See Husserl 1929; Spiegelberg 1965: I, 155.
[48] From Brentano 1874. Brief notice in the *Four Ages* (Deely 2001: 404 and 561n38); extended comment in Deely 1978a.
[49] Deely 1971a, 1975, 1978; cf. Deely 1968, 1972, 1972a.
[50] Heidegger 1927: 437.

first of all, but they have one species-specifically distinct feature of their Innenwelt or modeling system, a feature which was first brought to light in the postmodern context of semiotics, so far as I know, by Professor Sebeok,[51] namely, the ability to model objects *as things*. That is to say, the human modeling system or Innenwelt includes the ability to undertake the discrimination within objects of the difference between what of the objects belongs to the order of physical subjectivity[52] and what belongs wholly to the order of objects simply as terminating our awareness of them.[53] Perhaps you recall from your reading of Thomas Aquinas that he identified the origin of human experience in an awareness of being prior to the discrimination of the difference between *ens reale* and *ens rationis*, with the further point that this difference arises from within that awareness as species-specifically human and not by any addition to it?"

"Actually I don't recall any such discussion in St. Thomas."

"Fair enough, and we don't want to get completely off the track. Later on you might want to look up the point in Aquinas and give some consideration to the implications of his asseveration that "being is not a genus";[54] for it seems to me that what he is saying is that our original experience includes something of the world of things but definitively cannot be reduced to the order of *ens reale*. Comparative real-

---

[51] See, *inter alia*, Sebeok 1984a.

[52] *Entia realia.*

[53] *Entia rationis.*

[54] Indeed, Aquinas held that nothing could be added from without to the species-specifically constant awareness of being, although that awareness can be *contracted* to the consideration of the genus of *ens reale* or of *ens rationis*, and yet further sub-contracted within and between these genera in that virtually infinite semiosis that we have come in modern times to call "specialization".

ities and unrealities alike are discovered from within, not prior to, objectivity.[55] The experience of that contrast, indeed, is what transforms the generically animal Umwelt into a species-specifically human Lebenswelt[56] wherein even witches can be mistaken for realities of a definite type, and wherein it may be hard to realize that the mind-independent revolution of the earth around the sun is not unreal whereas the mind-dependent revolution of the sun around the earth is not real."

"What about Heidegger's objective distinction between the ready-to-hand and the present-at-hand?", my colleague pressed.

"Simple. This is a distinction that does not arise for any animal except an animal with a modeling system capable of representing objects (as such necessarily related to us) according to a being or features not necessarily related to us but obtaining subjectively and intersubjectively in the objects themselves (mistakenly or not, according to the particular case) – an animal, in short, capable of wondering about things-in-themselves and conducting itself accordingly. Now, since a modeling system so capacitated is, according to Sebeok, what is meant by language in the root sense, whereas the exaptation of such a modeling in action gives rise not to language but to linguistic communication,[57] and since 'language' in this derivative sense of linguistic communication is

---

55 In the *Four Ages* (Deely 2001), see the whole of Chapter 7, but esp. pp. 341–57, and the Table on p. 354.

56 This term is from Husserl 1936 in particular; in Aquinas's own manner of speaking, he calls the focus or "starting point" of species-specifically human awareness *ens primum cognitum*, which then subdivides over the course of experience into *ens reale* and *ens rationis*. See the *Four Ages* (Deely 2001), Chap. 7.

57 This distinction, taken from Sebeok, is one of the bases upon which the history of philosophy as a whole needs to be rewritten: see the *Four Ages*, Chapter 1.

the species-specifically distinctive and dominant modality of communication among humans, we have a difficulty inverse to that of the nonlinguistic animals, although we, unlike they, can overcome the difficulty."

"And what difficulty is that?"

"Within an Umwelt, objects *are* reality so far as the organism is concerned. But without language, the animals have no way to go beyond the objective world as such to inquire into the physical environment in its differences from the objective world. Within a Lebenswelt, by contrast, that is to say, within an Umwelt internally transformed by language, the reality so far as the organism is concerned is confused with and mistaken for the world of things. Objects appear not as mixtures of *entia rationis* with *entia realia*, but simply as 'what is', 'real being', 'the world of things'."

"That is the general assertion of 'realists'", my colleague mused. "It also reminds me of Reid's 'philosophy of common sense'."

"As well it might", I said.[58] "Descartes and Locke confused objects as suprasubjectively terminating relations with their counterposed subjective foundations or bases in the cognitive aspect of subjectivity, thereby reducing Umwelt to Innenwelt; Reid, in seeking to counter them and, especially, Hume after them, confused public objects with things, *ens primum cognitum* with *ens reale* (in the earlier terms of Aquinas), thereby reducing Umwelt to physical environment. But the physical universe of things is distinguished from within the world of objects as the sense of that dimension of objective experience which reveals roots in objects that do not reduce to our experience of the objects. Reality in this hardcore sense of

---

[58] See "What to do with common sense?", in the *Four Ages* (Deely 2001: 547–48).

something existing independently of our beliefs, opinions, and feelings is not 'given' to some magical faculty of 'common sense'. There is no 'gift of heaven' facilely discriminating 'the real' for our otherwise animal minds – a gift such as Reid avers,[59] which only bias or 'some mistaken religious principle' can mislead."

"So you are saying that the reality of objects within experience, for any animal, is a confused mixture of *entia realia* and *entia rationis*, but that this confusion only comes to light in the experience of human animals by means of a species-specific modeling of the world which you call language?"

"That is what I am saying."

"Well, it makes sense, I think; but it is a strange way of speaking. I need to digest this a bit before I can decide where to agree and where to differ. Enough of your *obiter dictum*. I want to get to the bottom of this objects presupposing signs business, and get some lunch."

"Back, then, to history", I urged. "You can see right off that every animal will use what it senses perceptually to orientate itself in the environment. Among these elements sensed some therefore will come to stand for something other than themselves. The most impressive of such sensory elements would be those manifesting the powers that hold sway over human existence, nature, on the one hand, and gods, on the other. So in the ancient consciousness arose the idea of σημεῖον, a natural event which generates in us the expectation of something else, an element of divination in the case of the gods, a symptom in the case of medicine.[60] This idea perme-

---

[59] Reid 1785: 604–5. A useful – if still presemiotic – discussion of "Thomas Reid and the Signs of the Times" is essayed in McInerny 2001: 52–56. A more explicitly semiotic discussion can be found in Henle 1983.

[60] See Sebeok 1984b on the latter point, Manetti 1993 on the former.

ates the ancient Greek writings. But, at the beginning of the Latin Age, Augustine unwittingly introduces a radical variant upon the ancient notion. I say 'unwittingly', not at all to disparage Augustine, but to mark the fact important in this connection that his ignorance of Greek prevented him from realizing what was novel about his proposal, and how much it stood in need of some explanation regarding its possibility.

"Augustine spoke not of σημεῖον but rather of *signum*. And instead of conceiving of it as a natural sensory occurrence or event, he conceived of it simply as a sensible event whether natural or artificial. At a stroke, by putting the word 'natural' under erasure, Augustine introduced the idea of sign as general mode of being overcoming or transcending the division between **nature and culture**. Specifically (and incredibly[61]), for the first time and ever after, human language (more precisely, the elements and modalities of linguistic communication) and culture generally came to be regarded as a system of signs (*signa ad placita*) interwoven with the signs of nature, the σημεῖα or, in Augustine's parlance, *signa naturalia*.

"To a man the Latins followed Augustine in this way of viewing the sign. But, gradually, problems came to light. In particular, at least by the time of Aquinas, if not a century earlier in Abaelard,[62] question arose as to which is the primary element in the being of sign: being sensible, or being in relation to another? For, the Latins noticed, all of our psychological states, the *passiones animae*, put us into a relation to what they themselves are not, and present this 'other' objectively in experience.[63] Is not this relation of one thing presenting another

---

[61] See the discussion of Markus 1972: 66 in the *Four Ages* (Deely 2001: 218–20, and esp. 406 n. 95).

[62] See "The So-Called Dark Ages", Chapter 6 of the *Four Ages* (Deely 2001: esp. 243–47).

[63] See the Index entries PASSIONS OF THE SOUL and FORMAL SIGN in the *Four Ages* (Deely 2001: 950 and 893–94, respectively).

than itself in fact more fundamental to being a sign than being a sensible element, whether natural or cultural? And if so, should not the passions of the soul, which, as effects of things necessarily provenate relations to what is objectively experienced, be regarded veritably as signs, even though they are not themselves directly sensible or, indeed, even outside of ourselves, outside of our subjectivity?

"So at another stroke was overcome the distinction between **inner and outer** as regards the means of signification, a landmark event paralleling Augustine's overcoming of the divide between nature and culture. The states of subjectivity whereby we cathect[64] and cognize objects, the scholastics

---

[64] Though my interlocutor raised no question about this term, and later in our discussion (see p. 201 below) manifested a thorough mastery of its usage as pertaining to semiotics, nevertheless, the term is important to the future of semiotics and sufficiently unfamiliar to most readers at the time this transcript was made to warrant a note of explication. An organism responds to an object not only by cognizing it but, at the same time, by *cathecting* that object as desirable, undesirable, or 'neutral', as we have said. The former relation arises from the cognitive representations (or 'ideas'), the latter from the emotional representations (or 'feelings') accompanying or evoked by the ideas. Thus cognition and cathexis are twin processes within zoö- and anthropo-semiosis, "simultaneously given and only analytically separable", as Parsons, Shils, and Olds best noted (1951: 68–69; see also their 1951a: 110).

The centrality of this idea for semiotics, particularly as regards the concept of Umwelt, appears from the following (Parsons, Shils, *et al.* 1951: 10n13): "A distinction between *affect* and *cathexis* is desirable for present purposes. *Affect* refers to a state of an organism – a state of euphoria or dysphoria or qualitative variants thereof. *Cathexis* refers to a state of an organism – a state of euphoria or dysphoria – *in relation to some object*. Thus the term *cathexis* is broader in its reference than the term *affect*; it is *affect plus object*. It is *object-oriented affect*. It involves attaching affective significance to an object; although it involves attachment to one or more properties of the object, as used

proposed, are themselves a type of sign, even though we do not access them by external sensation. Call them 'formal signs', they proposed, in contrast to the signs of which Augustine spoke, which they now proposed to call rather[65] 'instrumental' signs.

"But by now the discussion was no longer exclusively in the hands of the scholastic realists. The key distinction this time came rather from the nominalists after Ockham; and they were thinking exclusively of particular things, alone, according to their doctrine, belonging to the order of *ens reale*, in contrast to every relation which is as such an *ens rationis*.[66] Out of some two centuries of obscurity in which other issues held the center stage,[67] the Latin discussion of the 16th century took a turn in Iberia which was richly to vindicate Peirce's later thesis that an essential difference separated his Pragmaticism from the varieties springing up under his earlier label of Pragmatism, in that to the former scholastic realism is essential, while the latter remains compatible with nominalism.

"The decisive realization came cumulatively in the 16th and 17th centuries through the work of Soto (1529), Fonseca (1564), the Conimbricenses (1607), Araújo (1617), and finally Poinsot (1632a), in whose writing the decisive realization

---

here it does not itself refer to a property of the object, but to a *relation* between actor and object. Furthermore, there is no connotation either of activity or passivity in the actor's relation to the object implied in the concept." On the specifically Innenwelt side, see Murray 1951: 453 n. (The distinction Kluckhohn 1951: 395 attempts to draw between cathexis and valuation amounts to no more than the difference between cathexis within a generically animal Umwelt and a species-specifically human Lebenswelt.)

[65] See the discussion of this terminology in the *Four Ages* (Deely 2001: 390 n. 71).

[66] See Chapter 8 of the *Four Ages* (Deely 2001: esp. 385–93).

[67] "The Thicket", in the *Four Ages* (Deely 2001), pp. 394–408.

approximates unmistakable clarity.[68] This realization was twofold. One part[69] lay in the insight that not relation as such, but relation as triadic, constituted the being of the sign, while the sensible element (or, in the case of the formal sign, the psychological element) that occupied the role of other-representation is what we call a 'sign' in the common, loose way of speaking.[70] The other part[71] lay in the insight that it is not anything about relation as suprasubjective that determines whether it belongs to the order of *ens reale* or *ens rationis*, but wholly and solely the circumstances of the relation.[72] Whence one and the same relation, under one set of circumstances *ens reale*, by change of those circumstances alone could pass into an *ens rationis* without any detectable objective difference in the direct experience of the animal.

"Then came the virtual extinction of semiotic consciousness that we call modernity, a dark age that did not really end until Peirce returned to the late Latin writings and resumed the thread of their developing semiotic consciousness, first by explicitly naming the three elements or terms grounding the triadic sign relation, and then by shifting the emphasis from being to action with the identification of semiosis. The foreground

---

[68] The *Four Ages*, Chapters 9 & 10. In particular, see the Index entry SEMIOTIC CONSCIOUSNESS (Deely 2001: 988–89).

[69] Poinsot 1632a: *Treatise on Signs*, Book I, Question 3 (that the relation of sign to signified and the relation of sign to power are one single relation, thus irreducibly triadic).

[70] See the "hard distinction" introduced above, p. 104, text and n. 17; and also in Part I, Chap. 1, p. 5.

[71] Poinsot 1632a: *Treatise on Signs*, Book I, Question 2 (that the physical status of the sign to signified component of sign relations is determined by the context in which the sign functions).

[72] See "The Problem of the Nose of Wax" in the *Four Ages* (Deely 2001), Chapter 8, esp. 369–72 text and n. 24 p. 370.

element of other-representation in the sign relation Peirce termed the *representamen*.[73] This is what is loosely called a sign, but in reality is a sign-vehicle conveying what is signified to some individual or community, actual or prospective. The other represented or conveyed by the sign-vehicle Peirce traditionally termed the *significate* or *object signified* (in this two-word expression, to tell the truth, the first word is redundant[74]). Whereas the prospective other to which representation is made (emphatically not necessarily a person, as Peirce was the first to emphasize[75] and later semiotic analysis was to prove[76]) Peirce termed[77] the *interpretant*, 'the proper significate outcome' of the action of signs."

My colleague interrupted my historical excursus at this point.

"Do you really mean to call the period between Descartes and Peirce the semiotic dark ages?", he queried. "Isn't that a little strong?"

"Well", I half apologized, "the shoe fits. Nor do the semiotic dark ages simply end with Peirce, I am afraid. They extend into the dawn of our own century, though I am confident we are seeing their final hours. After all, a darkness precedes every full dawn."

"I saw an ad for a new book of yours comparing today's philosophical establishment with the judges of Galileo. That's not likely to get you job offers at the top", my colleague admonished.

---

[73] Latin derived, this term should be pronounced "rep-re-sen-tá-men", not "rep-re-sént-a-men", as the Anglophile Peirceans would have it, as we discussed in Part I, Chap. 1, p. 5 n. 4.

[74] Recall the discussion in Part I, Chap. 3, p. 43ff.

[75] Peirce 1904.

[76] Krampen 1981; Deely 1982b, 1989, 1993a, 1997, 1990, 1998, 2001b.

[77] Peirce c.1907: CP 5.473.

A *Sign Is* What?

"Yes", I sighed; "the ad drew on the *Aviso* prefacing my history of philosophy.[78] It was calculated, well or ill, to sell the book to those disaffected from the philosophical side of modernity, its 'dark side',[79] as distinguished from the glorious development of ideoscopic[80] knowledge that we call science."

"Ideoscopic?"

"Knowledge that cannot be arrived at or verified without experimentation and, often, the help of mathematical formulae", I explained.

"As opposed to what? Common sense?"

"No", I explained further, "as opposed to cenoscopic[81] knowledge, the systematic realization of consequences implied by the way we take 'reality' to be in those aspects wherein direct experimentation, and still less mathematization, isn't of much avail. In semiotics,[82] this distinction has been explained as the distinction between *doctrina* and *scientia* as the scholastics understood the point prior to the rise of science in the modern sense. Peirce himself[83] characterized the

---

[78] "Aviso", pp. vii–viii of the *Four Ages* (Deely 2001).

[79] See "Synthesis and Successors: The Strange Case of Dr. Jekyll and Mr. Hyde", Chapter 13 in the *Four Ages* (Deely 2001: 540–89, esp. 565–72).

[80] Also spelled "idioscopic". See the Index entry in the *Four Ages* (Deely 2001: 910); see above, Part I, Chap. 2, n. 16 p. 19.

[81] Also spelled "coenoscopic". See the Index entry in the *Four Ages* (Deely 2001: 865); see above, Part I, Chap. 2, n. 16 p. 19.

[82] The discussion began with Sebeok 1976, and was picked up in Deely 1976 and 1978 (the former an essay review of Eco 1976, the latter an essay review of Sebeok 1976). The point became an Appendix in Deely 1982: 127–30, an encyclopedia entry in Sebeok, Bouissac, Eco, Pelc, Posner, Rey, and Shukmad, Editors, 1986: I, 214, and is hardly regarded as controversial any longer among those cognizant of the discussion, as Petrilli and Ponzio have remarked (2001: *passim*).

[83] Peirce c.1902: CP 5.424.

distinction as 'cenoscopic' vs. 'ideoscopic', borrowing these terms from Jeremy Bentham."

"More strange terminology. Why can't semioticians talk like normal people? And by the way, is Peirce's usage faithful to that of Bentham, and is Bentham actually the originator, the coiner, of these terms?"

"Normal is as normal does", I said with mild exasperation. "How can you develop new ideas without new words to convey them? Of course old words used in unfamiliar ways can also serve, but tend to mislead in any case. Surely you won't deny that new insights require new ways of speaking? Perhaps you've been an undergraduate teacher too long.

"Point taken", my colleague allowed ruefully. "But what about the reliability of Peirce's usage vis-à-vis Bentham's coinage of these terms, if he did coin them?"

"As to the exact relation of Peirce's appropriation to the sense of Bentham's original coinage", I said, "I can't help you there. I have never looked into Bentham directly. But I find the distinction in Peirce useful, even crucial, to understanding the postmodern development of semiotics."

"You said just now", my colleague said, returning at this point to my interrupted historical excursus, "that what I would call the 'common sense' notion of sign, a particular thing representing something other than itself, Peirce called technically a *representamen*, and that this is not the sign itself technically speaking but what you rather termed a 'sign-vehicle', functioning as such only because it is the foreground element in the three elements whose linkage or bonding makes up the sign technically or strictly speaking."

"Yes", I allowed, "you have followed me well. What makes something appear within sense-perception as a sign in the common or loose sense is not anything intrinsic to the physical subjectivity of the sensed object as a thing but rather the fact that the objectified thing in question stands in the position of representamen within a triadic relation constituting a sign in its proper being technically and strictly. So that physical structure before the building in your line of vision that tells you this is no longer Monaghan House is a sign not strictly but loosely. Strictly it is the element of other-representation within a triadic relation having you with your semiotic web of experience and private semiosis as a partial interpretant, and this building here housing my office among other things as its signified object. Moreover, note that the physical structure of the particular thing appearing in your Umwelt as a sign may be subjected to ideoscopic analysis, but that that analysis will never reveal its sign-status as such. The recognition of signs as triadic relations in contrast to related things as subjective structures is a strictly cenoscopic achievement, although of course the semiosis of such things can well be developed ideoscopically by the social sciences, and philosophy will then be obliged to take such ideoscopic developments into account if it wishes to keep up with the reality of human experience as a whole."

"Now that is amazing." My colleague seemed delighted.

"What is amazing?"

"That I now see what you mean in saying that a sign is what every object presupposes. You mean that every object as an object depends upon a network of triadic relations, and that precisely these relations constitute the being of a sign strictly speaking. Hence without objects there would be isolated sensory stimuli, but no cathexis,[84] no cognition, establishing a

---

[84] In connection with our earlier note on this term "cathexis" (note 64, p. 196f., above), we may add here that the importance of introducing this term into semiotics is to provide a marker for Peirce's seminal idea (c.1907: 00035–36) that, within the life of animals, "every sign whatever that functions as such must have an emotional interpretant".

world of objects wherein some appear desirable (+), others undesirable (–), with still others as matters of indifference (0)."

"That is only part of it."

"Part of it?"

"Yes. Every sign acting as such gives rise to further signs. Semiosis is an open process, open to the world of things on the side of physical interactions and open to the future on the side of objects. Thus you need to consider further that all three sign-elements – sign-vehicles or representamens, objects signified or significates, and interpretants – can change places within semiosis. What is one time an object becomes another time primarily sign-vehicle, what is one time interpretant becomes another time object signified, and what is one time object signified becomes another time interpretant, and so on, in an unending spiral of semiosis, the very process through which, as Peirce again put it, 'symbols grow'."

"So signs have a kind of life within experience, indeed provide experience almost with its 'soul' in the Aristotelian sense of an internal principle of growth and development! One man's object is another man's sign, and an object one time can be an interpretant the next."

"Now you're getting the idea. Be careful. Next thing you know you'll claim to be a semiotist instead of a realist."

My colleague frowned a bit severely, as if to say that the crack was not appreciated; but all he actually said in as many words was: "So, signs strictly speaking are invisible."

"Yes, and inaudible and intactile, for that matter. By contrast, a sign *loosely speaking*, an element occupying the position of representamen in a renvoi relation vis-à-vis significate and interpretant, can indeed be seen and pointed to or heard. A great thinker of the 20th century once remarked,[85] perhaps

---

[85] Maritain 1957: 55: "So far we have spoken of genuine language. Let

without realizing the full depth of what he was saying,[86] that animals other than humans make use of signs, but those animals do not know that there are signs. The vehicles of signs can normally be perceived (as long as they are 'instrumental' rather than 'formal') and can become rather interpretants or signifieds; but the signs themselves are relations, like all relations irreducibly suprasubjective, but unique further in being irreducibly triadic. Signs, in short, strictly speaking can be *understood* but not *perceived*; while 'signs' loosely speaking can be *both* perceived *and* understood, but when they are fully understood it is seen that what we call signs loosely are strictly representamens, the foreground element in a given triadic relation through which alone some object other than the representamen is represented to some mind, actually or only prospectively."

"What do you mean 'prospectively'?"

I sighed. "You bring up another story for which the world is not yet prepared."

"I do?" My colleague looked worried, perhaps seeing lunch disappearing in a cloud of verbiage, and having had enough of the case of the giant rat of Sumatra on the table between us, still staring beady-eyed his way.

"Indeed you do. Remember a little while ago when the subject of evolution came up?"

"Indeed I do, and I can tell you that I am happy you didn't insist on going into it."

"Nor will I now, except to say this. Up to the present

us point out that the word 'language', when referring to animals, is equivocal. Animals possess a variety of means of communication but no genuine language. I have observed that animals use signs. But, as I also pointed out, no animal knows the relation of signification or uses signs as involving and manifesting an awareness of this relation." See this important article on the point *passim*.

[86] See the analysis in Deely 1986a.

evolution has been understood mainly as a *vis a tergo*, building up from below through individual interactions structures increasingly complex and far-flung.[87] I have a suspicion that this picture is incomplete in just the way that requires semiosis. For the action of signs is distinctive as compared with the action of things in that the action of things takes place only among actual physical existents, whereas semiosis requires at any given time only that two out of the three related elements actually exist. In physical interactions always the past shapes the future, but in semiosic interactions there is an influence of the future upon the present and even upon the past as bearing on the present, so to speak. My suspicion is that wherever you have evidence of such an influence you have semiosis, an action of signs. And since we can see from the semiosis of animal life that the very possibility of semiosis in general is rooted in the indifference of relation to its subjective ground on the one side and to the physical unreality of its object on the other side,[88] I venture to guess that a *physiosemiosis*, prior to and surrounding even the biosemiosis of which Sebeok speaks,[89] with its phytosemiosis, zoösemiosis, and anthroposemiosis as parts, will prove to be at the heart of what has heretofore been called, *faut de mieux*, evolution."

"Sebeok?" my colleague queried. "This is the second time you have spoken his name in this discussion. Who is he? And is he important for semiotics?"

I could not but chuckle at the relativity of fame. "Of the

---

87   Dennett 1995.

88   Poinsot 1632a: Second Preamble, Article 2, esp. 95/18–96/36; and Book I, Question 1, esp. 117/28–118/18.

89   Sebeok 2001a. But see also Sebeok and Umiker-Sebeok 1992; Emmeche 1994; Hoffmeyer 1996; Hoffmeyer and Emmeche 1999; Kull 2001. It is here the question of the "State of the Question" with which we opened this book in Part I, Chapter 1, pp. 3–9.

three most important figures in the later twentieth century development of semiotics", I averred, "Sebeok is the second most famous and the first in importance. He is to semiotics today what Mersenne was and more to philosophy in the time of Descartes. I am astonished you have not yourself heard of him or read something of his work, if not in semiotics then at least in linguistics, anthropology, or folklore."

"Does he accept your notion of sign as presupposed to object?"

"Well, I am reasonably confident that he would, although I have never put the question to him in just that way. After all, it is a formula I have stumbled upon only recently,[90] and I have not had a chance for extended discussions with Sebeok in quite some time, although I had hoped to arrange a visit this past summer. My main disagreement, if it can be called that, with Sebeok concerns not so much the question of objects in the sense we have discussed but concerns rather the bearing of semiosis upon the very idea of things in the universe. Over the last decade of the twentieth century and into this one,[91] Sebeok has envisioned a 'cosmos before semiosis'. In this way of thinking, the idea of 'nonbiological atomic interactions' as well as 'those of inorganic molecules' being 'semiosic' prior to the origin of life appears as 'surely metaphorical', in Sebeok's exact words."[92]

My colleague frowned. "Surely this Sebeok is right. Inorganic substances do not interpret signs, or involve themselves in *renvoi*!"

It was my turn to frown. "I am not so sure. I think that

[90] "A New Definition of *Signum*" in the *Four Ages* (Deely 2001: 434–35). But cf. Deely 1996b.
[91] "The Evolution of Semiosis", in Sebeok 1991a: 83–96 (reprinted in Sebeok 2001: 17–30).
[92] Ibid. 84 (or 2001: 18).

here Sebeok has been uncharacteristically hasty in his dismissal of a semiosis virtually active in the world of things. The whole question of the 'anthropic principle' is one that implies semiosis from the very beginning of the universe."

"An action of signs in the universe *prior even to the advent of life*? If that's not to indulge in metaphor I don't know what is", my colleague ventured.

"There is another alternative", I said, "a third way between metaphor and organic semiosis, a way suggested, in fact, by the father of systematic semiotics, if we may so speak of the first thinker theoretically to unify the notion of sign under the rubric of triadic relation or, as we are now inclined to say, 'renvoi'. According to Poinsot,[93] it suffices to be a sign virtually in order actually to signify. By this formula, even in the prima facie dyadic interactions of things relations are born sufficient to constitute a semiosis at work in the inorganic no less than organic layers of nature, and prior even to the advent of the organic layers – indeed, anticipatory of that advent. This is an argument I began in 1990[94] and have continued to develop since under the rubric 'physiosemiosis'."[95]

"Semiosis, signs at work in physical nature as such? That sounds crazy. No wonder some people regard semiotics as an imperialistic development!"

"Well, it is only a guess. But others besides me,[96] to say

---

[93] Poinsot 1632a: *Tractatus de Signis*, Book I, Question 1, "Resolution of Counter-Arguments", esp. 126/3–4, and 126/9–22.

[94] Deely, *Basics of Semiotics*, Chapter 5.

[95] On the term physiosemioc is, then, see Deely 1990, 1991, 1993a, 1997, 1998, and 2001e.

[96] E.g., Prodi 1977; Koch 1987; Kruse 1994; Corrington 2000. See the umbrella symposium convened by Nöth 2001 to open the new century.

nothing of Peirce before me,[97] have made analogous suggestions. Time will tell!"

"A discussion for another time. I hate to end a good discussion on a note of shibboleth, but let us go to eat."

I nodded in agreement and started to rise, when my friend
raised his hand to stay me.

"One last question, to be answered in the briefest of
terms."

"Go ahead."

"Are you saying that to know signs in the strict sense, to
thematize sign, as it were, requires a species-specifically
human Innenwelt?"

"Just so. For the imperceptible distinction between subjectivity and suprasubjectivity, between relations and related
things, is at the heart of linguistic communication so far as it
does not reduce to perceptible elements.[98] And it is the point
of departure for anthroposemiosis in its difference from all
zoösemiosis.[99] All animals are semiosic beings, but only
human beings can become semiotic animals – animals, that is
to say, that both use signs and know that there are signs."

"I like that. '*The semeiotic animal*': a new definition for
humanity as the postmodern age opens. Let us say goodbye
to the *res cogitans*, even as Descartes said goodbye to the *animal rationale*; and, like good semiotic animals, let us set out in
search of sign-vehicles which can lead us to objectified things

---

[97] Besides my own analysis of what I termed "Peirce's Grand Vision"
(Deely 1989), Nöth (2001: 16) observes that "renowned Peircean
scholars, such as Helmut Pape (1989), Klaus Oehler (1993), and Lúcia
Santaella-Braga (1994a, 1996, 1999), affirm that the origins of semiosis, according to Peirce, begin before life."

[98] Deely 1980, 2002.

[99] Such was the argument of Deely 1994, sharply focused in Deely 2002.

pleasant to eat. How about the Black Lab?" Now my colleague rose.

I rose with him, and together we set out in search of food. We had not far to go, for the Black Labrador is a rather good restaurant not two full blocks from the place of our discussion where my colleague's initial incredulity gave way to the conviction that, while there is yet more to be said, yet at least this much is certain even now: the sign is what every object presupposes.

Since what is last in discovery becomes first in exposition, the last discovery of the moderns in the person of Peirce has become the first theme postmodern philosophy and intellectual culture must come to terms with (since it defines them). It is not a bad discovery, even if compared to the late Latins it was only a rediscovery. Small wonder that, all thought being in signs, the objective universe is perfused with them – tends, indeed, to consist exclusively of them, each object blossoming into more and more signs within the semiotic spiral. It remains to see if even the physical universe may not as giving rise to us consist exclusively of signs. But first some lunch, in accord with the thinking of St. Thomas: *Primum est vivere, deinde philosophare*, "in order to philosophize, one has to live".

References, Historically Layered

Note on Reference Style: This work has been prepared in accordance with the Style Sheet of the Semiotic Society of America (*The American Journal of Semiotics* 4.3–4 [1986], 193–215; "Brief Version", *Semiotic Scene* [Winter, 1990], n.s. Volume 2, Number 3, 11–12), as modified to include page-bottom footnotes. This means basically three things. *First* that, barring some oversight, only those works are included in the final list of References which have actually been mentioned or cited, as distinguished from works read, consulted, or relevant to the various topics, as are often included in scholarly bibliographies. *Second* that punctuation marks are placed outside quotation marks except in those cases where the punctuation itself is part of the quoted material, a procedure that follows as a logical consequence of the purpose for which quotation marks are to be used: "to indicate the beginning and the end of a quotation in which the exact phraseology of another or of a text is directly cited" (see Deely, Prewitt, and Haworth 1990). *Third* that all the sources have been historically layered, i.e. (see Deely and Prewitt 1989), cited according to a primary reference date from within the lifetime of the author cited, with the relations to translations or later editions of the source work (the actual access volumes) set forth in the complete reference list. Under the authors of cited sources arranged alphabetically, the dates when those sources first came into existence can thus be seen at a glance, like geological layers in a rock or the age rings in a tree trunk; and since in fact human understanding itself is an historical achievement, the value of this bibliographical principle holds even for purely speculative and theoretical works in any field.

A main merit of this style of reference is that it establishes an invariant reference base of sources across all the linguistic, chronological, and editorial lines of access volumes used – an outcome so useful to the intellectual community as to recommend the adoption of historical layering as the organizing principle for all style sheets.

The specific conventions concerning the dating of works and authors that can be assigned only an approximate timeframe needs to be made explicit. In such cases the following prefixes are attached to assigned dates:

a. = *ante* or "before";

c. = *circa* or "approximately";

fl. = *floruit* or "the prime of life", "the time of flourishing";

i. = *inter* or "between";

p. = *post* or "after";

r. = the beginning of the period of occupation of an office, so = *regnat* or "rules";

s. = *usque* or "until", "up to the time of": used to indicate the outside date on which an author worked on a ms. left uncompleted.

Within references, the following abbreviations are used:

cf. = confer, consult, or compare;

q.v. = *quod vide* or "which see", a cross-reference.

ALLEN, Barry.
  1994. "Is Locke's Semiotic Inconsistent?", *The American Journal of Semiotics* 11.3/4, 23–31.

ANSHEN, Ruth Nanda, Editor.
  1957. *Language: An Enquiry into Its Meaning and Function* (New York: Harper & Bros.).

References, Historically Layered

AQUINAS, Thomas (1224/5–1274).

   i. 1252–1273. S. *Thomae Aquinatis Opera Omnia ut sunt in indice thomistico*, ed. Roberto Busa (Stuttgart-Bad Cannstatt: Frommann-Holzboog, 1980), in septem volumina:
  1. In quattuor libros Sententiarum;
  2. Summa contra Gentiles, Autographi Deleta, Summa Theologiae;
  3. Quaestiones Disputatae, Quaestiones Quodlibetales, Opuscula;
  4. Commentaria in Aristotelem et alios;
  5. Commentaria in Scripturas;
  6. Reportationes, Opuscula dubiae authenticitatis;
  7. Aliorum Medii Aevi Auctorum Scripta 61.

   c.1254/6. *In quattuor libros sententiarum Petri Lombardi*, in Busa ed. vol. 1.

   c.1256/9. *Quaestiones Disputatae de Veritate*, in Busa ed. vol. 3, 1–186.

   c.1266/73. *Summa theologiae*, in Busa ed. vol. 2, 184–926.

   c.1268/72. *In duodecim libros metaphysicorum Aristotelis expositio*, in Busa ed. vol. 4, 390–507.

   c.1269/72. *Quaestiones Quodlibetales, Quodlibet 4*, in Busa ed. 3, 438–501.

   i. 1271/3. *Summa theologiae tertia pars*, in Busa ed. 2, 768–926.

ARAÚJO, Francisco (1580–1664).

   1617. *Commentariorum in universam Aristotelis Metaphysicam tomus primus* (Burgos and Salamanca: J. B. Varesius, 1617). This rare, valuable survivor of the last Latin century exists in very few copies. The work itself contains one of the most extensive surveys we have, besides the *Disputationes Metaphysicae* of Francis Suárez, of late Latin positions, including a thematic discussion of sign; and it has the advantage of being Later than Suárez. A summary exposition of the metaphysical doctrine of this work has been published by Mauricio Beuchot (1987) as a stop-gap measure until an edition of the complete original can be published.

But until now the huge size of Araújo's work–over a thousand pages–has posed an insuperable economic obstacle. Fortunately, Beuchot has published a Spanish translation of the section on sign (to wit, Book III, quest. 2, art. 2, dubia 1–4, in Beuchot ed 1995: 51–106).

ARISTOTLE (384–322).

Note: our citations here are from the 12-volume Oxford edition prepared under W. D. Ross Ed. 1928–1952 (q.v.); for the convenience of the reader, after the abbreviation RM, we also give the pages where applicable to the more readily available one-volume edition of *The Basic Works of Aristotle* prepared by Richard McKeon using the Oxford translations (New York: Basic Books, 1941). Chronology for the works is based on Gauthier 1970, as follows:

c.360–330BC. *Organon*, i.e., Aristotle's writings on Logic, in Oxford Vol. I (RM 1–212). The title "Organon", which means "instrument", seems to have originally been assigned as a general title for these writings by either Andronicus of Rhodes in the 1st century BC or Diogenes Laertius in the 3rd century AD, and has been retained ever since: see Chapter 3 above, p. 89n66. The *Organon* consists of:

c.360BC.   *Categories* (trans. E. M. Edghill; RM 1–37 complete).

c.353BC.   *Topics* (trans. W. A. Pickard-Cambridge; RM 187–206 incomplete).

c.353aBC.   *Refuting Sophisms* (trans. Pickard-Cambridge; RM 207–12 incomplete).

c.348–7BC.   *Prior Analytics* (trans. Jenkinson; RM 62–107 incomplete).

c.348–7aBC.   *Posterior Analytics* (trans. G. R. C. Mure; RM 108–86 complete).

c.330BC.   *On Interpretation* (trans. Edghill; RM 38–61 complete).

It is worth noting that Arabic Aristotelian tradition

includes the *Rhetoric* (composed c.335–4BC) and the *Poetics* (c.335–4aBC) as part of the *Organon* itself, the part, specifically, pertaining to practical in contrast to theoretical discourse, i.e., discourse about what is to be made or done in contrast to discourse about the nature of things as transcending human action. Cfr. Lanigan 1969; Black 1990.

ASHLEY, Benedict.
  1985. *Theologies of the Body: Humanist and Christian* (Braintree, MA: The Pope John XXIII Research Center, 1985.

AUGUSTINE of Hippo (354–430).
  397AD. *Aureli Augustini Confessionum Libri Tredecim,* Latin text in O'Donnell 1992: I, 1–205; English text *Confessions Books I–XIII,* trans. F. J. Sheed, introduced by Peter Brown (Indianapolis, IN: Hackett Publishing Co.).
  i. 397–426. *De doctrina christiana libri quattuor* ("Four Books On Christian Doctrine"), in Tomus Tertius Pars
      Prior, pp. 13–151; also in *Patrologiae Cursus Completus,* ed. J. P. Migne, *Series Latina* (PL), Volume 34, cols. 15–122.

BACON, Roger (1214?–1294).
  c.1267. *De Signis,* ed. Fredborg, Nielsen, and Pinborg in *Traditio* Volume XXXIV (New York: Fordham University Press, 1978), pp. 81–136.

BAGGESEN, Jens.
  1800. "Napoleon. Un Voss. (1800.)", in *Jens Baggesen's Poetische Werke in Deutscher Sprache,* ed. Carl and August Baggesen (Leipzig: F. A. Brockhaus, 1836), pp. 92–103.

BAYLE, Pierre (1647–1706).
  1686/8. *Commentaire philosophique sur ces paroles de Jesus-Christ Contrain-les d'entrer; où l'on prouve par plusieurs raisons démonstratives qu 'l n'y a rien de plus-abominable que de faire des conversions par la contrainte, & l'on refute tous les sophismes des convertisseurs à contrainte, & l'apologie que S. Augustin a faite des persécutions.* This

work was issued pseudonymously as "Traduit de l'anglois du Jean Fox de Bruggs par M.J.F." and with a fictitious imprint: "A Cantorbery, Chez Thomas Litwel" (the actual publisher being Wolfgang of Amsterdam) details which serve to underline how fragile was the notion of "rights of conscience" as late as modernity's early years. The work appeared in four parts: Volumes I and II in October of 1686, Volume III in June of 1687, with a "Supplement" that appeared in January of 1688.

The two volumes of 1686 only have been translated and commented upon, with scattered references to the "Supplement", by Amie Godman Tannenbaum., *Pierre Bayle's Philosophical Commentary: a modern translation and critical interpretation* (New York : Peter Lang, 1987).

BENTHAM, Jeremy (1748–1832).

1816. *Chrestomathia: Being a Collection of Papers, Explanatory of the Design of an Institution Proposed to be Set on Foot Under the Name of the Chrestomathic Day School, or Chrestomathic School, for the Extension of the New System of Instruction to the Higher Branches of Learning, For the Use of the Middling and Higher Ranks in Life*, in *The Works of Jeremy Bentham*, ed. John Bowring (Edinburgh, 1838–1843; reproduced 1962 by Russell & Russell, Inc., New York), Vol. 8, pp. 1–191, esp. Appendix No. IV, the "Essay on Nomenclature and Classification", 63–128.

BERKELEY, Bishop George (1685–1753).

1710. *The Principles of Human Knowledge*, in *The Works of George Berkeley, Bishop of Cloyne*, ed. A. A. Luce and T. E. Jessop (London: Nelson, 1948ff.).

BEUCHOT, Mauricio.

1980. "La doctrina tomista clásica sobre el signo: Domingo de Soto, Francisco de Araújo y Juan de Santo Tomás", *Crítica* XII.36 (México, diciembre), 39–60.

References, Historically Layered

1983. "Lógica y lenguaje en Juan de Sto. Tomás", *Diánoia* 17.
1986. "Signo y Lenguaje en San Agustín", *Dianoia* (anuario de filosofia) 32, 13–26.
1987. *Metafísica. La Ontología Aristotélico-Tomista de Francisco de Araújo* (Mexico City: Universidad Nacional Autónoma de México).
1993. "La percepción sensible en Santo Tomás de Aquino", in *Percepción: Colores*, ed. Laura Benítez and José A. Robles (= La Filosofía y Sus Problemas; Mexico City: Universidad Nacional Autónoma, Instituto de Investigaciones Filosóficas), 11–29.
1994. "Intentionality in John Poinsot", in *ACPQ* 68.3 (Summer 1994), 279–96.
1995. *Algunas Teorías del Signo en la Escolástica Ibérica Post-Medieval*, selección de textos, introducción y traducción (Maracaibo y Caracas, Venezuela: Universidad del Zulia y Universidad Católica Andrés).
1998. "Bañez, Domingo (1528–1604)", entry in the *Routledge Encyclopedia of Philosophy*, ed. in 10 volumes by Edward Craig (London: Routledge, 1998), Vol. 1, pp. 647–49.

BEUCHOT, Mauricio, and John DEELY.
1995. "Common Sources for the Semiotic of Charles Peirce and John Poinsot", *Review of Metaphysics* XLVIII.3 (March), 539–66.

BLACK, Deborah Louise.
1990. *Logic and Aristotle's Rhetoric and Poetics in Medieval Arabic Philosophy* (Leiden: E. J. Brill).

BLACKWELL, Richard J.
1991. *Galileo, Bellarmine, and the Church* (Notre Dame, IN: University of Notre Dame Press).

BRENTANO, Franz.
1874. *Psychologie von Empirischen Standpunkt*, trans. Linda McAlister, A. Rancurello, and D. B. Terrell as *Psychology from an Empirical Standpoint* (New York: Humanities Press, 1963).

BURKS, Arthur W. (1915–).
    1958. "Bibliography of the Works of Charles Sanders Peirce", in *The Collected Papers of Charles Sanders Peirce, Volume VIII* ed. Arthur W. Burks (Cambridge, MA: Harvard University Press, 1958), 249–330.

CANCELLARIUS *see* PHILIP CANCELLARIUS

CASSIRER, Ernst (1874–1945).
    1921. *Kants Leben und Lehre* (2nd ed.; Berlin: Bruno Cassirer), trans. James Haden as *Kant's Life and Thought* (New Haven, CT: Yale University Press, 1981). Page references are to the English trans.

COBLEY, Paul, Editor.
    2001. *Routledge Critical Dictionary of Semiotics and Linguistics* (London: Routledge).

COLAPIETRO, Vincent (1950–), and Thomas OLSHEWSKY (1934–), Editors.
    1996. *Peirce's Doctrine of Signs* (Berlin: Mouton de Gruyter).

COLLINS, Arthur W.
    1999. *Possible Experience. Understanding Kant's Critique of Pure Reason* (Berkeley, CA: University of California Press).

CONIMBRICENSES.
    1607. "De Signis", being Chapter 1 of their commentary on Aristotle's *De Interpretatione*, in *Commentarii Collegii Conimbricensis et Societatis Jesu. In Universam Dialecticam Aristotelis Stagiritae. Secunda Pars* (Lyons: Sumptibus Horatii Cardon, 1607), pp. 4–67. An earlier edition minus the Greek text of Aristotle was published at Coimbra itself in 1606.

        This work has just been translated into English and published in a bilingual critical edition: see under Doyle Ed. 2001.

CORRINGTON, Robert S.
    2000. *A Semiotic Theory of Theology and Philosophy* (Cambridge, England: Cambridge University Press).

References, Historically Layered

DAWKINS, Richard.
 1986. *The Blind Watchmaker* (New York: Norton).
 1976. *The Selfish Gene* (New York: Oxford University Press).

DEELY, John.
 1968. "The Immateriality of the Intentional as Such", *The New Scholasticism* XLII no. 3 (Spring), 293–306.
 1969. "The Philosophical Dimensions of the Origin of Species", The Thomist XXXIII (January and April), Part I, 75–149, Part II, 251–342.
 1971. *The Tradition via Heidegger. An essay on the meaning of being in the philosophy of Martin Heidegger* (The Hague: Martinus Nijhoff).
 1971a. "The Myth as Integral Objectivity, *ACPA Proceedings* XLV, 61–76.
 1972. "The Ontological Status of Intentionality", *The New Scholasticism* Vol. XLVI, No. 2 (Spring), 220–33.
 1972a. "How Language Refers", *Studi Internazionali di Filosofia* IV, 41–50.
 1975. "Reference to the Non-Existent", *The Thomist* XXXIX.2 (April, 1975), 253–308.
 1976. "The Doctrine of Signs: Taking Form at Last", *Semiotica* 18:2, 171–93 (essay review of Eco 1976).
 1977. "'Semiotic' as the Doctrine of Signs", Ars Semeiotica 1/3, 41–68.
 1978. "What's in a Name?", *Semiotica* 22/1–2, 151–81 (essay review of Sebeok 1976).
 1978a. "Semiotic and the Controversy over Mental Events", *ACPA Proceedings* LII, 16–27.
 1980. "The Nonverbal Inlay in Linguistic Communication", in *The Signifying Animal*, ed. Irmengard Rauch and Gerald F. Carr (Bloomington, IN: Indiana University Press), pp. 201–17.
 1982. *Introducing Semiotic: Its History and Doctrine* (Bloomington: Indiana University Press); trans. by Vivina de Campos Figueiredo as *Introdução à*

Semiótica: historia e doutrina (Lisbon, Portugal: Fundação Calouste Gulbenkian, 1995).

1982a. "On the Notion 'Doctrine of Signs'", Appendix I in Deely 1982: 127–30.

1982b. "On the Notion of Phytosemiotics", in *Semiotics 1982*, ed. John Deely and Jonathan Evans (Lanham, MD: University Press of America, 1987), 541–54; reprinted with minor revision in Deely, Williams, and Kruse 1986: 96–103.

1984. "Semiotic as Framework and Direction", presented in the "Semiotic: Field or Discipline?" State-of-the-Art Conference organized by Michael Herzfeld at Indiana University (Bloomington) 8–10 October; published in Deely, Williams, and Kruse 1986: 264–71.

1985. "Editorial AfterWord" and critical apparatus to *Tractatus de Signis: The Semiotic of John Poinsot* (Berkeley: University of California Press), 391–514; electronic version hypertext-linked (Charlottesville, VA: Intelex Corp.; see entry under Poinsot 1632a below).

1985a. "Semiotic and the Liberal Arts", *The New Scholasticism* LIX.3 (Summer), 296–322. The "second epsilon" mentioned in this work is a blunder, for the "first epsilon" in the Greek "semeiotic" is not an epsilon but an eta, thus: Σημειωτική.

1986. "John Locke's Place in the History of Semiotic Inquiry", in *Semiotics 1986*, ed. John Deely and Jonathan Evans (Lanham, MD: University Press of America), 406–18.

1986a. "Semiotic in the Thought of Jacques Maritain", *Recherche Sémiotique/Semiotic Inquiry* 6.2, 1–30.

1986b. "Doctrine", terminological entry for the *Encyclopedic Dictionary of Semiotics*, ed. Thomas A. Sebeok et al. (Berlin: Mouton de Gruyter), Tome I, p. 214.

1986c. "A Context for Narrative Universals. Semiology as a *Pars Semiotica*", *The American Journal of Semiotics* 4.3–4, 53–68.

1986d. "Idolum. Archeology and Ontology of the Iconic Sign", in *Iconicity: Essays on the Nature of Culture*, Festschrift volume in honor of Thomas A Sebeok, edited by Paul Bouissac, Michael Herzfeld, and Roland Posner (Tübingen: Stauffenburg Verlag), 29–49.

1989. "The Grand Vision", presented on September 8 at the September 5–10 Charles Sanders Peirce Sesquicentennial International Congress at Harvard University, in Colapietro and Olshewsky eds 1996: 45–67. This essay was first published in the *Transactions of the Charles S. Peirce Society* XXX.2 (Spring 1994), 371–400, but, inexplicably, after the submission of corrected proofs, the journal repaged the whole and introduced such extreme errors as to make the text unreadable at some points. The correct version has appeared as Chapter 7 of Deely 1994a: 183– 200.

1990. *Basics of Semiotics* (Bloomington, IN: Indiana University Press).

1990a. "Logic Within Semiotics", in *Symbolicity*, ed. Jeff Bernard, John Deely, Terry Prewitt, Vilmos Voigt, and Gloria Withalm (Lanham, MD: University Press of America, 1993), 77–86; *Symbolicity* is bound together with *Semiotics 1990*, ed. Karen Haworth, John Deely, and Terry Prewitt as a single volume.

1991. "Semiotics and Biosemiotics: Are Sign-Science and Life-Science Coextensive?", in *Biosemiotics. The Semiotic Web 1991*, ed. Thomas A. Sebeok and Jean Umiker-Sebeok (Berlin: Mouton de Gruyter, 1992), 45–75. Since revised as Chapter 6 "How Do Signs Work?" in Deely 1994a: 151–82.

1992. "From Glassy Essence to Bottomless Lake", in *Semiotics 1992*, ed. John Deely (Lanham, MD: University Press of America, 1993), 151–58.

1993. "Locke's Proposal for Semiotic and the Scholastic Doctrine of Species", presented at the 3rd Midwest Seminar in the History of Early Modern Philosophy held at the University of Chicago 9–10 November 1991; published in *The Modern Schoolman* LXX (March 1993), 165–88.

1993a. "How Does Semiosis Effect Renvoi?", the Thomas A.

Sebeok Fellowship Inaugural Lecture delivered at the 18th Annual Meeting of the Semiotic Society of America, October 22, 1993, St. Louis, MO; published in *The American Journal of Semiotics* 11.1/2 (1994), 11–61; text available also as Ch. 8 of Deely 1994a: 201–4.

1994. *The Human Use of Signs; or Elements of Anthroposemiosis* (Lanham, MD: Rowman & Littlefield).

1994a. *New Beginnings. Early Modern Philosophy and Postmodern Thought* (Toronto, Canada: University of Toronto Press).

1994b. "Why Investigate the Common Sources of Charles Peirce and John Poinsot?", in *Semiotics 1994*, ed. C. W. Spinks and John Deely (New York: Peter Lang Publishing, 1995), 34–50.

1994c. "Locke's Philosophy versus Locke's Proposal for Semiotic", *The American Journal of Semiotics* 11.3/4, 33–37.

1995. "Ferdinand de Saussure and Semiotics", in *Ensaios em Homagem a Thomas A. Sebeok*, quadruple Special Issue of *Cruzeiro Semiótico*, ed. Norma Tasca (Porto, Portugal: Fundação Eng. António de Almeida), 75–85; later version of same title in *Semiotics 1995*, ed. C. W. Spinks and John Deely (New York: Peter Lang, 1996), 71–83.

1995a. "Quondam Magician, Possible Martian, Semiotician: Thomas Albert Sebeok", in Tasca ed. 1985: 17–26.

1996. *Los Fundamentos de la Semiótica*, trans. José Luis Caivano (Mexico City, Mexico: Universidad Iberoamericana). An expanded text of Deely 1990.

1996a. "The Four Ages of Understanding between Ancient Physics and Postmodern Semiotics", in *Semiotics 1996*, ed. C. W. Spinks and J. N. Deely (New York: Peter Lang Publishing, Inc., 1997), pp. 229–40.

1996b. "A New Beginning for the Sciences", *Semiotics as a Bridge between the Humanities and the Sciences*, ed. Paul Perron, Marcel Danesi, Paul Colilli, and John Wattanabee (proceedings of the 2–6 November 1995 Symposium organized at Victoria College by Prof. Danesi; Ottawa: Legas Press, 2000), pp. 95–108.

References, Historically Layered

1997. "How Is the Universe Perfused with Signs?", in *Semiotics 1997*, ed. C. W. Spinks and J. N. Deely (New York: Peter Lang Publishing, Inc., 1998), pp. 389–94.

1997a. "Quid Sit Postmodernismus?", in *Postmodernism and Christian Philosophy* (a Proceedings of the American Maritain Association; Washington, DC: Catholic University of America Press), 68–96.

1998. "Physiosemiosis and Semiotics", in *Semiotics 1998*, ed. C. W. Spinks and J. N. Deely (New York: Peter Lang Publishing, Inc., 1999).

1998a. "The Ethics of Terminology", in the *American Catholic Philosophical Quarterly* Special Issue on Peirce guest-edited by Vincent Colapietro, LXXII.2, 197–243.

2000 *The Beginning of Postmodern Times, or: Charles Sanders Peirce and the Recovery of Signum* (University of Helsinki, Finland: Department of Musicology, booklet prepared for November 2, 2000, meeting of The Metaphysical Club under chairmanship of Erkki Kilpinen of the Finnish Academy).

2000a. "The Latin Foundations for Semiotic Consciousness: Augustine (5th century AD) to Poinsot (17th century AD)", *Recherches Semiotiques/Semiotic Inquiry* 20.1–2–3, 11–32.

2001. *Four Ages of Understanding. The first postmodern history of philosophy from ancient times to the turn of the 21st century* (Toronto, Canada: University of Toronto Press).

2001a. "John Locke (1632–1704)", entry in Cobley Ed. 2001: 217–18, q.v.

2001b. "Physiosemiosis in the Semiotic Spiral. A Play of Musement", in Nöth 2001.

2001c. "A New Determination of the Middle Ages", Foreword to Doyle Ed. 2001.

2001d. "Sebeok's Century", thematic preface to *Semiotics 2000*, ed. Scott Simpkins and John Deely (Ottawa, Canada: Legas Publishing, 2001), xvii–xxxiv.

2001e. "A Sign is *What*?", *Sign Systems Studies* 29.2, 705–43.

2001f. "Umwelt", *Semiotica* 134–1/4, 125–35.

2002. *What Distinguishes Human Understanding?* (South Bend, IN: St. Augustine's Press).

2002a. "On the Word Semiotics", forthcoming.

DEELY, John N., Brooke WILLIAMS, and Felicia E. KRUSE, editors.
    1986. *Frontiers in Semiotics* (Bloomington: Indiana University Press). Preface titled "Pars Pro Toto", pp. viii–xvii; "Description of Contributions", pp. xviii– xxii.

DELEDALLE, Gérard.
    1992. "Peirce's Sign: Its Concept and Its Use", *Transactions of the Charles S. Peirce Society* (Spring), XXVIII.2, pp. 289–301.
    1990. "Traduire Charles S. Peirce. Le *signe*: le concept et son usage", *TTR: Traduction, Terminologie, Rédaction* 3.1 (Trois Rivières: Université du Quebec), pp. 15–29.
    1987. "Quelle philosophie pour la sémiotique peircienne? Peirce et la sémiotique grecque", *Semiotica* 63.3/4, 241–51.
    1981. English and French Versions of C. S. Peirce's "The Fixation of Belief" and "How To Make our Ideas Clear", *Transactions of the Charles S. Peirce Society* (Spring) XVII.2, 141–52. This article is substantially and essentially the English equivalent of the 1980a entry following.
    1980. "Avertissement aux lecteurs de Peirce", *Langages* 58 (June), pp. 25–27.
    1980a. "Les articles pragmatistes de Charles S. Peirce", *Revue philosophique* CLXX, pp. 17–29. See gloss on 1981 entry following.

DENNETT, Daniel C.
    1995. *Darwin's Dangerous Idea* (New York: Simon & Schuster).

DOYLE, John P.
    1984. "The Conimbricenses on the Relations Involved in Signs", in *Semiotics 1984*, ed. John Deely (Proceedings of the Ninth Annual Meeting of the Semiotic Society of America; Lanham, MD: University Press of America, 1985), 567–76.

References, Historically Layered

1994. "Poinsot on the Knowability of Beings of Reason", in *American Catholic Philosophical Quarterly* LXVIII. 3 (Summer 1994), 337–62.

DOYLE, John P., Editor and Translator.
2001. *The Conimbricenses. Some Questions on Signs* (Milwaukee, WI: Marquette University Press), bilingual critical edition of Conimbricenses 1607, q.v.

DRAKE, Stillman.
1983. "Galileo and the Church", reprinted from *Revista di Studi Italiani* 1.1 (June), 82–97, in *Essays on Galileo and the History of Science*, selected and introduced by N. M. Swerdlow and T. H. Levere (Toronto, Canada: University of Toronto Press, 1999), Vol. 1, pp. 153–66.

ECO, Umberto.
1976. *A Theory of Semiotics*, trans. David Osmond-Smith (Bloomington: Indiana University Press).
1987. "The Influence of Roman Jakobson on the Development of Semiotics", in *Classics of Semiotics*, ed. Martin Krampen, Klaus Oehler, Roland Posner, Thomas A. Sebeok, and Thure von Uexküll (New York: Plenum Press), 109–27.
2000. *Kant and the Platypus. Essays on Language and Cognition* (New York: Harcourt, Brace & Co.), English trans. in consultation with author by Alastair McEwen of *Kant e l'ornitorinco* (Milano: Bompiani, 1997).

ECO, Umberto, and John DEELY.
1983, May 30–June 24. "Historiographical Foundations of Semiotics", course team-taught at ISISSS '83 (Indiana University, Bloomington campus). This course exists in a series of twenty-six untranscribed casettes created by students in the course.

ECO, Umberto, Roberto LAMBERTINI, Costantino MARMO, and Andrea TABARRONI.
1986. "Latratus Canis or: The Dog's Barking", in Deely, Williams, and Kruse 1986: 63–73; see the editorial note on the background of this text, ibid. p. xix.

EMMECHE, Claus.
  1994. *The Garden in the Machine* (Princeton, NJ: Princeton University Press).
FISCH, Max H. (1900–1995)
  1978. "Philodemus and Semiosis (1879–1883)", Section 5 of the essay "Peirce's General Theory of Signs", in *Sight, Sound, and Sense*, ed. Thomas A. Sebeok (Bloomington, IN: Indiana Univ. Press), 31–70.
FONSECA, Petrus ("Pedro da").
  1564. *Institutionum dialecticarum libri octo* (Coimbra: Apud haeredes Joannis Blauij). The most important edition of this work thus far is the bilingual presentation comparable to Poinsot 1632a (q.v.) of Joaquim Ferreira Gomes, *Instituicoes Dialecticas (Institutionum dialecticarum libri octo)*, 2 vols. (Instituto de Estudos Filosoficos da Universidad de Coimbra, 1964).
FRENCH, Anthony Philip, and KENNEDY, P. J., Editors.
  1985. *Niels Bohr, A centenary volume* (Cambridge, MA: Harvard University Press).
GIGANTE, Marcello.
  1995. *Philodemus in Italy: The Books from Herculaneum*, trans. Dirk Obbink (Ann Arbor: University of Michigan Press) from the original French (1987) and revised Italian (1990) editions.
GILSON, Étienne (13 June 1884–1978 September 19).
  1952. *Being and Some Philosophers* (2nd ed., corrected and enlarged; Toronto: Pontifical Institute of Mediaeval Studies).
GOTTLIEB, Anthony.
  2001. *The Dream of Reason: A History of Philosophy from the Greeks to the Renaissance* (New York: Norton, W. W. & Company, Inc.).
GOULD, Stephen J., and Elisabeth S. VRBA.
  1982. "Exaptation–A Missing Term in the Science of Form", *Paleobiology* 8.1 (Winter), 4–15.

References, Historically Layered

GROTE, George (1794–1871).

1872. *Aristotle*, posthumous ed. by Alexander Bain and G. Croom Robinson (London: J. Murray), 2 vols.

GUAGLIARDO, Vincent (1944–1995).

1993. "Being and Anthroposemiotics", in *Semiotics 1993*, ed. Robert Corrington and John Deely (Lanham, MD: University Press of America, 1994), 50–56.

1994. "Being-as-First-Known in Poinsot: A-Priori or Aporia?", *American Catholic Philosophical Quarterly* 68.3 "Special Issue on John Poinsot" (Summer), pp. 363–93.

HANDYSIDE, John, Translator. *See further* Kemp Smith 1929, below.

1929 (posthumous). *Kant's Inaugural Dissertation and Early Writings on Space*, being an introduction to with translations of Kant 1768 and 1770, posthumously prepared for publication by Norman Kemp Smith, who added to Handyside's papers his own translation of selected passages from Kant 1747, included in the volume (Chicago: The Open Court Publishing Co.).

HARDWICK, Charles S., Editor, with the assistance of James Cook.

1977. *Semiotics and Significs. The Correspondence between Charles S. Peirce and Victoria Lady Welby* (Bloomington: Indiana University Press).

HEGEL, G. W. F. (1770–1831)

1802. "Glauben und Wissen oder die Reflexionsphilosophie der Subjektivität", from the *Journal der Philosophie*, Band II, Stück 1, as reprinted in the *Sämtliche Werke*, ed. Hermann Glockner (Stuttgart: Frommann, 1958), Vol. I, pp. 278–33.

1807. *Phänomenologie des Geistes*, trans. A. V. Miller as *Phenomenology of Spirit*, analysis of the text and foreword by J. N. Findlay (Oxford : Clarendon Press, 1977).

1812. *Wissenschaft der Logik. Erster Teil: Die Objektive Logik*, in *Sämtliche Werke*, Vol. 4 (Stuttgart: Frommann, 1958).

1817. *Encyclopädie der philosophischen Wissenschaften*, ed.

Georg Lasson (Leipzig: Felix Meiner, 1930), with a table, pp. V–VIf, correlating all the elements of this original publication with what appears further in later editions, notably the two that appeared within Hegel's lifetime in 1827 and 1830, respectively.

1821. *Naturrecht und Staatswissenschaft im Grundrisse; Grundlinien der Philosophie des Rechts* ("Foreword" ["Vorrede"] completed June 25, 1820), trans. as *Hegel's Philosophy of Right* by T. M. Knox (Oxford: Clarendon Press, 1952, corrected sheets 1957).

1830. *Die Logik,* being the *Erster Teil* of *System der Philosophie,* in *Sämtliche Werke,* Vol. 8 (Stuttgart: Frommann, 1964), i.e., Part I of the 3rd edition of *Enzyklopädie der philosophischen Wissenschaften,* first published in 1817.

1830a. *Die Philosophie des Geistes,* being the *Dritter Teil of System der Philosophie,* in *Sämtliche Werke,* Vol. 10 (Stuttgart: Frommann, 1958), i.e., Part III of *Enzyklopädie der philosophischen Wissenschaften,* first published in 1817.

HEIDEGGER, Martin (1889–1976).

1927. *Sein und Zeit,* originally published in the *Jahrbuch für Phänomenologie und phänomenologische Forschung,* ed. E. Husserl. Page references in the present work are to the 10th edition (Tübingen: Niemeyer, 1963).

1947. "Brief über den Humanismus", in *Platons Lehre von der Wahrheit* (Bern: Francke Verlag). A separate and independent edition of the so-called "Letter on Humanism" was published in 1949 by Klosterman of Frankfurt.

HENLE, Robert J. (1909–2000)

1983. "Thomas Reid's Theory of Signs", in *Semiotics 1983,* ed. Jonathan Evans and John Deely (Lanham, MD: University Press of America, 1987), 155–68.

HILL, Archibald A.

1948. "The Use of Dictionaries in Language Teaching", *Language Learning* 1, 9–13.

References, Historically Layered

1958. *Introduction to Linguistic Structures. From sound to sentence in English* (New York: Harcourt, Brace).

HOFFMEYER, Jesper.
1996. *Signs of Meaning in the Universe* (Bloomington, IN: Indiana University Press), trans. by Barbara J. Haverland of *En Snegl På Vejen: Betydningens naturhistorie* (Copenhagen: Rosinante, 1993).

HOFFMEYER, Jesper, and Claus EMMECHE, Guest-Editors.
1999. *Biosemiotics*, Special Issue of *Semiotica* 127.

HUME, David (1711–1776)
1748. *An Enquiry Concerning Human Understanding* (originally published under the title *Philosophical Essays concerning the Human Understanding*, but retitled as of the 1758 edition), ed. P. H. Nidditch (3rd ed.; Oxford, 1975).

HUSSERL, Edmund (1859–1938).
1929. *Cartesian Meditations. An Introduction to Phenomenology*, trans. by Dorion Cairns (The Hague: Martinus Nijhoff, 1960), of a work that appeared in Husserl's lifetime only in French.
1936. *The crisis of European sciences and transcendental phenomenology. An introduction to phenomenological philosophy*, trans. with an Introduction by David Carr (Evanston, ILL: Northwestern University Press, 1970) of *Die Krisis der europaischen Wissenschaften und die transzendentale Phanomenologie; eine Einleitung in die phanomenologische Philosophie*, posthumously edited by Walter Biemel and published in German 1954.

JACOB, François.
1982. *The Possible and the Actual* (Seattle, WA: University of Washington Press).

JAKOBSON, Roman (1896–1982).
1974. "Coup d'oeil sur le devéloppement de la sémiotique", in *Panorama sémiotique/A Semiotic Landscape*, Proceed-

ings of the First Congress of the International Association for Semiotic Studies, Milan, June 1974, ed. Seymour Chatman, Umberto Eco, and Jean-Marie Klinkenberg (The Hague: Mouton, 1979), 3–18. Also published separately under the same title by the Research Center for Language and Semiotic Studies as a small monograph (= Studies in Semiotics 3; Bloomington: Indiana University Publications, 1975); and in an English trans. by Patricia Baudoin titled "A Glance at the Development of Semiotics", in *The Framework of Language* (Ann Arbor, MI: Michigan Studies in the Humanities, Horace R. Rackham School of Graduate Studies, 1980), 1–30.

KANT, Immanuel (1724–1804).

1747. Selected passages from Kant's first published writing, *Thoughts on the True Estimation of Living Forces*, trans. by Norman Kemp Smith and included in the posthumous ed. he prepared for press of Handyside Trans. 1929 (q.v.): 3–15.

1768. *On the First Ground of the Distinction of Regions of Space*, in Handyside Trans. 1929: 19–29.

1770. *De Mundi Sensibilis atque Intelligibilis Forma et Principiis. Dissertatio pro loco professionis log. et metaph. ordinariae rite sibi vindicanda*, trans. as *Dissertation on the Form and Principles of the Sensible and Intelligible World*, in Handyside Trans. 1929: 33–85.

1781. *Kritik der reinen Vernunft* (Riga: Johann Friedrich Hartknoch).

1783. *Prolegomena zu einer jeden künftigen Metaphysik, die als Wissenschaft wird auftreten können*, ed. Rudolf Malter (Stuttgart: Philipp Reclam, 1989). I have used the English trans. *Prolegomena to Any Future Metaphysics [which will be able to come forth as science]* by Mahaffy (1872) after Richardson (1836), as edited in English by Carus (1902) and extensively revised, finally, by Lewis White Beck (Indianapolis, IN: The Bobbs-Merrill Co., 1950); with an Introduction by Lewis White Beck.

References, Historically Layered

1787. *Kritik der reinen Vernunft* (Zweite hin und wieder verbesserte Auflage; Riga: Johann Friedrich Hartknoch); English trans. by Norman Kemp Smith, *Kant's Critique of Pure Reason* (New York: St. Martin's Press, 1963).

1790. *Kritik der Urteilskraft*, 2 vols. in 1, trans. and ed. James C. Meredith as *Critique of Judgment* (Oxford, 1957).

KEMP SMITH, Norman (1872–1958).
1929. "Preface" to, and selected passages from Kant 1747 in, Handyside Trans. 1929: v–vi and 1–15, respectively.

KLUCKHOHN, Clyde.
1951. "Values and Value-Orientation in the Theory of Action", in Parsons and Shils Eds. 1951: 388–433.

KOCH, Walter A.
1987. "A Plea for Evolutionary Cultural Semiotics", in *A Plea for Cultural Semiotics* (Bochum: Brockmeyer), pp. 53–131.

KRAMER, Heinrich ("Henricus Institutoris"), and Jacob SPRENGER.
1486. *Malleus Maleficarum* ("Hammer of Witches"), trans. with Introduction, Bibliography, and Notes by Montague Summers (London: Pushkin Press, 1951).
     This work appeared with a singular Preface, to wit, the Papal Bull *Summis desiderantes affectibus* of 9 December 1484 (the very first year of the Pontificate of Innocent VIII), a document of highest authority in which Kramer and Sprenger are named specifically as the already-delegated Inquisitors in the matter of witchcraft with renewed emphasis: "By our supreme authority we grant them anew full and complete faculties" throughout the German territories, including, as circumstances warrant, "the help of the secular arm". To this Preface was added an Official Letter of Approbation of the work from the Faculty of Theology of the University of Cologne, dated 19 May 1487.

Summers, in his Introduction (p. xiv) notes that, for nearly three centuries after its appearance, "the *Malleus* lay on the bench of every judge, on the desk of every magistrate. It was the ultimate, irrefutable, unarguable authority. It was implicitly accepted not only by Catholic but by Protestant legislature."

KRAMPEN, Martin (1928–).
  1981. "Phytosemiotics", *Semiotica*, 36–3/4, 187–209. Substantially reprinted in Deely, Williams, and Kruse 1986: 83–95.

KRUSE, Felicia E.
  1994. "Is Cosmic Evolution Semiosis?", in *From Time and Chance to Consciousness: Studies in the Metaphysics of Charles Peirce*, ed. Edward C. Moore and Richard S. Robin (Oxford, England: Berg), 87–98.

KULL, Kalevi, Guest-Editor.
  2001. *Jakob von Uexküll: A Paradigm for Biology and Semiotics*, a Special Issue of *Semiotica* 134–1/4.

LANGER, Susanne K. (1895–1985).
  1971. "The Great Shift: Instinct to Intuition", in J. F. Eisenberg and W. S. Dillon, Eds., *Man and Beast: Comparative Social Behavior* (Smithsonian Annual III; Washington, DC: Smithsonian Institution Press), 313–32.

LANIGAN, Richard.
  1969. "Aristotle's Rhetoric: Addendum to the Organon", *Dialogue* 11.2 (November), 1–6.

LIDDELL, Henry George (1811–1898), and Robert SCOTT (1811–1887).
  1846. *Greek-English Lexicon, based on the German work of Francis Passow, by Henry George Liddell, M.A., and Robert Scott, M.A., with corrections and additions, and the insertion in alphabetical order of the proper names occurring in the principal Greek authors by Henry Drisler, LL.D.* (1st American ed.; New York: Harper & Brothers, 1846).

References, Historically Layered

1940, 1968. *A Greek-English Lexicon* compiled by Henry George Liddell and Robert Scott (original ed. 1843), revised and augmented throughout by Sir Henry Stuart Jones (1867–1939) with the assistance of Roderick McKenzie (1887–1937) (9th ed., 1940) with a Supplement (1968) by E. A. Barber with the assistance of P. Maas, M. Scheller, and M. L. Left (Oxford University Press).

LYOTARD, Jean-François.
   1984. *The Postmodern Condition: A Report on Knowledge* (Minneapolis, MN: University of Minnesota Press), trans. Geoff Bennington and Brian Massumi of *La Condition postmoderne: rapport sur le savoir* (Paris: Editions Minuit, 1971).

MacKINNON, D. L., Translator.
   1926. *Theoretical Biology*, being an attempted translation of von Uexküll 1920 (New York: Harcourt Brace & Co.). Hopefully, another attempt will be made, this time within the perspective of semiotic.

MANETTI, Giovanni.
   1993. *Theories of the Sign in Classical Antiquity* (Bloomington, IN: Indiana University Press), trans. by Christine Richardson of *Le teorie del segno nell'antichità classica* (Milan: Bompiani, 1987).
   1996. "The Concept of the Sign from Ancient to Modern Semiotics", in Manetti Ed. 1996, q.v.: 11–40.
   1997. "Sign Conceptions in Grammar, Rhetoric, and Poetics in Ancient Greece and Rome", in Posner, Robering, and Sebeok, Eds. 1997: 876–92.
   1997a. "Sign Conceptions in Natural History and Natural Philosophy in Ancient Greece and Rome", in Posner, Robering, and Sebeok, Eds. 1997: 922–39.
   2002. "Philodemus' 'De Signis': An Important Ancient Semiotic Debate" (review of Gigante 1995), *Semiotica* 138–1/4, 279–97.

MANETTI, Giovanni, Editor.
1996. *Knowledge through signs. Ancient semiotic theories and practices* (Bologna: Brepols).

MARITAIN, Jacques (18 November 1882–1973 April 28).
Note: the writings of Maritain are so diverse and have appeared in so many translations with so many modifications that it needs to be noted that in the thirteen years spanning 1983 and 1995 the Cercle d'Etudes Jacques et Raïssa Maritain (in the persons of Jean-Marie Allion, Maurice Hany, Dominique and René Mougel, Michel Nurdin, and Heinz R. Schmitz) established the definitive text of all the writings and brought them to publication in 15 volumes entitled *Jacques et Raïssa Maritain. Oeuvres Complètes* (Editions Universitaires Fribourg Suisse et Editions Saint-Paul Paris, 1983–1995). In citing Maritain from this set, I will abbreviate it to OC (for *"Oeuvres Completes"*) followed by volume number in Roman numerals and pages in Arabic numbers.

1921. *Theonas, ou les Entretiens d'un Sage et de Deux Philosophes sur Diverses Matières Inégalement Actuelles* (Paris: Nouvelle Librarie Nationale). In OC II 765–921.

1937–1938. "Sign and Symbol", trans. Mary Morris for the *Journal of the Warburg Institute* I, 1–11.

1938. "Signe et Symbole", *Revue Thomiste* XLIV (April), 299–330.

1943. "Sign and Symbol", English trans. by H. L. Binsse of 1938 entry above q.v., but with footnotes separated from the text proper at the end of the volume, in *Redeeming the Time* (London: Geoffrey Bles), text pp. 191–224, Latin notes pp. 268–76.

1956. "Le Langage et la Theorie du Signe", Annexe au Chapitre II of *Quatre Essais sur l'Esprit dans sa Condition Charnelle* (nouvelle edition revue et augmentee; Paris: Alsatia), 113–24. (The *Chapitre II* to which this Anex is added is the text of the entry for 1938 above).

References, Historically Layered

1957. "Language and the Theory of Sign", in *Language: An Enquiry into Its Meaning and Function*, ed. Ruth Nanda Anshen (New York: Harper and Brothers), 86–101. Text of 1956 entry preceding, but with several paragraphs added near the beginning to make the essay self-contained when published apart from the 1938 main essay text. These added paragraphs summarize the section "The Theory of the Sign" in 1943: 191–95, to which the extensive Latin notes drawn from Poinsot's 1632a treatise on signs are appended. See further the posthumous 1986 entry below: page references in Part III of the present book are based on the 1986 reprint as the most definitve English version.

1968. "Philosophy and Ideosophy", in *The Peasant of the Garonne*, trans. Michael Cuddihy and Elizabeth Hughes (New York: Holt, Rinehart and Winston), 98–102.

1986 (posthumous editing). Reprint of "Language and the Theory of Sign" (1957 entry, above) with the addition of a full technical apparatus explicitly connecting the essay to Maritain's work on semiotic begun in 1937 (entry above) and to the text of Poinsot 1632a (on which Maritain centrally drew, entry below) in Deely, Williams and Kruse, Eds., *Frontiers in Semiotics* (Bloomington, IN: Indiana University Press, 1986), pp. 51–62, the most definitve English version of this seminal text from Maritain.

MARKUS, Robert Austin (1924–)
1972. "St. Augustine on Signs", in *Augustine. A Collection of Critical Essays*, ed. R. A. Markus (Garden City, NY: Doubleday & Co.), pp. 61–91.

McINERNY, Ralph.
2001. "Thomas Reid and the Signs of the Times", a subsection of Lecture IV of McInerny's 1999–2000 Gifford Lectures, *Characters in Search of Their Author* (Notre Dame, IN: University of Notre Dame Press), 52–56.

MEIER-OESER, Stephan.
　1995.　Entry "Semiotik, Semiologie" in the *Historisches Wörterbuch der Philosophie*, ed. Joachim Ritter and Karlfried Gründer (Basel: Schwabe), Band IX, cols. 601–8.
　1997.　*Die Spur des Zeichens. Das Zeichen und seine Funktion in der Philosohie des Mittelalters und der frühen Neuzeit* (Berlin: Walter de Gruyter).

MERGUET, H.
　1887.　*Lexikon zu den Philosophischen Schriften Cicero's, mit Angabe sämtlicher Stellen* (2nd ed.; Hildesheim: Georg Olms Verlag, 1987 reproduction of the 1887 Jena edition), in 3 Vols.

MURRAY, Henry A.
　1951.　"Toward a Classification of Interaction", in Parsons and Shils Eds. 1951: 434–64.

NÖTH, Winfried, Organizer.
　2001.　German-Italian Colloquium "The Semiotic Threshold from Nature to Culture", Kassell, Germany, 16–17 February at the Center for Cultural Studies, University of Kassel; papers published together with the Imatra 2000 Ecosemiotics colloquium in *The Semiotics of Nature*, a Special Issue of *Sign System Studies* 29.1, ed. Kalevi Kull and Winfried Nöth. (This journal, founded by Juri Lotman in 1967, is the oldest contemporary journal of semiotics, and, interestingly, appeared in its first three issues under the original version of Locke's coinage, Σημίωτική rather than Σημείωτική: see the extended discussion of the matter in the *Four Ages* Chapter 14.)

OEHLER, Klaus.
　1993.　*Charles Sanders Peirce* (München: Beck).

PAIS, Abraham.
　1991.　*Niels Bohr's Times, in Physics, Philosophy, and Polity* (Oxford: Clarendon Press).

PAPE, Helmut.
  1989. *Erfahrung und Wirklichkeit als Zeichenprozess* (Frankfurt am Main: Surkamp).

PARSONS, Talcott, and Edward SHILS, Editors.
  1951. *Toward a General Theory of Action* (Cambridge, MA: Harvard University Press).

PARSONS, Talcott, Edward SHILS, Gordon W. ALLPORT, Clyde KLUCKHOHN, Henry A. MURRAY, Robert R. SEARS, Richard C. SHELDON, Samuel A. STOUFFER, and Edward C. TOULMIN.
  1951. "Some Fundamental Categories of the Theory of Action: A General Statement", in Parsons and Shils Eds. 1951: 3–29.

PARSONS, Talcott, and Edward SHILS, with the assistance of James OLDS.
  1951. "Categories of the Orientation and Organization of Action", in Parsons and Shils Eds. 1951: 53–109.
  1951a. "Personality as a System of Action", in Parsons and Shils Eds. 1951: 110–58.

PEIRCE, Charles Sanders (1838–1914).
  Note: all eight volumes of *The Collected Papers of Charles Sanders Peirce*, Vols. I–VI ed. Charles Hartshorne and Paul Weiss (Cambridge, MA: Harvard University Press, 1931–1935), Vols. VII–VIII ed. Arthur W. Burks (same publisher, 1958), are now available in electronic form in an edition prepared by John Deely in collaboration with Mark Rooks (Charlottesville, VA: Intelex Corporation, 1994).
  1867. "On a New List of Categories", *Proceedings of the American Academy of Arts and Sciences 7* (presented 14 May 1867), 287–98; in CP 1.545–59, with "notes on the preceding" continuing to 1.567 (Burks p. 261).
  c.1897. A fragment on semiotics, partially printed in CP 2.227–29, 2.244 n. 1.

1898. Lecture series, "Detached Ideas on Vitally Important Topics" (the passage in CP 4.1 is from Lect. 2).

c.1902. "Minute Logic", draft for a book complete consecutively only to Chapter 4. Published in CP in extracts scattered over six of the eight volumes, including 1.203–83, 1.575–84; 2.1–202; 4.227–323, 6.349–352; 7.279, 7.374 n. 10, 7.362–87 except 381 n. 19. (For fuller detail, see Burks 293–94.)

1903. "The Ethics of Terminology", from *A Syllabus of Certain Topics of Logic* (Boston: Alfred Mudge & Son), pp. 10–14; reprinted in CP 2.219–2.226 continuing 1.202 (Burks p. 295).

1903a. Lowell Lectures, "Some Topics of Logic Bearing on Questions Now Vexed", esp.: lect. IIIA, "Lessons from the History of Philosophy", CP 1.15–26; draft 3 of lect. 3 entitled "Degenerate Cases", in CP 1.521–44; lect. 8, "How To Theorize", CP 5.590–604 (Burks p. 295); and the section published in CP 4.510–529 under the title "The Gamma Part of Existential Graphs".

1904. "On Signs and the Categories", from a letter to Lady Welby dated 12 October, in CP 8.327–41 (Burks p. 321). This letter in full can be found in in *Semiotics and Significs. The correspondence between Charles S. Peirce and Victoria Lady Welby*, ed. Charles S. Hardwick (Bloomington, IN: Indiana University Press, 1977), 22–36.

1905. "What Pragmatism Is", *The Monist* 15 (April), 161–81; reprinted in CP 5.411–37, with 5.414–5.435 being editorially headed "Pragmaticism" in CP.

1905a. "Issues of Pragmaticism", *The Monist* 15 (October), 481–99; reprinted in CP 5.438–63, except 448 n. 1, which is from 1906 [see Burks, entry for 1905(d), p. 298] (Burks p. 297). Also reprinted in *The Essential Peirce*, ed. Nathan Houser et al. (Bloomington, IN: Indiana University Press, 1998; hereafter EP) 2.346–59.

c.1905. Unsigned letter addressed to Signor Calderoni, in CP 8.205–13.

References, Historically Layered

1907. "Pragmatism", Reading 28 in EP 2.398–433.

c.1907. Ms. 318 in Robin 1967: 36–7, numbered ISP 00002–00350: one of the most important of Peirce's literary remains, this many-layered ms. has never been published in full. Where I have drawn on unpublished sections I have used a photocopy bearing the sheet numbers stamped by the Texas Tech Institute for Studies in Pragmaticism (hence: ISP nos.) on the electroprint copy Ketner with associates had made from microfilm, and then checked against the original in the Harvard archives. Further subdivisions and rearrangements have been made since. Originally an untitled letter-article to the editor of *The Nation*, this ms. has several partial draft endings signed "Charles Santiago Peirce", but no single, consecutive, complete draft as a whole.

CP 5.464–96, under a title supplied by the editors of the volume, "A Survey of Pragmaticism" (cf. Burks p. 299) is from this ms. 318. NEM III.1: 481–94 presents a small segment under the title "From Pragmatism". EP 2.398–433, under the title "Pragmatism" (the 1907 entry immediately above), is the most complete, though still partial, presentation of this document.

PEIRCE, Charles Sanders, Editor.

1883. *Studies in Logic by members of the Johns Hopkins University* (Boston: Little, Brown, and Co.), 1–11. Facsimile reprint with an Introduction essay by Max H. Fisch and a Preface by Achim Eschbach as Volume 1 in the series "Foundations in Semiotics" under the general editorship of Eschbach (Amsterdam/Philadelphia: John Benjamins Publishing Co., 1983).

PENCAK, William.

1993. *History, Signing In! Essays in History and Semiotics* (New York: Peter Lang).

PETRILLI, Susan, and PONZIO, Augusto.

2001. *Thomas Sebeok and the Signs of Life* (USA: Totem Books).

PHILIP CANCELLARIUS (c.1160/1185–1236, "Philip the Chancellor")

c.1225/8. *Philippi Cancellarii Parisiensis Summa de Bono*, critical ed. by N. Wicki (Bern: Corpus philosophorum medii aevi II, 1985). Earliest treatise introducing the medieval doctrine of the transcendental properties of being.

PHILODEMUS (c.110–c.40BC).

i. 54–40BC. Περὶ σημειώσεων (*De Signis*), trans. as *On the Methods of Inference* in the ed. of Phillip Howard De Lacy and Estelle Allen De Lacy, rev. with the collaboration of Marcello Gigante, Francesco Longo Auricchio, and Adele Tepedino Guerra (Naples: Bibliopolis, 1978), Greek text pp. 27–87, English 91–131.

Manetti's comments (2002: 282) are worth adding here as a gloss on this important text: "The first critical edition of the papyrus containing this work of Philodemus (Pherc. 1065) was published by T. Gomperz, who significantly gave it the title *Philodem Über Induktions-schlüsse* (1865). The current standard edition is the text published by Phillip and Estelle Allen De Lacy, *On Methods of Inference* (1978). This is a revised version of an earlier edition (1941), now improved by the contributions of Marcello Gigante who, together with Francesca Longo Auricchio and Adele Tepedino Guerra, made an inspection of the papyrus with microscopic binoculars, allowing them to recover many previously unrecognized readings of the text." Manetti's review bears reading in full, particularly for making clear for semioicians why (p. 296) "it is safe to say that [Philodemus' text] has not yet revealed all its secrets to us, and remains an extremely rich source for further study and reflection".

POINSOT, John.

Note. A complete table of all the editions, complete

and partial, and in whatever language, of Poinsot's systematic works in philosophy and theology is provided in Deely 1985: 396–97. A complete breakdown of the contents of the original volumes of Poinsot's *Cursus Theologicus* and of the relation of that content to the volumes of the principal modern editions is provided in Deely 1994a: 284. The principal modern edition utilized in this work (besides the *Tractatus* itself) is abbreviated R followed by a volume number (I, II, or III) and pages, with column (a or b) and line indications as needed = the *Cursus Philosophicus Thomisticus*, ed. by B. Reiser in 3 volumes (Turin: Marietti, 1930, 1933, 1937).

1631. *Artis Logicae Prima Pars* (Alcalá, Spain). The opening pages 1–11a14 of this work and the "Quaestio Disputanda I. De Termino. Art. 6. Utrum Voces Significant per prius Conceptus an Res" pages 104b31–108a33, relevant to the discussion of signs in the *Secunda Pars* of 1632 (entry following), have been incorporated in the 1632a entry (second entry following, q.v., pp. 4–30 and 342–51 "Appendix A. On the Signification of Language", respectively), for the independent edition of that discussion published by the University of California Press. From R I: 1–247.

1632. *Artis Logicae Secunda Pars* (Alcalá, Spain). From R I: 249–839.

1632a. *Tractatus de Signis*, subtitled *The Semiotic of John Poinsot*, extracted from the *Artis Logicae Prima et Secunda Pars* of 1631–1632 using the text of the emended second impression (1932) of the 1930 Reiser edition (Turin: Marietti), and arranged in bilingual format by John Deely in consultation with Ralph A. Powell (First Edition; Berkeley: University of California Press, 1985). Pages are set in matching columns of English and Latin, with intercolumnar numbers every fifth line.

(Thus, references to the volume are by page number, followed by a slash and the appropriate line number of the specific section of text referred to – e.g., 287/3–26.) This work, the first systematic treatise on the foundations of semiotic, is also available as a text database, stand-alone on floppy disk or combined with an Aquinas database, as an Intelex Electronic Edition (Charlottesville, VA: Intelex Corp., 1992).

1633. *Naturalis Philosophiae Prima Pars* (Madrid, Spain). In R II: 1–529.

1633a. By reason of its importance for the contemporary discussion of semiotic categories, I give a separate listing here to Poinsot's treatment *De primo cognito*, "of being-as-first-known", within his *Philosophiae naturalis prima pars* (*Part I of Natural Philosophy*), as follows: Quaestio 1, "De Scientia Philosophiae et Ordine Cognoscendi" ("On Philosophical Knowledge and the Order of Knowing"), articulus 3, "Utrum magis universale, atque adeo ipsum ens ut sic, sit primo cognitum ab intellectu nostro" ("Whether the more universal, and therefore being itself as such, is primarily known by human understanding"), Reiser ed. vol. II, 20a2– 33b38.

The most important commentary on this text is to be found in Guagliardo 1994.

1634. *Naturalis Philosophiae Tertia Pars* (Alcalá, Spain); in R vol. II: 533–888. (On the suppressed *Secunda Pars Philosophiae Naturalis*, Poinsot's treatment of astronomical questions, see Deely 1985: 402–4).

1635. *Naturalis Philosophiae Quarta Pars* (Alcalá, Spain); in R vol. III: 1–425.

POSNER, Roland, Klaus ROBERING, and Thomas A. SEBEOK, Eds.
1997. *Semiotik – Semiotics: Ein Handbuch Zu Den Zeichentheoretischen Grundlagen Von Natur Und Kultur – a Handbook on the Sign-Theoretic Foundations of Nature and Culture*, Volume I (Berlin: Walter de Gruyter, Inc.).

References, Historically Layered

POWELL, Ralph A.
2000. "'That a State Establishment of Any Religion Claiming Divine Revelation Is Contrary to Natural Law': The Semiotics of Separation of Church and State", in *Semiotics 2000*, ed. Scott Simpkins and John Deely (Ottawa, Canada: Legas Publishing, 2001), 455–69.

PRODI, Giorgio.
1977. *Le basi materiali della significazione* (Milano: Bompiani).

RASMUSSEN, Douglas B., and Douglas J. Den UYL.
1991. *Liberty and Nature* (La Salle, IL: Open Court).

RAUCH, Irmengard.
1983. "'Symbols Grow': Creation, Compulsion, Change", Presidential Address to the eighth Annual Meeting of the Semiotic Society of America (Snowbird, Utah), subsequently published in *The American Journal of Semiotics* 3.1 (1984), 2–23.
1999. *Semiotic Insights* (Toronto: University of Toronto Press).

REDPATH, Peter.
1997. *Cartesian Nightmare: An Introduction to Transcendental Sophistry* (Amsterdam: Rodopi).
1997a. *Wisdom's Odyssey. From Philosophy to Transcendental Sophistry* (Amsterdam: Rodopi).
1998. *Masquerade of the Dream Walkers. Prophetic Theology from the Cartesians to Hegel* (Amsterdam: Rodopi).

REID, Thomas.
1785. *Essays on the Intellectual Powers of Man*, ed. Baruch Brophy (Boston: MIT Press, 1969).

ROMEO, Luigi.
1976. "Heraclitus and the Foundations of Semiotics", *Versus* 15.5 (dicembre), 73–90. Reprinted without the brief section on philological sources (pp. 75–79) in Deely, Williams, & Kruse 1986: 224–34.
1977. "The Derivation of 'Semiotics' through the History of the Discipline", in *Semiosis* 6, Heft 2, 37–49.

1979. "Pedro da Fonseca in Renaissance Semiotics: A Segmental History of Footnotes", *Ars Semeiotica* (1979) II.2, p. 190ff.

RUSSELL, Anthony F. (1922–1999).
1981. "The Logic of History as a Semiotic Process of Question and Answer in the Thought of R. G. Collingwood", in *Semiotics 1981*, ed. John N. Deely and Margot D. Lenhart (New York: Plenum, 1983), pp. 179–89.
1982. "The Semiosis Linking the Human World and Physical Reality", in *Semiotics 1982*, ed. John Deely and Jonathan Evans (Lanham, MD: University Press of America, 1987), 591–600.
1984. *Logic, Philosophy, and History. A study in the philosophy of history of R. G. Collingwood*, with a Foreword by Brooke Williams (Lanham, MD: University Press of America).
1987. "The Semiotic of Causality and Participation: A New Perspective on the Cajetan–Fabro–Montagnes Controversy over the Analogy of Being", in *Semiotics 1987*, ed. John Deely (Lanham, MD: University Press of America, 1988), 467–72.
1999. "In Response to G. E. Moore: A Semiotic Perspective on R. G. Collingwood's Concrete Universal", in *Semiotics 1999*, ed. C. W. Spinks, Scott Simpkins, and John Deely (New York: Peter Lang Publishing, 2000).

RUSSELL, Bertrand (1872–1970).
1959. *My Philosophical Development* (New York: Simon and Schuster).

SANTAELLA-BRAGA, Lúcia.
1991. "John Poinsot's Doctrine of Signs: The Recovery of a Missing Link", *The Journal of Speculative Philosophy*, New Series, 5.2 (1991), 151–59.
1992. *A Assinatura das Coisas* (Rio de Janeiro: Imago Editora).

References, Historically Layered

1994. "The Way to Postmodernity", preface in Deely 1994a: xv–xvi

1994a. "Peirce's Broad Concept of Mind", *European Journal for Semiotic Studies* 6, 399–411.

1996. "Semiosphere: The Growth of Signs", *Semiotica* 109, 173–86.

1999. "A New Causality for Understanding of the Living", *Semiotica* 127, 497–518.

SAUSSURE, Ferdinand de (1857–1913).

1916. *Cours de Linguistique Général* (Paris: Payot, 1916). Lectures delivered at the University of Geneva i.1906–1911 and posthumously published from auditors' notes by Charles Bally and Albert Sechehaye with the collaboration of Albert Riedlinger.

SCHRADER, George.

1967. "The Thing in Itself in Kantian Philosophy", in *Kant. A Collection of Critical Essays*, ed. Robert Paul Wolff (Notre Dame, IN: University of Notre Dame Press), pp. 172–88.

SEBEOK, Thomas A.

1971. "'Semiotic' and Its Congeners", in *Linguistic and Literary Studies in Honor of Archibald Hill, I: General and Theoretical Linguistics*, ed. Mohammed Ali Jazayery, Edgar C. Polomé, and Werner Winter (Lisse, Netherlands: Peter de Ridder Press), 283–95; reprinted in Sebeok 1985: 47–58, and in Deely, Williams and Kruse 1986: 255–63.

1975. "The Semiotic Web: A Chronicle of Prejudices", *Bulletin of Literary Semiotics* 2, 1–63; reprinted "with essential corrections and additions" in Sebeok 1976: 149–88, to which reprint page numbers in the present monograph are keyed.

1975a. "Zoösemiotics: At the Intersection of Nature and Culture", in *The Tell-Tale Sign*, ed. T. A. Sebeok (Lisse, the Netherlands: Peter de Ridder Press), pp. 85–95.

1976. *Contributions to the Doctrine of Signs* (=Sources in Semiotics IV; Lanham, MD: University Press of America, 1985 reprint with a new Preface by Brooke Williams of the original book as published by Indiana University, Bloomington, and The Peter De Ridder Press, Lisse).

1977. "Neglected Figures in the History of Semiotic Inquiry: Jakob von Uexküll", reprinted in *The Sign & Its Masters* (reprinted with new front matter but unchanged pagination; Lanham, MD: University Press of America, 1989), pp. 187–207.

1977a. "Ecumenicalism in Semiotics", in *A Perfusion of Signs*, ed. Sebeok (Bloomington, IN: Indiana University Press, 1986), 180–206.

1978. "'Talking' with Animals: Zoösemiotics Explained", *Animals* 111.6 (December), 20–23, 38; reprinted in Sebeok 1981a: 109–16.

1979. "Semiosis in Nature and Culture", as reprinted in Sebeok 1979a/1989: 3–26.

1979a. *The Sign & Its Masters* (original ed.; Austin, TX: University of Texas Press). See 1989 entry below.

1979b. "Prefigurements of Art", *Semiotica* 27–1/3, 3–73; reprinted in Sebeok 1981a: 210–59.

1981. "The Ultimate Enigma of 'Clever Hans': The Union of Nature and Culture", in *The Clever Hans Phenomenon: Communcation with Horses, Whales, Apes and People* (Annals of the New York Academy of Sciences Vol. 364), 199–205.

1981a. *The Play of Musement* (Bloomington, IN: Indiana University Press).

1984. "Vital Signs", Presidential Address delivered October 12 to the ninth Annual Meeting of the Semiotic Society of America, Bloomington, Indiana, October 11–14; subsequently printed in *The American Journal of Semiotics* 3.3, 1–27, and reprinted in Sebeok 1986: 59–79.

References, Historically Layered

1984a. "The Evolution of Communication and the Origin of Language", lecture of June 3 in the June 1–3 ISISSS '84 Colloquium on "Phylogeny and Ontogeny of Communication Systems". Published under the title "Communication, Language, and Speech. Evolutionary Considerations", in Sebeok, *I Think I Am A Verb. More Contributions to the Doctrine of Signs* (New York: Plenum Press (New York: Plenum, 1986), pp. 10–16.

1984b. "Symptom", Chapter 10 of *New Directions in Linguistics and Semiotics*, ed. James E. Copeland (Houston: Rice University Studies), 212–30.

1985. *Contributions to the Doctrine of Signs* (=Sources in Semiotics IV; reprint of 1976 original with an extended Preface by Brooke Williams, "Challenging Signs at the Crossroads" [Williams 1985], evaluating the book in light of major reviews; Lanham, MD: University Press of America).

1986. *I Think I Am A Verb. More Contributions to the Doctrine of Signs* (New York: Plenum Press).

1986a. "Toward a Natural History of Language", in *The World & I* (October 1986), 462–69.

1987. "Language: How Primary a Modeling System?", in *Semiotics 1987*, ed. John Deely (Lanham, MD: University Press of America, 1988), 15–27.

1987a. "Toward a Natural History of Language", *Semiotica* 65, 343–58 (expanded from the 1986a review article, above), as reprinted in Sebeok 1991a: 68–82.

1989. *The Sign & Its Masters* (= Sources in Semiotics VIII; Lanham, MD: University Press of America). Corrected reprint with a new author's Preface and editor's Introduction of the University of Texas Press 1979 original imprint.

1991. *Semiotics in the United States* (Bloomington, IN: Indiana University Press).

1991a. *A Sign is Just a Sign* (Bloomington, IN: Indiana University Press).

1991b. "Indexicality", in Sebeok 1991a: 128–43.
1992. "Galen in Medical Semiotics", as finally published in Sebeok 2001: 44–58 (see the bibliographical note on p. 44 bottom).
1992a. "'Tell Me, Where Is Fancy Bred?': The Biosemiotic Self", in *The Semiotic Web 1991*, ed. T. A. Sebeok and J. Umiker-Sebeok (Berlin: Mouton de Gruyter), 333–43 (reprinted also in Sebeok 2001: 120–27).
1995. "Semiotics as Bridge between Humanities and Sciences", in the volume of this same title ed. Paul Perron, Leonard G. Sbrocchi, Paul Colilli, and Marcel Danesi (Ottawa, Canada: Legas Publishing, 2000), 76–100. Reprinted under the title "Signs, Bridges, Origins", in Sebeok 2001: 59–73, with the addition of a brief concluding eight-line "Erato's Coda".
1996. "Galen in Medical Semiotics", *Interdisciplinary Journal for Germanic Linguistics and Semiotic Analysis* 1.1 (Spring), 89–111.
2000. "Some Reflections on Vico in Semiotics", in *Functional Approaches to Language, Culture and Cognition*, ed. D. G. Lockwood, P. H. Fries, and J. E. Copeland (Amsterdam: John Benjamins), 555–68; as reprinted in Sebeok 2001: 135–44, to which reprint page refernces in this essay are keyed.
2001. *Global Semiotics* (Bloomington, IN: Indiana University Press).
2001a. "Biosemiotics: Its Roots, Proliferation, and Prospects", in Kull Guest-Ed. 2001: 61–78.

SEBEOK, Thomas A., Editor.
1977. *A Perfusion of Signs* (Bloomington: Indiana University Press).

SEBEOK, Thomas A., General Editor; Paul BOUISSAC, Umberto ECO, Jerzy PELC, Roland POSNER, Alain REY, Ann SHUKMAN, Editorial Board.
1986. *Encyclopedic Dictionary of Semiotics* (Berlin: Mouton de Gruyter), in 3 Volumes.

References, Historically Layered

SEBEOK, Thomas A., and Jean UMIKER-SEBEOK, Editors.
1992. *Biosemiotics. The Semiotic Web 1991* (Berlin: Mouton de Gruyter).

SOKAL, Alan, and Jean BRICMONT.
1998. *Fashionable Nonsense. Postmodern intellectuals abuse of science* (New York: Picador USA).

SOMMERS, Mary Catherine.
2001. "Imaging the Contemplative Life in Thomas Aquinas", in *Semiotics 2001*, ed. Scott Simpkins and John Deely (Ottawa, Canada: Legas Publishing, 2002).

SOTO, Dominicus ("Domingo de") (1494–1560).
1529, 1554. *Summulae* (1st ed., Burgos; 2nd ed., Salamanca; 3rd rev. ed., Salamanca; Facsimile of 3rd ed., Hildesheim, NY: Georg Olms Verlag).

SPIEGELBERG, Herbert (1904–).
1965. *The Phenomenological Movement* (2nd ed., rev.; The Hague: Martinus Nijhoff), 2 volumes.

STEVENSON, Robert Louis (1850–1894).
1885/6. *Strange Case of Dr. Jekyll and Mr. Hyde* (London: Longman). The first edition was actually prepared late in December of 1885, but deemed too late for the Christmas book trade and therefore postponed to a January 1886 release. On the original printed copies from Longman, the date is actually hand-corrected from 1885 to read 1886. Note the absence of *The* at the beginning of the original title, commonly inserted in later editions. I have used the text of Michael Hulse, *Strange Case of Dr. Jekyll and Mr. Hyde and other stories* (Cologne: Könemann Verlagsgesellshcaft mbH, 1995), 5–78, which is based in turn on the Edmund Gosse London edition of 1906.

TASCA, Norma, Editor.
1995. *Ensaios em Homagem a Thomas A. Sebeok*, quadruple Special Issue of *Cruzeiro Semiótico*,(Porto, Portugal: Fundação Eng. António de Almeida).

von UEXKÜLL, Jakob.

1899–1940. *Kompositionslehre der Natur. Biologie als undogmatische Naturwissenschaft*, selected writings edited and with an introduction by T. von Uexküll (Frankfurt a. M.: Ullstein).

1920, 1928. *Theoretische Biologie* (Berlin; 2nd ed. 1928, reprinted Frankfurt a. M.: Suhrkamp 1970). Attempted English translation by MacKinnon 1926, q.v.

1934. *Streifzuge durch die Umwelten von Tieren und Menschen* (Berlin), trans. by Claire H. Schiller as "A Stroll through the Worlds of Animals and Men" in *Instinctive Behavior: The Development of a Modern Concept*, ed. by Claire H. Schiller (New York: International Universities Press, Inc., 1957), 5–80.

1940. "Bedeutungslehre", Bios 10 (Leipzig), trans. by Barry Stone and Herbert Weiner as "The Theory of Meaning" in *Semiotica* 42.1 (1982), 25–82.

von UEXKÜLL, Thure.

1981. "The Sign Theory of Jakob von Uexküll", in *Classics of Semiotics* (English edition of *Die Welt als Zeichen: Klassiker der modernen Semiotik*, Berlin: Wolf Jobst Siedler Verlag), ed. Martin Krampen, Klaus Oehler, Roland Posner, Thomas A. Sebeok, and Thure von Uexküll (New York: Plenum Press, 1987), 147–79.

1982. "Semiotics and the Problem of the Observer", in *Semiotics 1982*, ed. John Deely and Jonathan Evans (Lanham, MD: University Press of America, 1987), 3–12.

VICO, Giambattista (1668–1744).

1744. *Scienza Nuova* (3rd ed.; Naples), as edited by Fausto Nicolini (Bari: Laterza, 1928), and presented in the rev. trans. by Thomas Goddard Bergin and Max Harold Fisch, *The New Science of Giambattista Vico* (Ithaca, NY: Cornell University Press, 1968).

WEINBERG, Julius Rudolph.

1965. *Abstraction, Relation, and Induction: three essays in the history of thought* (Madison, WI: University of Wisconsin Press).

WILLIAMS, Brooke.

1983. "History as a Semiotic Anomaly", in *Semiotics 1983*, ed. Jonathan Evans and John Deely (Lanham, MD: University Press of America, 1997), 409–19; reprinted under the title "History in Relation to Semiotics" in Deely, Williams, and Kruse 1986: 217–23.

1984. "Preface" to *Logic, Philosophy, and History* (A. F. Russell 1984).

1985. "Challenging Signs at the Crossroads", prefatory essay to Sebeok 1985: xv–xlii.

1985a. *History and Semiotic* (Toronto Semiotic Circle Monograph, No. 4; Victoria University of the University of Toronto).

1985b. "What Has History to Do with Semiotic", *Semiotica* 54.3/4, 267–333.

1990. "Uma década de debates: História e Semiótica nos annos 80", *Face* 3.1 (janeiro/junho), 11–28.

1990a. "Re-posing the Objectivity Question," in *Semiotics 1990*, ed. Karen Haworth, John Deely, Terry Prewitt (Lanham, MD: University Press of America, 1991), 87–95

1991. "History and Semiotics in the 1990s", *Semiotica* 83.3/4, 385–417.

WILLIAMS, Brooke, and William PENCAK, Guest Editors.

1991. "Special Issue: History and Semiotics", *Semiotica* 83–3/4.

WOJTYLA, Karol Jósef.

1998, September 14. *Fides et Ratio*, encyclical letter on the relationship between faith and reason (Rome, Italy: Vatican City).

Index

This index covers both terms and proper names, and some propositions. The whole is arranged alphabetically, including such propositional subentries as occur. Names which provide historical landmarks in intellectual history have been given with dates included for the convenience of readers. In addition, index entries likely to be of special help to readers in grasping the content of the work have been highlighted with **bold-faced** type.

Index

Index

Index

Index

Index

Index

Index

Index